THE COMPANION
TO MEDIEVAL SOCIETY

THE COMPANION
TO MEDIEVAL SOCIETY

FRANCO CARDINI

Translated by Corrado Federici

McGill-Queen's University Press
Montreal & Kingston • London • Ithaca

International Copyright © 2012
by Editoriale Jaca Book SpA, Milano

ISBN 978-0-7735-4103-0

Legal deposit third quarter 2012
Bibliothèque nationale du Québec

The translation of this book has been funded by SEPS –
Segretariato Europeo per le Pubblicazioni Scientifiche
(Via Val d'Aposa 7 – 40123 Bologna, Italy, www.seps.it, seps@seps.it).

McGill-Queen's University Press acknowledges the support of the Canada Council
for the Arts for our publishing program. We also acknowledge the financial support
of the Government of Canada through the Canada Book Fund for our publishing activities.

Library and Archives Canada Cataloguing in Publication

Cardini, Franco
    The companion to medieval society / Franco Cardini; translated by Corrado Federici.

Translation of: La societa medievale.
ISBN 978-0-7735-4103-0

1. Civilization, Medieval. I. Federici, Corrado II. Title. III. Title: Medieval Society.

CB351.C2913 2012   940.1   C2012-902768-5

This book was typeset by Interscript in 11/13 Garamond.

Selection of images and page layout
Graphic SrL, Milan

Printing and binding
Grafiche Flaminia, Foligno (Pg), Italy
July 2012

CONTENTS

THE COMPANION
TO MEDIEVAL SOCIETY

1

1

WHAT ARE THE MIDDLE AGES?

THE MIDDLE AGES AND MEDIEVALISM

Interest in the ten centuries usually defined as "medieval" can be divided into two kinds, which are distinct but not necessarily separate. One is "medieval studies," the study of the Middle Ages from historical, philological, artistic, philosophical, religious, and literary perspectives. The other is "medievalism," which is the sum of interests and attitudes that manifested themselves largely during the nineteenth century and aimed at reviving, sometimes humorously and at other times in nostalgic or evocative ways, an essentially imaginary "Middle Ages." We have been using and abusing the word "medieval" for three centuries. but there is still discussion as to whether, apart from the conventional dates, the word has specific, identifiable meanings. These would distinguish it from, for example, those uses typical of the so-called *ancien régime,* which stretch it beyond most accepted chronological endpoints into a so-called "long Middle Ages," or perhaps the "moyen-áge des profondeurs" (the Middle Ages of the Depths) proposed by Jacques Le Goff.

The fact remains that these days the term, which enjoys a well-established place in the area of specialized research in history and philology, too often refers to an ambiguous and confused object: a "Middle Ages" that is arbitrarily conceived and proposed, requiring us to analyze the user's intentions, the methods and materials used to create this object, the degree of historical accuracy, and accuracy in general. However ill-defined, the phrase itself, whatever the particular meaning attributed to it, is found everywhere in the mass media and seems to generate a great deal of business. Like the pyramids and the mysteries of the pharaohs, the Middle Ages is inescapable, appearing on the shelves of bookstores, in toy stores and kiosks, on movie and television screens, in stories of the quest for Holy Grail, books on the secrets of the Templars, and "cloak-and-dagger" novels. Given this, it might seem that its most important aspect is as a medieval period for lovers of the esoteric and the occult.

There are other Middle Ages, such as the one popularized by Umberto Eco's *The Name of the Rose,* with its satirical and provocative passages targeting the Middle Ages of "traditionalists" – the Middle Ages broadly inspired by the "reactionary" spirit of a Jorge Borges, on the one hand, and by the writings of such figures as French author René Guénon (1886–1951) or Italian Jules Evola (1898–1974), on the other. Then there is the Middle Ages reinvented in best-sellers, like those of Ken Follett and Michael Crichton, and, finally, we have the evocative, popular Middle Ages associated with the great festivals and the search for a Romantic-nationalist identity or roots, which is also inspired by revivalism and thus is a part of the tourism industry as well as the "nostalgia industry" – both typical features of a consumer society. This is a Middle Ages on its way to becoming part of the collective experience, daily life, and its pageants, as are the festival of Calendimaggio (The Ides of May) in Assisi, the chivalrous contests in Asti, Ascoli-Piceno, Narni, and Foligno, the "reconstructions"

2

1. Francesco Azzurri, *Study for the Atrium of the Palazzo Pubblico* (Parliament Building) *of San Marino,* watercolour on paper, n.d. (1883?). State Archives, Republic of San Marino.

2. Attributed to Francesco Azzurri, *Perspective View of the Parliament Building of San Marino,* watercolour and diluted Indian ink on paper, April 1883. State Archives, Republic of San Marino.

9

of "medieval" times and settings in Bevagna, the festivals celebrated in Brisighella or Città del Sole, the historical re-creations of the era of Empress Matilda in Parma or the Battle of Legnano waged against Emperor Frederick Barbarossa, "Medieval Week" in San Marino, and many other festivals (leaving out the Palio of Siena, which has a complex history and acquired a medieval aspect only recently).

A BRIEF HISTORY OF A REVIVAL

This "fashion" or passion for the medieval age is not new. The history of Middle Ages revivals in the eighteenth, nineteenth, and twentieth centuries, in other words "medievalism," is essentially a "history of taste," to use a phrase from Kenneth Clark's well-known and important work on the Gothic Revival. Clearly social factors cannot be ruled out as an element in the production of taste; however, keep in mind that the establishment of, and variations in, fashion often follow a cultural logic and are only in part directly connected to the political and social conditions of a given period.

It is customary to date the start of the Gothic Revival from the 1750s, with Horace Walpole's construction of Strawberry Hill at Twickenham, outside London. To design his residence, Walpole established a "Committee of Taste," headed by him, which was to direct the project, using information from books and prints. The results were quite imaginative, owing as much to Rococo and Georgian styles as to the French Gothic. With respect to the latter, what is especially striking is the absence of the pointed arch as a structural element. This feature was used instead as a decorative element in the interior of Strawberry Hill and the arches were built using materials such as wood and stucco, which runs counter to their original function. From 1760 onward, several more or less professional architects took up Walpole's ideas and applied them to the construction and reconstruction of many buildings in the countryside.

Between the end of the eighteenth century and the beginning of the nineteenth we find another example of a significant variation in neo-Gothic architectural style in Fonthill Abbey, completed between 1796 and 1812, designed by James Wyatt

3. Johann Heinrich, *Strawberry Hill, Twickenham*, view from the south, c.1755–59.

4. Humphrey Repton, example of the transformation of the landscape, from one of his *Red Books*. With his landscape gardening projects, Repton was one of the first interpreters of Horace Walpole's vision and sensibility.

5

6

5. John Constable, *Salisbury Cathedral*, view from the bishop's garden, oil on canvas, 1826. The Frick Collection, New York.

6. Interior view of Fonthill Abbey, designed by James Wyatt, 1795–1807.

for the eccentric billionaire William Beckford. Beckford originally wanted to build only faux ruins of a Gothic abbey but Wyatt's work went much further, creating a complete building and an immense tower. The tower collapsed a few years after it was built, crashing down on the building; apparently, creating Gothic architectural structures was not easily mastered.

Wyatt went on to apply his theories in other work, dedicating himself particularly to very ambitious restorations of cathedrals, such as that of Salisbury at the end of the 1700s. The English architect thought of his interventions on the interiors as efforts to "clean and colour" old medieval Gothic structures. Although his intentions do not seem to have been prescriptive, Wyatt is credited with having introduced a taste for the Gothic such that it no longer served merely as superficial decoration, a revival of details, as was the case in Strawberry Hill, but instead as a reinvention of Gothic monumentality. The road was then open for the construction of entirely new churches designed in that style. Within a few decades of the start of the 1800s, thanks to the Church Building Act, more than 200 churches in neo-Gothic style were built in England alone. It is commonly believed that this development in architecture parallels developments in literature, such as that from Walpole's *The Castle of Otranto* to the historical novels of Walter Scott, in other words, from an interpretative fantasy not based on actual research on the subject to more accurate writing that is attentive to historical truth.

7

Between the seventeenth and eighteenth centuries, the cultural relationships between England and North America, despite the political situation, were fairly close. Interest in the Gothic, in both literature and architecture, easily permeated the ex-colonies, although it cannot be said that it had a dramatic effect on North American society and culture. Literature written during this period indicates a clear interest in Gothic taste, but architects were probably somewhat distrustful of a tradition that was felt to be profoundly European and tied to a culture that was – or was imagined to be – medieval, papist, superstitious, and restricted.

Soon, however, the English influence became more pervasive as the result of a growing number of North Americans travelling to Europe and the success of Walter Scott's novels, which no longer depicted a medieval world of austerity and suffering but one of heroism and chivalry. The figure of the knight, interpreted in a profoundly anti-historical fashion as a solitary and self-reliant champion, could be compared to the new American, the pioneer, the hero of the frontier in the novels of James Fenimore Cooper. This led to such phenomena as the complex transfer and reconstruction of a Spanish monastery on the shores of the Hudson River near New York (The Cloisters) and the "medievalist" inspiration behind much of the American and Canadian architecture of the period.

THE DEBATE ON THE MIDDLE AGES

7. Cloister, interior view. The Cloisters Museum and Gardens, Metropolitan Museum of Art, New York.

But what are the "Middle Ages" that fill the imagination and create so much discussion? As is often the case, the best way to begin to define something is to trace the history of the word. (Many scholars have already done this, starting with the

8, 9. Augustus Welby Northmore Pugin, *Contrasts: A parallel between the noble edifices of the fourteenth and fifteenth centuries and similar buildings of the present day. Showing the present decay of taste.* London, 1836.

Facing-page:
10. Gold medallion depicting the bust of Theodoric. National Museum of Rome.

11. Domenico Ghirlandaio, detail of a fresco in the Sassetti Chapel, with Lorenzo the Magnificent in the centre, 1482–85, Santa Trinita, Florence.

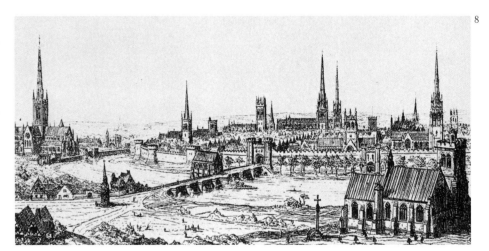

8

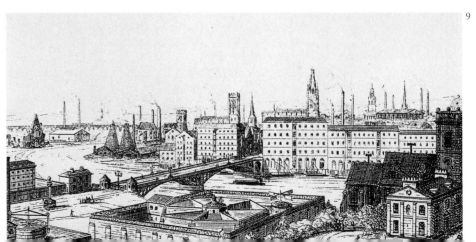

9

10

great Italian medievalist Giorgio Falco, whose classic book *La polemica sul medioevo* (The debate on the Middle Ages), published in 1933, can still be read profitably and with pleasure) One of the important factors in the complexity and confusion of this debate, which has lasted for several centuries, is the fact that the so-called "Middle Ages" cover an entire millennium, from the fall of the Western Roman Empire in 476 A.D. to the discovery of America in 1492 – a millennium during which a great many things occurred. Is it possible to speak of such figures as Theodoric the Goth and Lorenzo the Magnificent in the same breath simply because they can both be defined as "medieval"? Is it possible and appropriate to speak of "medieval man," "medieval society," "medieval culture," etc., as though they were unified and coherent entities? Clearly, the answer is no.

Even the conventional phrase "Middle Ages" is puzzling. The person who invented the expression meant to provide a non-definition rather than a definition: to indicate an in-between age, a transitional period between the only two ages that matter – the ancient and the modern. The term was invented by fifteenth-century humanists who expanded on Petrarch's idea (which has famous ancient antecedents) of the decline of civilization and his novel and insightful conclusion that the world of great culture, the peak of which was marked by the Roman Empire and the birth of Christ, had come to an end. The recognition that there had been a break with the ancient age and that the resulting decline must be reversed by restoring or reviving the ancient splendour in new forms (in what would come to be called the Renaissance) led the humanists to consider the many centuries "in

12. Scene depicting Creusa preventing Aeneas from returning to the battle, as well as Ascanius and Anchises, fourth-fifth century, from Vergil, *Complete Works*, Vat. Lat. 3225, parchment, fol. 75, Vatican Apostolic Library, Rome.

13. Portrait of Vergil, sixth century, from *Virgilio Romano* (Roman Vergil). Vatican Apostolic Library, Rome.

between" as a *media aetas* (middle age), *media tempestas* (middle time), or *media tempora* (middle period).

An important assumption underlying the humanist cult of antiquity involved their awareness that the ancient world had ended and that, therefore, that world was foreign relative to the society in which the humanists lived. The idea of a presumed break between antiquity and the medieval world did not exist prior to the 1300s. Yet, strange as it may seem, this was entirely logical. In the fifth century the Roman Empire still effectively continued to exist, a successor to Augustus ruled in Constantinople, and people everywhere adhered to the Christian Church – which was born in the empire of Constantine – and spoke and wrote in the language of Rome, Latin. For the entire period that we refer to as medieval, Europeans felt that they were connected to the ideals of the Church and the empire, and used the works of Latin authors such as Ovid, Lucan, and Statius alongside the Bible in their schools and universities. The Roman legacy as a whole was used without making too many chronological, stylistic, or philosophical distinctions. The main idea was that the ancients, because of the valuable legacy they had left behind, were seen as authorities. God himself, who had spoken to humankind, favouring the people of Israel,

14

15

had also communicated His truth in mysterious ways to the ancients. Thus myths such as those of Orpheus and Dionysus contained figures who anticipated Christ, and Vergil – who, in Eclogue IV speaks of a child that would be born to a Virgin at the beginning of the new era – could be considered a prophet, like those in the Bible.

The sense that antiquity had come to a close began to grow among the privileged classes in Italy during the fourteenth century. Rome had been abandoned by the popes, the Roman-Germanic Empire was on its way to becoming a Germanic kingdom, the Byzantine Empire had already become a small Greek kingdom threatened by the Turks. Pilgrims who went to Rome saw the ruins of the ancient empire. The beauty of those monuments, as well as the difference between those structures and the ones being erected by the "moderns" (as the people of the 1300s came to define themselves) were sources of amazement, inspiring people to reproduce them. In the meantime, lay intellectuals, who were employed by the state chancelleries to produce elegant letters, became increasingly concerned with the issue of the Latin language as the "language of literature" and therefore with reproducing it stylistically, which necessitated a choice of which version of Latin to use as a model. The wars between cities and factions, which were frequent in fourteenth-century Italy, were interpreted

14. Portrait of Orpheus in a floor mosaic in the Baptistery of Aquileia. In the transition to Christianity, the image of Orpheus is transformed until it becomes that of the Good Shepherd.

15. Orpheus with a stringed instrument, wearing Greek attire, and surrounded by animals, from a tomb floor mosaic, probably dating to the sixth century.

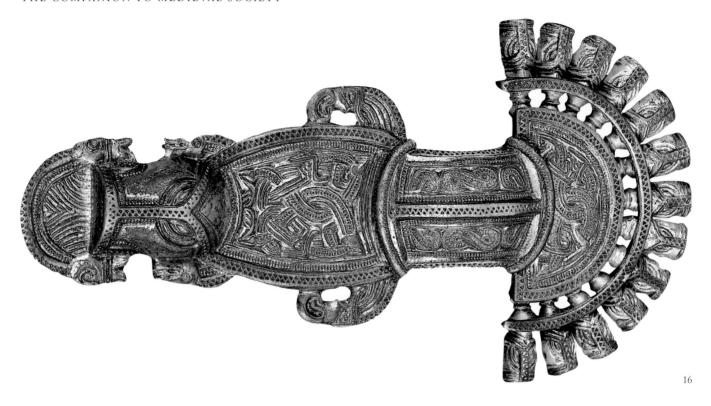

16

16. Bow fibula from the necropolis at Nocera Umbra, sixth-eighth century, Museum of the Late Middle Ages, Rome.

in light of Roman history from the time of Marius and Sulla, Caesar and Pompey. Thus awareness of the break with antiquity implied a desire to restore the ideals of beauty, freedom, and rationality identified with the Rome of a period perceived to have been supreme in its long history.

During the 1500s, both Catholic and Protestant scholars and polemicists – Cardinal Baronio and the Centuriators of Magdeburg, for example – continued a fierce debate over the same issue. Although they accepted the idea that the centuries following the fall of the Roman Empire were long periods of barbarism and ignorance, each group blamed the other for the decline. For the Catholics, the culprits were the Northern peoples, who would also be responsible for that other great misfortune, the Reformation, while for the Protestants, the cause of the fall was the corruption of the Holy See.

In the eighteenth-century Enlightenment, the term "medieval" was synonymous with all forms of superstition, fanaticism, and ignorance. In nineteenth-century Romanticism, on the contrary, there was a tendency to see in it faith, beauty, spontaneity, and the joy of living. In a sense, we are all children of Voltaire and Novalis when we continue to debate these questions, using these age-old arguments.

CONCEPTS AND PERIODIZATION

The purpose of the pages that follow is to provide a possible meaning for the term "medieval," starting not from a rigid chronology but rather from themes that help us to define, to the extent this is possible, the different ways of imagining and experiencing an epoch, the different conventional images that have emerged, and the persistence of both a discontinuity and occasionally a true break with the past.

17

A triple premise is necessary, however. In the first place, we need to remember that the "medieval" label applies solely to the Western world, comprising Europe and the Mediterranean, and can be applied to other geographical and historical contexts only in a metaphorical or figurative sense. Secondly, the term does not correspond to a unified concept but varies with the historiographic and ideological attitudes of the person using the term. Finally, it is not really possible to treat the entire Middle Ages in the same way – the common way of understanding it – since the period is very long, spanning as it does the fourth to eighth centuries as well as the fourteenth to fifteenth. (According to other less well-known interpretations, the period begins in the second to third century and concludes in the eighteenth). In this immense stretch of time (a thousand years more or less, according to the "classic" definition, and from seven to fifteen centuries, according to others, institutions, structures, living conditions, territorial configurations, ways of thinking about the world, etc., underwent profound changes throughout Europe. It is therefore very difficult (and also dangerous) to claim that something is "absolutely" medieval. Doing so runs the risk of generalizing certain concepts and problems that do not really belong to the Middle Ages as a whole but only to one phase or a specific aspect of its dynamic flow or to one way of interpreting it.

17. Piero della Francesca, *The Flagellation of Christ*, mid-fifteenth century, National Gallery of Marche, Urbino.

2

THE "SILENT COLLAPSE" OF THE WESTERN ROMAN EMPIRE

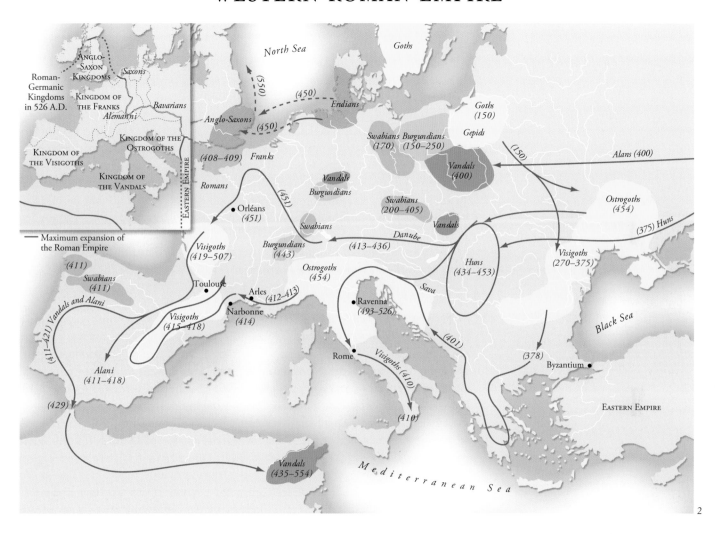

Roman-Germanic Kingdoms in 526 A.D.

Anglo-Saxon Kingdoms
Kingdom of the Franks
Alemanni
Bavarians
Kingdom of the Ostrogoths
Kingdom of the Visigoths
Kingdom of the Vandals
Eastern Empire
Saxons

— Maximum expansion of the Roman Empire

North Sea

Goths

Goths (150)
Gepids
(150)
Swabians (170)
Burgundians (150–250)
Vandals (400)
Erulians
(450)
Alans (400)
Ostrogoths (454)
Anglo-Saxons (450)
(550)
Franks (408–409)
Romans
Vandals
Burgundians
(451)
Swabians
Swabians (200–405)
Vandals
Danube
(413–436)
Huns (375)
Visigoths (270–375)
Visigoths (419–507)
Burgundians (443)
Orléans (451)
Ostrogoths (454)
Sava
Huns (434–453)
(378)
Byzantium
Black Sea
(411)
Swabians (411)
Toulouse
Arles (412–413)
Narbonne (414)
Visigoths (415–418)
Ravenna (493–526)
(401)
(411–421) Vandals and Alani
Alani (411–418)
Rome
Visigoths (410)
Eastern Empire
(429)
(410)
Vandals (435–554)
Mediterranean Sea

2

FROM THE NORTH AND THE EAST

The Latin word *barbarus*, derived from the Greek *barbaros*, was applied to foreigners and had a somewhat pejorative connotation in that, onomatopoetically, it appears to refer to the difficulty foreigners had in pronouncing the Greek (or Latin) language. Up to the second and third centuries, the "barbarians" par excellence for the Romans were the Persians and Scythians, who were considered to be fierce peoples devoted to obscure magic rituals. Caesar, however, had come into

1. Scenes depicting the war against the Dacians, detail of Trajan's Column, c.113, Trajan's Forum, Rome.

2. The migrations and settlements of the Germanic tribes in the fifth to eighth centuries.

3

3. The hammer, a symbol of the god Thor, relief from a stone carving.

4. The god Thor holding his hammer, which represents lightning, model for a tenth-century bronze statuette. National Museum, Copenhagen.

contact with other barbarians, the Germanic tribes and the Celts. He provides us with a picture of them intended to promote understanding and even compassion, as Tacitus had done in *Germania,* where he praised the Germanic peoples for their courage, simplicity, and rugged way of life and contrasted them with the Romans, who he felt had become morally corrupt.

In the second century A.D., other Germanic peoples appeared on the borders of the Roman Empire in hopes of infiltrating it. Their push into the empire intensified in the two centuries that followed. By the middle of the fourth century, the Germanic tribes were exerting great pressure on the *limes* (limit), the area of the Rhine and Danube Rivers. Pushed by a Ural-Altaic tribe, the Huns (identifiable as the Hsiung-Nu who, according to Chinese sources, had laid siege to the Great Wall about one century earlier) moved from the steppe in search of a space that the Roman Empire was no longer willing to defend, as did the groups known as the Alemanni, Swabians, Burgundians, Franks, Vandals, Ostrogoths, and Visigoths.

In large or small groups, the barbarians entered the territory of the Roman Empire, generally as auxiliaries of the army. In exchange for their services, they often obtained the right to settle in certain areas and work the land, thus transforming themselves from shepherds and nomadic or semi-nomadic hunters into farmers and contributing, at least in part, to resolving the crisis created by people abandoning their fields. However, we should not think of the Germanic world as a compact and homogenous whole. There must have been profound differences among the various tribes because of the influence exerted on them by other cultures, such as Greek, Latin, Slavic, Celtic, Ugro-Finnic, and Scythian-Sarmatic.

INVASIONS, INCURSIONS, AND MIGRATIONS

What were for a long time referred to as the "barbarian invasions," which German historians more correctly call *Volkerwanderungen* or migrations of peoples, are in reality vast movements carried out over long periods of time whose epicentre was located approximately in the steppes of Central Asia.

In 410, the Visigoths, led by Alaric, succeeded in occupying and sacking Rome, although the emperor of the Western Roman Empire, Honorius, remained secure and protected in Ravenna, the city that he had chosen as his capital in 402. The sack of Rome by Alaric was not in itself an overly dramatic event. There was of course violence, but the king of the Visigoths was a Christian and he paid homage to the tombs of the Apostles, thereby underscoring the nascent respect that the people who followed him had for the name and prestige of the *caput mundi* or "head of the world," as Rome was known. However, the episode inspired St Augustine to undertake his most ambitious work, *De civitate Dei* (The city of God), in which he reflects on the reasons why God had allowed such a terrible event as the profanation of the *Urbe* (city).

Having made peace with the empire, which they had no intention of fighting, much less overthrowing, the Visigoths were granted imperial permission to settle in southern Gaul and Spain. Meanwhile, other Germanic peoples migrated throughout the western part of the empire, establishing the ethnographic foundations of south-western Europe, including the Burgundians in what is today Burgundy, the Alemanni in the Middle Rhine Valley, the Vandals in southern Spain, from where they moved on to Africa, and the Angles and the Saxons in Britannia, which would later assume the name England.

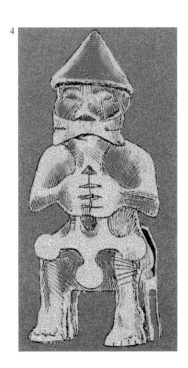

4

5

5. Funerary stele from the seventh century. The bas-relief shows Odin on horseback carrying a sword and lance.

6. Depiction of the Yggdrasil tree. Note the eagle among thick branches, the squirrel climbing down, the four deer eating the leaves, and the roots that grow in three directions.

In the mid-fifth century, after residing on the Balkan Peninsula for a short time and following an incursion into Gaul, the Huns also arrived in Italy. They were led by a figure traditionally known as Attila (c.400–453), a man of legendary ferocity, but also a man of exceptional military and political ability as well as culture. Having been in contact with the court in Constantinople for some time, he spoke Greek well and was the leader not only of the Huns but of a federation of Germanic, Nordic, and Slavic peoples. He marched on Rome and Emperor Valentinian III (419–455), whose sister Honoria he wanted to marry, was unable to stop him. The imperial general and "barbaric" tutor, the Illyrian Ezio (Flavius Aetius), who had had mercenary Huns under his command and knew them well, defeated Attila in 451 at Champs Catalauniques near Châlons-sur-Marne, but managed only to push him toward Italy. In 452, however, Attila inexplicably stopped at the Mincio River (Lombardy) while on his way to Rome and returned to the Roman province of Pannonia. He probably feared a counter-attack by the army of the Eastern Roman Empire but, according to tradition, Pope Leo I went out to meet him and persuaded him not to profane what, by then, had become the capital of Western Christendom.

6

While the pagan Attila had not dared to profane the city walls of Rome, such respect did not deter Gaiseric the Christian (who was, as were many Germanic peoples, of the Arian confession), king of the Vandals, from swooping down on the city and its ships in 455. The second "sack of Rome," which was more dramatic than the one inflicted by Alaric, was at least ostensibly caused by Gaiseric's outrage over the news that Emperor Valentinian III had been killed by usurper Petronius Maximus, a scheming official who had encouraged Valentinian to murder General Flavius Aetius with his own hands the year before.

THE WORLD OF THE GERMANIC "BARBARIANS"

Our knowledge of Germanic mythology and religion has several gaps due to the scarcity of sources: archeological finds, runes, and poems are often difficult to decipher, while accounts left by Latin and Greek chroniclers are hardly objective because the authors found it difficult to fully understand cultures that were so different from their own.

In general, we can say that the principal Germanic cults revolved around a group of deities and a few basic myths: the god Thor, whose attribute is a weapon (the hammer) associated with lightning, appears to represent a cult of the sun and the heavens. It is more difficult to understand the nature of the Odin/Wodin divinity with his shamanic features: he is in charge of magic (he can change himself into an animal, foretell the future, and compose dirges), magical inscriptions (runes), poetry, law, and war. Both Thor and Odin/Wodin are part of the pantheon of Aesir divinities, even though Odin/Wodin's complexity seems to endow him with chthonic characteristics: he is the leader of a hellish army of warriors who died in battle. The gods and goddesses associated with the cult of Earth-Mother and fertility belong to the pantheon of Vanir deities, such as Nerthus-Njordhr and Freyer-Freya, who dispense riches, peace, and the fecundity of the sea and the earth.

Writing in the first century, Tacitus claims (in *Germania* IX) that the Germanic peoples had neither a true priestly caste nor a set of sanctuaries or sacred places. In addition, he says that they did not attribute anthropomorphic features to their divinities, which is not entirely accurate, even if the most conspicuous feature of their religion was the apparent prevalence of the cult of "natural" elements. Trees and woods seem to have played an important role in the myths and rituals of the Germanic peoples. According to Tacitus, for example, during the time they had a settlement near the mouth of the Elba River, one of the tribes most familiar to us, the Lombards, belonged to a confederation of peoples who venerated the goddess Nerthus. The ritual celebrated in her honour took place on an island where a sacred grove grew. The goddess would descend from the heavens in a cart drawn by heifers and, as the cart proceeded from place to place, the faithful paid homage to the deity. At the end of the ceremony, all the items involved were washed in the purifying waters of a consecrated lake.

In the eleventh century, the chronicler Adam of Bremen speaks of a sacred grove. In the Scandinavian Peninsula, pagans who lived in the region of what is now Uppsala in modern-day Sweden sacrificed humans and animals, hanging them from the branches of the trees in a sacred grove. The ritual was probably associated with

7. Bust of Emperor Honorius (384–423).

7

8

the god Odin/Wodin, whose initiation into the power of the sacred runes occurs in accordance with the Hávamál, a sort of epic-magical incantation that is part of the *Eddas* (which were composed during the thirteenth century in Norse, the language of the Norwegian colonizers of Iceland, who had been converted to Christianity but whose work contains examples of the myths of the pagan era nonetheless). The initiation rite involves being suspended from a sacred tree, the Yggdrasil or "The Ash Tree of the World." This similarity between the initiation of Odin/Wodin and the crucifixion of Christ was used by missionaries who, from the eighth to the tenth century, converted the Germanic peoples in central-eastern and northern Europe to Christianity. (Those living in the southern and western regions of the continent had been converted between the fourth and sixth-seventh centuries.) One of the principal cosmological themes of the Germanic-Scandinavian world revolves around the sacred Yggdrasil tree, which other Germanic tribes knew as the Irminsul ("Mighty Pillar"). This is the Primordial Tree (ash or yew), which grows from the earth, nourished by the waters and stretching toward the sun or the top of the world. As the Axis of the World, the sacred tree maintains the stability of the cosmos and upholds

8. Raphael Sanzio, *Meeting of Pope Leo the Great and Attila*, fresco, 1513–14. Room of Heliodorus, Vatican Museums, Rome.

9

9. Coin with the image of Odoacer in profile.

10. Exterior view of the Mausoleum of Theodoric, Ravenna.

10

its order. In the Germanic tradition, cosmic order is destroyed at the end of time in the Ragnarok or final battle in which the Aestir gods are defeated and the cosmos is swallowed up by the wolf Fenrir. This analogy with the Christian Apocalypse was also used by the missionaries.

With regard to social structure, the nucleus of the Germanic peoples consisted of families united by kinship (*Sippe*). In general, property was not owned by individuals but administered collectively. Each group of *Sippen*, associated with a particular territory (*gau* or *pagus*), identified itself with a larger group that the Romans called *civitas* (citizenship) and which could be considered a "people." Each people had freemen, who had the right to bear arms and were called Arimans. During wartime, it was they (especially the Adelings or those of noble blood) who elected the king. Below the Arimans were the semi-free Aldi, and below them the slaves.

COEXISTENCE

In 476, another barbarian, who was also leader of a mercenary army in the Roman military at the time, the Erulian Odoacer, brought the Western Empire to an end by deposing and exiling its last Roman emperor, young Romulus Augustulus. Breaking with the custom of appointing puppet rulers, Odoacer sent the imperial insignia to Zeno (c.426–491), emperor of the Eastern Roman Empire, with the message that one emperor was sufficient for the whole empire. Zeno responded by conferring on Odoacer the title of *patricius* (nobleman), which allowed him to rule Italy as a public servant until 493, when he was defeated and killed by another barbarian king, the Ostrogoth Theodoric.

In a sense, the Goths had opened the way for later migrations. In the mid-fifth century, they were the subjects of the Huns and settled in the Pannonia Valley (roughly today's Hungary). They then became *foederati* (allied states) of the Eastern Empire and, as such, settled in Macedonia. The ruler of Constantinople, however, preferred not to have them on his borders and so he encouraged them to head toward Italy, conferring on their king, Theodoric (c.454–526), the title of *patricius*.

From his residence in the capital city of Ravenna, Theodoric, after having defeated and killed Odoacer, instituted a policy that was original in many respects in that it aimed at bringing about the peaceful coexistence of Goths and Romans, based on a separation of responsibilities; he was also careful to avoid actions that might provoke aggression and friction. In institutional terms, Theodoric was the only Goth who, as *patricius*, could hold Roman citizenship. Otherwise Goths and Romans coexisted within distinct legal systems. As *foederati* of the empire, the Goths concerned themselves only with the administration of military matters and the Romans only with civil matters. The fact that the Goths were Arians, while the "Latins" (as they were increasing called because of their official language) practised Christianity, following the Council of Nicaea, encouraged the development of parallel lives in the respective communities, each with its own places of worship, clergy, and liturgy.

Theodoric augmented this wise and balanced internal policy with extremely dynamic relationships with the other Roman-Barbaric kingdoms. Through a series of political marriages, he allied himself with the Visigoths of Spain, the Franks of Gaul, and the Burgundians. His actions gradually led to the creation of a Germanic

11

11. Interior of
Sant'Apollinare Nuovo,
Ravenna.

federation of western tribes, but he did not abandon the venerable Roman traditions, which fascinated him, and continued to behave as a servant and ally of Rome. He reformed the laws, adorned his capital, Ravenna, with sumptuous monuments, and entrusted his chancellery to a series of brilliant Roman intellectuals, such as Cassiodorus, Boethius, and Simmachus. Theodoric's policy, however, ultimately failed because of plots hatched by the imperial rulers of Rome, who in the 520s began to eye the western part of the empire with renewed interest and worked to sow discord among the Goths and the Latins, and because of intransigence on the part of many Goth leaders who preferred to reduce the Latins to slavery rather than respect their property and customs. After Theodoric's death in 526, wars of dynastic succession took place but there was no one capable of resisting re-conquest of the west by the eastern emperors. At the end of the long series of conflicts between the Eastern Roman Empire and the Ostrogoth Kingdom of Italy known as the Gothic War (535–53), which stands as one of the most tragic events in the history of the peninsula, Italy fell under the control of Constantinople, although for most of the territory this lasted for only a short period, as the Lombards began their conquest of the peninsula in 568.

1

3

CHRISTIANIZATION OF EUROPE

FIRST STEPS

Communities of believers in Christ (the *ekklesiai* or "churches") formed freely in various places as conversions increased in numbers. Initially, their structure was rather simple: the faithful gathered around *presbyteroi* (Greek, literal meaning "elders"), who assumed responsibility for teaching the Sacred Scriptures, in particular the Gospels, and for the commemorative celebration of the "holy supper" in memory of the meal Christ shared with his Apostles. The Latin translation of the Bible, which was essential to the spread of the new faith, was begun several times. We have fragments of an "African" version from the second century and of an "Italic" version from the second-third century. Finally, St Jerome (347–c.420) visited the Holy Land expressly for this purpose and between 385 and 405 produced a translation known as the *Vulgate*, based on the original Hebrew Old Testament and the Greek New Testament.

The first archeologically confirmed examples of *domus ecclesiae* (house churches), that is, private homes adapted for congregation and worship, date from the second-third century. From the early fourth century, as attested by Eusebius of Caesarea (c.265–c.339), the type of building called "basilica" began to be adapted for Christian worship.

As early as the third century, as Christian churches established themselves and spread, disputes began to arise not only with the Jewish communities but also with pagan thinkers, especially Neoplatonists. Despite the controversies, the new faith absorbed many philosophical and ethical elements from other beliefs, especially Neoplatonism and Stoicism. There is a fairly large body of pagan anti-Christian literature (Porphyry, Celsus, Julian the Apostate) and Christian anti-pagan literature, referred to as "apologetic" (principal apologists include Origen, Clement of Alexandria, Marcus Minucius Felix, Lactantius, and St Jerome). Both, however, show that there was constant dialogue and identification of shared affinities. The philosopher Justin Martyr, martyred in 165, had begun a rigorous discussion on the possibility of conciliation between Christianity and Neoplatonism. Origen and

1. View of the left aisle looking east, Church of Santa Sabina, Rome.

2. Image of a basilica bearing the inscription ECCLESIA MATER or "Mother Church," from a fifth-century mosaic in a Christian tomb. Tabarka, Tunisia.

3. Antonello da Messina, *The Penitence of St Jerome*. National Museum of Magna Grecia, Reggio, Calabria.

4. Eusebius of Caesarea, detail of a twelfth-century miniature in a Lives of the Saints. Public Library, Troyes.

5

5. Emperor Constantine and his mother, Helena, eleventh-century mosaic. Monastery of Hosios Loukas. Phocis, Greece.

later Jerome developed an original system of thought according to which it was appropriate to accept the pagan cultural heritage to enrich the Christian world, just as Exodus describes how the Jews in the time of Moses, fleeing the Egypt of the pharaohs, took possession of its treasure by divine will. In the fifth century, these ideas opened the way for Cassiodorus and Augustine, staunch defenders of the Greek and Latin cultures.

HERESIES

In 313 the Emperor Constantine put an end to the persecution of Christians and in the decades that followed it appears that he was determined to support the new faith, although the meaning of his own conversion remains a topic of debate. In 380, the Edict of Thessalonica affirmed the adoption of Christianity as the state religion. In the edict, Emperor Theodosius declares: "I want all those who are born as our subjects to adhere to the religion that the apostle Peter taught to the Romans." What had been the only cult systematically persecuted by the Roman state now became the only cult of worship allowed and, given its monotheistic nature, the state could not allow other religions to survive. It was therefore necessary to organize the Church as a universal entity, although divided into a number of diocesan churches, as well as to establish the core tenets of the faith and the truths held to be "revealed" (the objects of Revelation) and therefore beyond discussion, accepted on faith (the dogma). Dissent about these statements of faith was now declared to be "heresy" – the support of opinions believed to undermine Christian unity and peace and therefore a grave error. In its turn, the state declared heresy to be a crime, which is logical since the Church was considered to be an organ of the state.

The first and principal heresies were "Christological"; in other words, they pertained to the person and nature of Christ, His humanity, and His relationship with divinity. But others, deeper and more general, were related to the fact that from the first century on the original Christian dogmas were challenged by influences and problems created by contact with Hellenistic philosophy as well as with different traditions (Syrian, Indo-Persian, and Egyptian).

The foundation of this complex ferment of ideas was Gnosis (*gnosis* is Greek for "knowledge"). Gnostics taught that knowledge acquired through initiation was a necessary condition for salvation; therefore they believed that any faith that supported an independent religious practice that ignored this knowledge was baseless. Nonetheless, elements of mysticism and gnostic philosophy spread into Christian communities, as is apparent in the forty-four works from second-century Egypt preserved in papyrus manuscripts discovered in 1946 in the Nag Hammadi oasis in Upper Egypt.

Other sets of religious beliefs that the Christian churches and council decrees declared to be "heresies" were found in the writings of thinkers who came to be known as the "Church Fathers," such as the Modalism of Sebelius (third century), who contended that the components of the divine Trinity are not "persons" but transitory modes of being in which the divine expresses itself, and Docetism, which denied the material reality of the suffering and death of Jesus on the cross and held that these were merely appearances (its name derives from the Greek *dokein* or "to seem").

In the fourth century, the most important heretical doctrine was preached by the presbyter Arius of Alexandria and called "Arianism." According to Arius, Christ was the beloved Son of God and similar to Him, but not identical. Thus, he denied the doctrine of the divinity of Christ and God's sacrifice of Himself for humanity. Arius's

doctrine was discussed and repudiated at the Council of Nicaea and by decree the Nicene Symbol (the text of which later became that of a fundamental Christian prayer, the Nicene Creed) affirmed the doctrine of the consubstantiation of the Father and the Son. While remaining three distinct "persons" (that is, three different aspects of the same substance), the Father, Son, and Holy Spirit were not three different Gods: they were all God and, as such, parts of a single substance. With this, the dogma of the Trinity was established.

As well as Arianism, other heresies proposed by different theologians were multiplying. Among these was one formulated by Nestorius (381–451), the patriarch of

6. A sixteenth-century icon depicting the first Council of Nicaea and the condemnation of Arius. Monastery of St Catherine, Mount Sinai.

7. St Athanasius of Alexandria, in a fifteenth-century icon originating in Novgorod; he strenuously defended the principles endorsed by the Council of Nicaea even before Constantine, who was more interested in religious peace.

8. Baptism of Jesus, and Apostles, fourth-century cupola mosaic in the Arian Baptistery, Ravenna.

9. Map illustrating the Roman Empire and the spread of Arianism at the end of the fourth century.

10

8

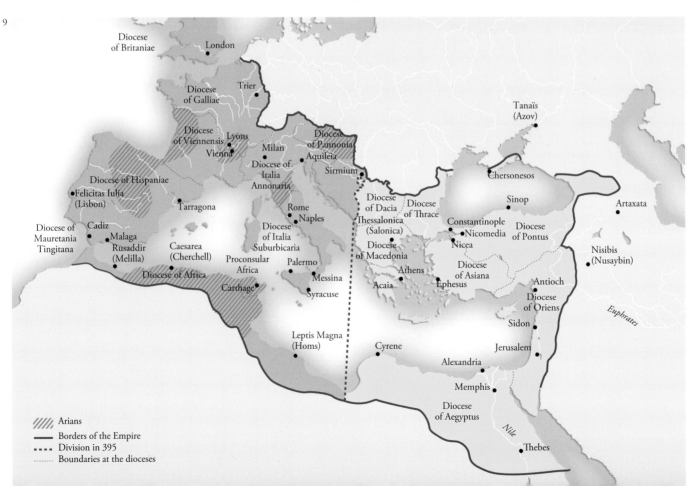

9

///// Arians
——— Borders of the Empire
- - - Division in 395
········ Boundaries at the dioceses

10. Icon from about the sixth century in Santa Maria in Trastevere, Rome. The Virgin, wearing royal Byzantine drapery, is depicted as *Theotokos*, the Mother of God.

11. Map showing the spread and variety of eastern churches.

12. Stone funerary cross from the Noraduz cemetery, Armenia.

Constantinople from 427 to 431, who held that there was a simultaneous presence of two distinct persons in Christ, one divine and the other human. It was especially important in the authoritative theological school in Antioch. The other was Monophysitism, taught by the Greek monk and theologian Eutychus (c.378–after 454), which, rigorously opposed to Nestorianism, denied Christ any human nature or personhood, claiming that his only nature was divine and his human nature was only an appearance.

The heads of the Church convened a series of councils as part of their attempt to defeat the various heresies. They issued pronouncements against the Arian heresy at the Council of Nicaea in 325, against Nestorianism at the Council of Ephesus in 431, from which the cult of the Virgin Mary as *Theotokos* or "Mother of God" originated, and against Monophysitism at the Council of Chalcedon in 451. However, decrees issued by the councils were certainly not sufficient to eliminate the heresies. The two centuries during which they spread were also those in which the separation of the Western and Eastern parts of the Roman Empire occurred. Furthermore, in those same centuries, new peoples were converted to Christianity by missionaries who sometimes adhered to one set of beliefs and at other times to a different set. As a result some Germanic tribes converted to Arianism, while Monophysitism took root in Syria, Egypt, and Ethiopia, and Nestorianism spread throughout the Middle East, from Arabia, Mesopotamia, and Persia to India and China.

12

11

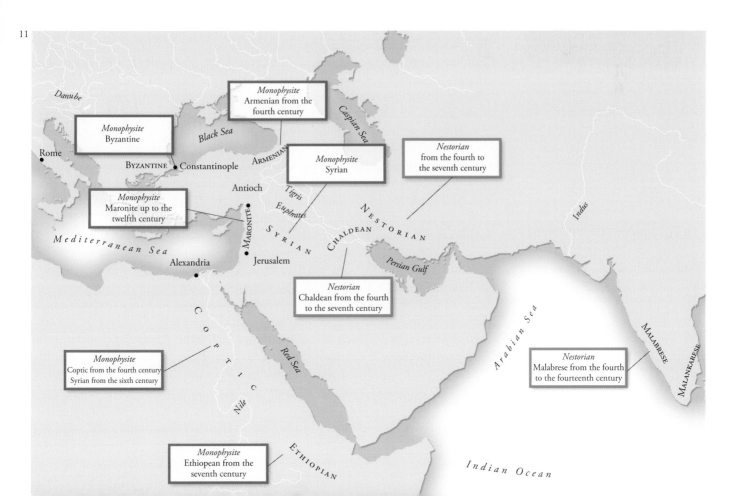

13

14

13. Part of an ivory diptych, with the figure of St Gregory the Great. Museum and Treasury of Monza Cathedral.

14. Christ in the centre of a fourth-century floor mosaic, from the Hinton St Mary villa. British Museum, London.

15. Ruins of a monastery on the island of Skelling, near the southern coast of Ireland, the area where St Patrick and his fellow missionaries began the work of Christianization in the fifth century.

ROME AND THE MISSIONS

In the west, the bishop of Rome promoted the spread of Christianity among the barbarian peoples; the conversion of the Franks to Christianity in the fifth to sixth century in accordance with Roman customs was particularly important. However, the activity of missionaries who dedicated themselves to the Christianization of Europe between the sixth and eighth centuries was not limited to a single centre. Monasteries and bishoprics also contributed to this work and, starting at the end of the eighth century, so did some dynastic rulers. In 596, Pope Gregory the Great sent Augustine, accompanied by forty monks from his own monastery, to England, which had been invaded by Angles, Saxons, Frisians, and Jutes. When they arrived on the island, Augustine asked for support from Ethelbert, king of Kent, whose wife was already a Christian. The ruler himself did not convert, but he allowed the monks to settle in Doruvernis, today the city of Canterbury. From there, conversion missions spread throughout the region. Soon after establishing a settlement in Canterbury, Augustine, who had been made a bishop, founded the first church.

Augustine subsequently brought Christianity to the whole of Anglia. He was supported in this activity by Pope Gregory, who wrote to King Ethelbert asking him to destroy pagan temples and idols, which were still venerated by his subjects. However, this did not come about until 640, when another king of Kent, the Christian Earconbert, ordered his people to reject paganism and to destroy the images and temples of their ancestral faith. In the second half of the seventh century, despite the occasional recurrence of paganism, the Christianization of the Angles and

16. Image of St Columbanus from a thirteenth-century manuscript. Public Library, Douai, France.

17. St Patrick's cross, Kells.

16

17

Saxons made great strides. Canterbury remained the most important religious centre in the land, but several dioceses were established, the most important being those of London and Eboracum (York). It was in Eboracum in the seventh century that another great evangelist, Bishop Paulinus, came to prominence. Paulinus is described by the venerable historian Bede as having been especially zealous in destroying the material vestiges of paganism, as well as in building churches.

In what was almost a competition with the missionaries sent out by Rome, Irish monks, who had developed their own autonomous Church, headed for other lands to proselytize among the peoples living there. The Caledonia of the Celts (who lived in the area that corresponds roughly to modern-day Scotland) had remained immune to the influence of the Roman Empire. Their deeply rooted traditions made them hostile to the influence of Christianity as well. A few of the disciples of the famous Irish monk Columbanus dedicated themselves to the conversion of the Celts to Christianity, constructing their monastery on the island of Iona, which they had received in a grant from the king. Moving beyond Scotland, Irish monasticism also spread toward the continent. The most notable of the many missionaries who played a role in this process were Columbanus himself and his confrere Gall. Together they journeyed south between the sixth and seventh centuries and then separated, each continuing the work of proselytization on his own. Both distinguished themselves by establishing important monasteries, such as those at Bobbio, Luxeuil, and St Gall, which were destined to become centres of spiritual and cultural reform.

It was from England that the Christian triumph over the Germanic tribes in the northern and eastern portions of the kingdom of the Franks began. With the backing

Map 18 — Christianity in the British Isles (labels):

Orkney Islands

Shetland Islands

Atlantic Ocean

Abercorn
Glasgow
Lindisfarne
Scotland
North Sea
Withorn
Hexham
Clogher
Armagh
Isle of Man
Ripon
York
Ardagh
Trim
Kildare
Glendalough
St Asaph
Bangor
Elmham
Lichfield
Worcester
Leicester
Hereford
Dunwich
Emly
Ferns
Sletty
Dorchester
Barking
St Davids
Thames
Rochester
Sherborne
Winchester
Canterbury
Selsey
Bodmin
English Channel

- ✝ Celtic bishopric
- • Celtic monastery
- ✝ Anglo-Saxon bishopric
- • Anglo-Saxon monastery

18

20

18. Christianity in the British Isles
up to the ninth century.

19. Map showing the travels and institutions founded
by Sts Columbanus, Willibrord, and Boniface.

19

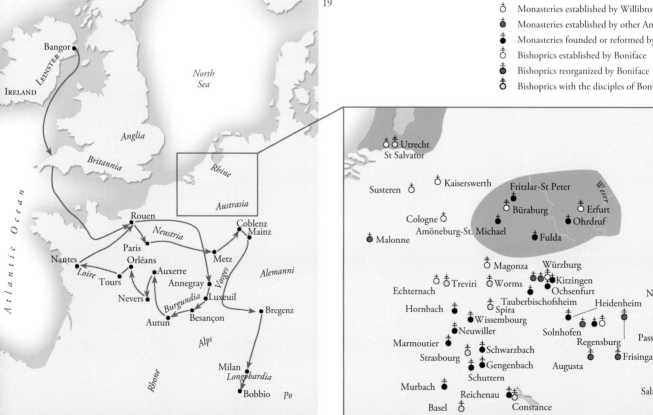

Map 19 (labels):

Bangor
LEINSTER
IRELAND
North Sea
Anglia
Britannia
Rhine
Atlantic Ocean
Austrasia
Rouen
Coblenz
Mainz
Neustria
Paris
Metz
Nantes
Orléans
Auxerre
Alemanni
Loire
Tours
Annegray
Vosges
Nevers
Luxeuil
Burgundia
Bregenz
Autun
Besançon
Alps
Milan
Longobardia
Rhone
Bobbio
Po

Inset (labels):

Utrecht
St Salvator
Susteren
Kaiserswerth
Fritzlar-St Peter
Weser
Cologne
Büraburg
Erfurt
Malonne
Amöneburg-St. Michael
Ohrdruf
Fulda
Magonza
Würzburg
Treviri
Worms
Kitzingen
Echternach
Ochsenfurt
Hornbach
Spira
Tauberbischofsheim
Heidenheim
Niederaltaich
Neuwiller
Wissembourg
Solnhofen
Passau
Marmoutier
Regensburg
Strasbourg
Schwarzbach
Frisinga
Murbach
Gengenbach
Augusta
Schuttern
Basel
Reichenau
Salzburg
Constance

of the majordomo (mayor), Pippin of Herstal, the Northumbrian monk Willibrord reached Frisia in 690 and became the first archbishop of Utrecht. From there, he directed his missionary work toward Flanders and northern Germany. At the same time, a noble Saxon from Wessex, Wynfrith, who was born around 675, felt himself swept up by a vocation to proselytize among his brothers on the continent who were still pagans, namely, the Saxons of Germany. In 719, his name was changed by Pope Gregory II and he became known as Boniface.

As he had strong ties with Willibrord, in 723–25, Boniface went to Thuringia, where he converted many pagans, eventually summoning other monks from England. Shuttling between these lands and Rome, he founded the dioceses of Passau, Ratisbon, Freising, and Strasburg in the southern regions of the Germanic lands, and in 740 he held the first synod of the German Church. Having established the faith in the southern part of the Germanic kingdom, Boniface returned to Hesse and Thuringia where, in 744, he founded the famous Benedictine abbey in Fulda, which

20. Monks traveling on a boat, detail from a fourteenth-century illustration for a moral poem. Royal Library, Brussels.

21. Interior of the Carolingian church of St Michael, Fulda, the abbey founded by St Boniface in 744.

22. Funerary statue of St Boniface Mainz, Cathedral.

23. Detail of a Romanesque bishop's crosier from the convent of Boscherville, Normandy, in which we see the Christian adoption of Celtic and pre-Christian motifs and symbols.

24. Königswinter-Niederdollendorf stele, near Bonn, seventh century. It depicts a corpse defending itself with a large dagger against a serpent with two heads, one at each end of its body, symbolizing the underworld.

was destined to become a true centre of German Christian culture. Upon his return to Frisia, he was martyred in 754 along with a group of his followers.

CONVERSION OF THE GERMANIC PEOPLES TO CHRISTIANITY

It is difficult to say with any certainty to what type of "Christianity" the people of the High Middle Ages were converted. The methods of religious instruction were cursory and may have emphasized ceremonies and the sacraments at the expense of doctrinal education. For example, it was difficult to convert the proud Germanic peoples, for whom war was a holy experience, to the truth of a loving and peaceful God. Thus in the Europe of the Early Middle Ages, there remained "pockets" of pagans who were only superficially Christians, using the new religion to clothe their ancient customs and rituals. The Church tolerated this situation, preferring to deal with it through the instrument of confession. Several manuals used by confessors, called *Poenitentialia*, still exist and are important sources of anthropological information about the Christianity of the peoples of the forests and steppes, providing access to a true "cultural folklore."

From the twelfth century on, literature records traces of this lore. Germanic mythology, for instance, emphasized the "magic" performed by the gods and the relationship between that magic and the kingdom of the dead. Certain traditions – handed down to us through the mediation of the Latin people or by Scandinavian mythology, which, in its turn, was influenced by Christianity – seem to be related to the cult of the dead and their relationship with some deities. These are known in medieval as well as modern Europe, especially in terms of folklore. For instance, the tradition of the *wuttende Heer* or the army of dead heroes selected by the Valkyries (the "choosers of the slain") to live with Odin in the afterlife (Valhalla, which can be translated as "the hall of combat") survives in demonized form in the *wilde jagd* or "wild hunts" (or "fantastic hunts") that appear in numerous medieval sources. Tacitus spoke of the *feralis exercitus* (deadly army), that is, the ghosts of ancestors who, at night, magically came to help Germanic warriors in distress. The restless souls that wander at the crossroads and among houses have either a threatening or a benevolent (the "dead who bring gifts," are also found in Nordic tradition) attitude toward the living.

SPREAD OF CHRISTIANITY INTO THE COUNTRYSIDE

It was not only the Christianization of the Germanic tribes, however, that proved to be difficult. In Romanized areas, away from the cities and great network of roads, there were fields and mountainous zones where innovation arrived slowly, and where the memory of pre-Christian ancient cults and traditions persisted. The religious beliefs of the frontier regions were rooted in the physical places (mountains, forests, springs, rivers, borders, etc.) and traditional cycles (birth, death, marriage, the harvest) that brought people into close contact with one another and on which they often depended. This explains their conservatism and tendency toward syncretism, in which the new was accepted without the old necessarily being discarded. It was difficult for the promoters and ministers of the new faith to make clear that the God of the Christians demanded exclusive worship, which meant abandoning the old deities and traditions that communities had followed previously.

The bishops' councils held during the fourth to fifth century consistently stress the need to eradicate pagan customs. They mention the veneration of trees, springs, and rocks, which were probably consecrated to pagan gods. Ethnic groups were condemned if they continued to make sacrifices to the gods even after being baptized. Between the fifth and the sixth centuries, the sermons of Bishop Caesarius of Arles provide a good picture of the unorthodox beliefs and rituals that were commonly practised. For instance, Caesarius describes magical devices used by women, instead of prayer, in order to achieve conception. "Herbs" were used – which suggests the popularity of natural medicine – together with "symbols" or "ligatures," which were probably amulets or talismans of some sort.

In other homilies, Caesarius speaks of baptized individuals who negate the value of the received sacrament by continuing to perform pagan rituals, such as making votive offerings to trees, springs, and ancient sanctuaries, as well as continuing the practice of ritual banquets. This suggests that the bishop of Arles had to deal not only with the persistence of pagan customs but also with the refusal, or at least reluctance, of peoples accustomed to a syncretic religion to accept a strictly monotheistic religion like Christianity. This impression is confirmed, though indirectly, by another sermon against wild celebrations on the occasion of the January Calends, in which Caesarius lists the deities of classical paganism (Mars, Mercury, Jupiter, Venus, Saturn), emphasizing their lascivious, impious, and sacrilegious nature.

25. Stone painting preserved in the Historical Museum, Stockholm, originating in Gotland, c.700. In the scene Sleipnir, Odin's horse with eight hooves, rides toward Valhalla, where a Valkyrie awaits.

26. Popular masked feast from an illustration of the *Roman de Fauvel* (Romance of Fauvel), an allegorical poem written by Gervais du Bus between 1310 and 1314. The satire is directed in part at political figures, but especially at certain prelates as well as the Dominican and Franciscan orders. MS. 146, fol. 34. National Library of France, Paris.

27. The benefits of the turnip according to the *Remedium Sanitatis* (Health remedies); it stimulates fertility and is more effective if it is black and wrinkled.

27

26

1

2

3

4

A WORLD TO BE REORGANIZED (EIGHTH TO TENTH CENTURIES)

ORATORES, BELLATORES, LABORATORES:
THE FICTIONAL AUTOBIOGRAPHY OF MEDIEVAL SOCIETY

What did the social structure look like in the centuries around the first millennium? What image of itself did that society have? "In this vale of tears, some pray, others fight, and still others work. The three groups are interconnected and cannot stand alone, so that the function of one group relies on the works of the other two, and in turn, all three ensure mutual assistance." With these words, written around 1030 in a poem addressed to King Robert the Pious, Adalberon, bishop of Laon, gives us a portrait of European society around the year 1000. This portrait is based on the concept of three primary social functions, which represent the earthly order that God willed and, at the same time, are the elements that ensure harmony in society: *oratores, bellatores*, and *laboratores*. The first group of men prayed so that the stability of the Christian world would be maintained, the second fought so that society could enjoy security, and the third supported the other two "orders" with its work. (The Latin term *labor* referred essentially to farm work or agriculture.)

This division of responsibilities and duties corresponded to a precise division of labour and wealth. In a society in which each individual was responsible for him/herself in an economy of subsistence in which agriculture was the most important element, it was natural for labour to be conceptualized in terms of servitude. In a society where money did not circulate, it was logical for the Church to consider any type of profit not derived directly from the sweat of one's brow as suspicious and damnable because it was the product of usury, and to disapprove of loans (banned as forms of as "usury") and commercial transactions.

In the second half of the 1900s, a great philologist and "historian of mythology," Georges Dumézil, produced a general theory of Indo-European societies (the societies that emerged from the great migrations of peoples in the second millennium B.C. from the Eurasian steppes into the Caucasus, Anatolia, Persia, and the Indus basin, which was the definition of "Indo-European" at the time) in which he identified the triple-function structure as a common feature. Because the *oratores* often represent the order entrusted with the task of maintaining and writing down the mythic memories of the peoples, the praying function appears to be the most important and most sacred, since on an ideal scale of values it comes closest to the majesty of the heavens, with which it mediates on behalf of the other two orders. This structure is the basis of an ancient rivalry, or at least tension, between the priest function and the warrior function, which is evident, for example, in the conflict between the *sacerdotum* (priesthood) and the *imperium* (empire) during the time of Pope Gregory VII and Emperor Henry IV. The dispute between the two most important elite social

1. Detail of a fierce battle in a fifteenth-century illustration in Vincent de Beauvais's *Speculum Historiale* (Mirror of history), from the thirteenth century. Conde Museum, Chantilly.

2. Mother Church, detail of the *Mater Ecclesia* (Exultet hymn) from the mid-thirteenth century preserved in the Diocesan Museum, Salerno.

3. Farm work, depicted in an eleventh-century miniature preserved in the Abbey of Monte Cassino.

4. *Death of the Usurer*, illustration in a volume originating in Heidelberg. Private collection.

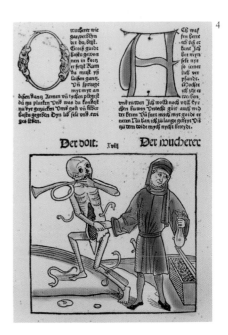

4

5. The abbot of Cluny asks that the custom of hospitality be respected even during the harsh dispute between the factions loyal to the pope and to Emperor Henry IV, miniature from *I principi di Canossa* (Vita di Matilda). Vatican Apostolic Library, Rome.

6. Otto II hands the bishop's crosier to St Albert, an example of lay investiture of an ecclesiastical office, detail of the bronze portal from the twelfth century. Gniezno Cathedral, Poland.

classes, that of the priests and the warriors, constitutes a recurring theme in the history of Europe, from ancient, to medieval, to modern times, which comes to an end in the late 1700s, when the French Revolution brings about the abolition of the three "estates," the direct descendants of the original three functions.

THE MANORIAL ECONOMY

The sixth to ninth centuries, and in general the so-called Early Middle Ages, can be described as a "manorial economy," a transition phase from the Roman villa economy to the seigneurial system of the feudal age. The manorial model most often mentioned by historians is the one established in the region between the Loire and the Seine Rivers, i.e., the kingdom of the Franks. But this model is not necessarily more instructive than others – it is only better documented. In reality, these property relationships and manorial modes of production, with a few variants, took root in much of western Europe during the early medieval period.

The villa or *curtis* (manorial court) was a large housing and production centre; it consisted of dairy farm, crop farm, workshop, and a residential area for the *dominus* (lord) and his servants, that is, those who worked the land and who, in order to maintain their theoretically free status, placed themselves under the lord's protection in times when there was no public authority. The manor was a series of structures that functioned as dwellings, stables, storehouses, etc., and a variety of parcels of land; the size of the manor ranged from a few dozen to tens of thousands of hectares. The lord's residence was surrounded by the most important buildings: hunting stables, mills, presses, haylofts, wells, and a church. The manorial court contained all the resources necessary to produce the goods needed for subsistence: fabrics, utensils, crockery, tools, and armaments. Certain areas were designated for the preparation of food and there were stocks of supplies for the transformation of raw materials into finished products. In times of danger along the highways, decline in commercial trade, or scarcity of money, which during this period was often counterfeit and almost non-existent, manorialism became a closed and autocratic system.

With regard to the administration of the land, the *curtis* was divided into a *pars dominica*, (owner's portion) administered by the lord directly, and a *pars massarica* (peasant's portion) administered by the free workers or serfs and divided into demesnes – productive units of varying sizes (according to the type of crop grown, the altitude of the property, the condition of the soils, the latitude, etc.) that were sufficient to provide subsistence for a family of peasants. The workers gave the lord a portion of their produce and were also obliged to provide free labour on the *pars dominica*. This division of property was already practised by the Romans, although in their day the practice was used during periods of recession caused by a crisis in the supply of slave labour, the abandonment of the cities, and their resulting decline as economic and manufacturing centres, a demographic crisis that necessitated the "valorization" of the slaves through the offer of conditions for self-sufficiency (benefices).

7. Image of the prosperous estate of *Dominus Iulius*, fourth-century mosaic. Bardo National Museum, Tunis.

8

8. The month of March, showing well-organized fields and peasants at work in the shadow of the imposing ducal castle, miniature from *Les Très Riches Heures du Duc de Berry*, 1413–16. Conde Museum, Chantilly.

LORDS AND VASSALS

A variably sized group of friends, subjects, and bodyguards provided protection for the *dominus*. He was the *senior* (lord) – a term used by the bands of warriors, which would later develop into the equivalent of *dominus*. The French "seigneur" and the Italian "signore" are derived from this noun. These acolytes were his *antrustiones* or *fideles* (trust). Historical sources use different names to refer to them, but the most common is *vassi*, derived from a Celtic word that means roughly "dependents." The *vassi* swore fealty to the *senior* and in return received *beneficia* or benefits in the form of valuable objects, arms, and lands to cultivate (as noted, money was almost never used at the time). It is not easy to say which of the two elements in this relationship came first: the need on the part of a person who, finding himself in the socially subordinate position of relying on the protection of someone else, swears loyalty to him and offers his services as a warrior, or the need on the part of the lord to compensate his bodyguards. The "vassalage" institutions, based on a relationship of personal loyalty (understood to be mutual) and on the use of goods – increasingly land – belonging to the lord, became a fundamental feature of the Early Middle Ages and an integral part of the so-called feudal system.

Speaking generally, there are three basic elements in the "feudal" or "vassal-benefice" system, First, there is a real element, namely, *honor* or *beneficium*, which is the tangible object (lands, houses, and various remunerative offices) provided by the *dominus* or *senior* (lord, seigneur, or "elder," the leader of a *comitas* of knights) to the *vassus*. Then there is the personal element, the "vassalage," which is the personal loyalty sworn in a commendation ceremony, the *homagium*, by means of which the *vassus* proclaims himself *homo* or *fidelis* of his *dominus* or *senior*; and, last, there is the legal element, which is immunity, the landowner leaving the vassal undisturbed in possession of the fief. (In relationships among high-ranking aristocrats, immunity also involved concession of the *districtus* or "jurisdiction," the right to wield judicial power and to enjoy the benefits deriving from that exercise.)

The Medieval Latin term "feudum" (fief) derives from the Franconian word "feh" (livestock) and "od" (property), which represented conspicuous wealth in the world of nomads. Following the great migrations of the third to sixth centuries, after which the Germanic tribes became sedentary, the same term became more or less synonymous with the concept of "good," "possession," and "wealth." Historians tend to agree that the feudal system is based on goods (animals, arms, valuable objects) that the Germanic princes of the age of the barbarians offered to their warriors, who were members of what Tacitus calls *comitatus*. With the transition from a nomadic to a sedentary way of life, the lords began to give their followers – from whom they expected service as warriors – parcels of land that were either uncultivated (useful for hunting or raising animals) or cultivated. The beneficiary became the holder of these lands but not their owner: the lord granted him the right to hold and use the land, but not to own it outright. This meant that, originally, the fief could not be sold or alienated in any way (not even given as a gift) and it could not be left to descendants as inheritance. Of course, the fief was not always in the form of land; sometimes it involved money, a sort of salary. "Classic" feudalism, however, is characterized by the subdivision of lands – which at first often involved the public concessions of the Carolingian age, in other words, the marches (frontiers) and counties – into smaller or larger feudal seigneuries.

The personal element in the feudal system is called vassalage. One could be the vassal of a sovereign, an important lord, a member of the petty nobility, or, rarely,

9. The commendation ceremony described in a fourteenth-century codex. University Library of Heidelberg.

10. Edward of Woodstock, the *Black Prince*, pays homage to Edward III for receiving the Duchy of Aquitaine, detail of a miniature. British Library, London.

a small landowner. The vassalage relationship was established privately between two individuals, one of whom (the vassal) declared himself *homo* of the other. This contract was formalized in a ceremony called "homage," during which the vassal placed his folded hands (from which the Western Christian prayer gesture originates) in those of the lord and swore fealty to him. In exchange, the lord offered the vassal his protection and, in some cases, provided him with a fief through the ceremony of "investiture," during which the good offered as a fief was symbolized by an object (a clump of earth, a fistful of straw, or a pennant in cases where the fief was associated with a jurisdictional right).

11. The labours of the ancestors, detail of a bas-relief to the right of the San Zeno Cathedral portal in Verona.

12. Farm work, miniature in the *Speculum Virginum* (Mirror of virgins), 1190–1200. Dombibliothek, Trier.

Vassalage clearly met the widespread need for protection on the part of private citizens in times when public authority was absent. Originally, it did not necessarily involve the acquisition of a fief. One became someone's vassal simply to be protected. However, the custom of retaining one's vassals and asking for their services, which assumed a certain economic base, soon led to the practice of homage or investiture becoming inseparable from vassalage.

The strictly legal element of the feudal system consisted in immunity and, in the larger fiefs, the concession of a jurisdictional right. Immunity meant that the holders of the fief were exempt from the control of public authorities within the borders of the lord's property. In addition, the most important lords also received proxy jurisdictional right, which was the right to administer public justice and to enjoy part of the economic proceeds from that activity (in those days the penalties could be either corporeal or monetary).

THE REORGANIZATION OF AGRICULTURE

In the eighth century, coinciding with the end of waves of plague, the economy began to improve, a trend that would continue until the early part of the fourteenth century. Economic progress seems, however, to have been due less to an extension of the trade network than to improvements in the primary sector, agriculture. The introduction of the practice called "triennial crop rotation," was particularly important. In the previous system, used by the Romans, one half of the land was cultivated while the other half was left fallow to allow the land to recover. Now arable land began to be divided into three zones, allowing annual plantings of winter cereal crops (such as wheat) and summer cereal crops (such as oats), while one-third of the arable land remained fallow, providing an annual harvest from two-thirds of the land as opposed to just half.

Other improvements in agricultural technology include the widespread introduction of the water mill, the heavy plough with mouldboard – which permitted the farmer to plough the field more deeply than he could using the older Roman plough, which remained in use in the Mediterranean territories – as well as the shoulder harness for draught animals, which allowed the animals to use their power more effectively than was possible with the old collar, which choked them. Reclamation and deforestation projects were promoted in order to produce more arable land. At the same time, many uncultivated areas, which were increasingly being reduced, were privatized by the lords. It must be emphasized that the general improvement in the economy did not automatically create advantages for workers in the agricultural sector, who had fewer opportunities to use products resulting from their activities on uncultivated terrain (the products of hunting, fishing, and gathering) and were forced to adopt a more monotonous diet.

Technological progress was accompanied and perhaps assisted by an improved climate, which is remarked on in the early part of the tenth century and which caused the Arctic Sea ice to melt, thereby allowing the Vikings' agile, light boats to reach Iceland and Greenland. The improved climatic conditions of the tenth century may have affected society by promoting demographic growth in two ways: due to more abundant harvests and the end of the famines caused by inclement weather, and also due to a reduction in illnesses associated with cold climates, which strike children especially. The warmer temperatures and the qualitative and quantitative improvements in the food supply not only reduced infant mortality (which was very high throughout the pre-industrial age), but also raised the general level of life expectancy. The less harsh living conditions also encouraged people to have larger families.

14

13. Work scene, bas-relief on the south side of the façade of San Pietro church in Spoleto, from the end of the twelfth century.

14. The labours of Adam and Eve, detail of a relief on the façade of the Cathedral of Modena.

13

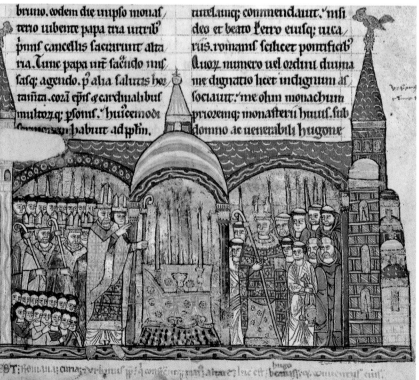

THE CHURCH

THE ORIGINAL ORGANIZATION

Beginning in the fourth century, local "churches" were joined together in "dioceses" or territorial entities modelled on the districts of the Roman Empire. The head of each diocese was the *episkopos* or "supervisor" (bishop). The prelates (including the "patriarchs" of the four bishoprics that claimed to be founded by the Apostles: Rome, Constantinople, Antioch, and Alexandria) met periodically in large general assemblies or local assemblies called councils in order to deliberate on all the problems, both spiritual and practical, that faced the communities of believers in Christ. The councils could be either "ecumenical" (involving the entire Church) or "regional" (involving only some dioceses, located in the vicinity of a metropolis). The administration of justice within each diocese was entrusted to synods, which brought together the clergy of a diocese. The first ecumenical council, celebrated in 325 in Nicaea, was held in the presence of Emperor Constantine.

From that point forward, the community of the faithful gradually made a distinction between the "clergy" (from the Greek *kleros*, meaning "separate portion," i.e., the part of the priestly order that had developed from the *presbyteroi*) and the "laity," from the Greek *laos* or "people of the same stock," the so-called "people of God." (In the Greek and Hellenistic world, the *leitourghia* or "public work" was an institution that placed the onus of carrying out financial initiatives and events of common interest, such as plays and banquets, on the wealthier citizens.)

This separation occurred during a time in which the distance between ordinary presbyters or deacons and bishops grew steadily and religious ceremonies became increasingly characterized by previously unknown liturgical spectacle. Christians began reading biblical descriptions of complex religious ceremonies and sacrifices performed by the Jews. The protagonists of the Hebrew liturgy were the priests, but in the Jewish tradition the priesthood had come to an end with the destruction of the Temple of Solomon. Christians revived the priesthood, taking as a model the priestly role of Christ, who had instituted the sacraments as tangible signs of the conferral of divine grace. The clergy was organized on the basis of mystical knowledge into canonical orders divided into "minor" (distributor of the Eucharist, reader, exorcist, or acolyte) and "major" (sub-deacon, deacon, and priest). The "priests," who were usually the elders (*presbiteros*), thus became *sacerdoces* and the "holy supper," a commemorative ceremony that became the sacrament of the Eucharist, evolved into the Mass. During the fourth century, the structure of the Mass was organized in three parts: the liturgy of the word (Bible readings), the offertory (the offering of gifts), and the canon (the Eucharist liturgy and dismissal).

The influence the Church exerted on cultural life became increasingly important. At the same time, the spheres of action of the old aristocracy became increasingly restricted as the key roles in administrative sectors were now performed by men from

4

1. Sixth-century mosaic on the triumphal arch in the Roman basilica of San Lorenzo fuori Le Mura (St Lawrence outside the Walls), showing Christ in majesty flanked by Sts Peter and Paul and, from the left, a bishop, Pope Pelagius II, Peter, Paul, St Stephen, and the presbyter Hippolytus.

2. St Benedict, fresco from the end of the twelfth century, detail of the altar of the Oratory of St Benedict, Civate, Lecco.

3. Pope Urban II consecrates the high altar of the church of Cluny in 1095, twelfth-century miniature from the *Chronicon cluniacense* (Chronicle of Cluny). National Library of France, Paris.

4. The structure of the church is organized around the celebration of the Eucharist. Abel and Melchisedek as priests, mosaics found in the Baptistery of San Vitale, Ravenna.

5

6

5. Image of St Anthony, the monk of the desert, preserved in the Coptic Museum.

6. St Anthony's grotto behind the present monastery that bears his name in Egypt.

7. View of the Monastery of St Anthony, Egypt.

8. View of the present cenobitic monastery in the region of Fayyum, Egypt.

the army or the cavalry. The importance of the churchmen, however, grew as they began to welcome more and more highly cultured individuals into their ranks.

SECULAR AND REGULAR CLERGY

In addition to the organization of its realm into provinces, dioceses, and parishes, which mirrored the administrative organization of the state, Christianity was able to offer an alternative way of living and of configuring the communal experience, namely, monasticism. The "clergy" was, in fact, divided into secular (destined to remain in the *saeculum* or "of the world," in contact with the faithful) and regular (destined to organize itself into monastic orders, each living in conformity to a specific set of prescribed norms: the Rule).

To understand the monastic movement, we need to keep in mind that the Christian religion had developed through the ongoing dialectic between two aspirations: on the one hand, that of fleeing from the world in order to find refuge in the contemplation of the divine word, which taught one to disdain earthly goods, especially power and wealth; on the other hand, that of loving one's neighbour and performing acts of charity, which led to engagement with the earthly life. The word "monk" derives from the Greek *monos*, meaning "alone" or "solitary." The quest for solitude was not new, having been part of the history of various religious communities or philosophical sects. Both Hinduism and Buddhism, for example, have long and illustrious monastic traditions. Christian monasticism also came from the Orient, having developed especially in third-century Egypt and then spreading to Syria and Palestine. This was "anachoretic" or eremitic monasticism, involving isolated individuals who lived in the desert and devoted themselves to prayer, fasting, and rituals.

The Church, however, did not look favourably upon such monastic experiences, which often led to uncontrollable deviations from dogma. It favoured, instead, "cenobitic" or communal monasticism, whose first great model was the monastery

7

9. St Ephrem, who is associated with the Syrian anachoretic tradition, twelfth-century miniature preserved in the Syrian Orthodox Patriarchal Library, Damascus.

10. St Basil the Great, a reformer of original monasticism making it communal; his ideas influenced nascent western monasticism as well, eighteenth-century icon. Church of St Nicholas, Tripoli, Lebanon.

11. Interior of a monolithic monastic church in Cappadocia.

founded by St Pachomius (292–346). Pachomius gathered a community of followers in the desert of Thebes (Upper Egypt), organizing their life in common in accordance with a Rule that established the norms of behaviour for both the spiritual and the material life. Another important monastic centre was established by St Basil the Great (c.330–370) in Cappadocia, in the centre of the Anatolian Peninsula. The pragmatic nature of cenobitic monasticism was more readily accepted by the West than was the mysticism underlying anachoretism.

In Ireland, which was converted to Christianity in the fifth century by St Patrick, an original form of monasticism that incorporated elements of the Celtic culture took root and village communities that were also monasteries were established. Faithful to the old monastic principle according to which eremetism is a more perfect form of cenobitism, the Irish created an original form of the anachoretic life centered on performing pilgrimages. Descendants of brave Celtic navigators, these pilgrims set sail in small, fragile boats and, in the sixth century, managed to reach the Far Oer Islands, Scotland, the Orkney Islands, and Iceland; later, travelling on foot once on the continent, they reached France, Flanders, Germany, and Italy.

THE DEVELOPMENT OF WESTERN MONASTICISM

During the harsh years of the fifth to ninth centuries, which coincided with a widespread depression on the continent, Benedictine monasteries dotted the whole of Europe with their organizational and cultural network, changing agricultural production and protecting the monuments of ancient thought, bringing security and, to the extent possible, peace to the disoriented peasants of the period. It is certainly no coincidence that Benedict had such an exceptional biographer as Pope Gregory the Great, who was a determined organizer of a Church that he wanted to be vigilant in spiritual matters but also sensitive to the material needs of the faithful. We owe the portrait we have of Benedict to Pope Gregory's *Dialoghi* (Dialogues), which show

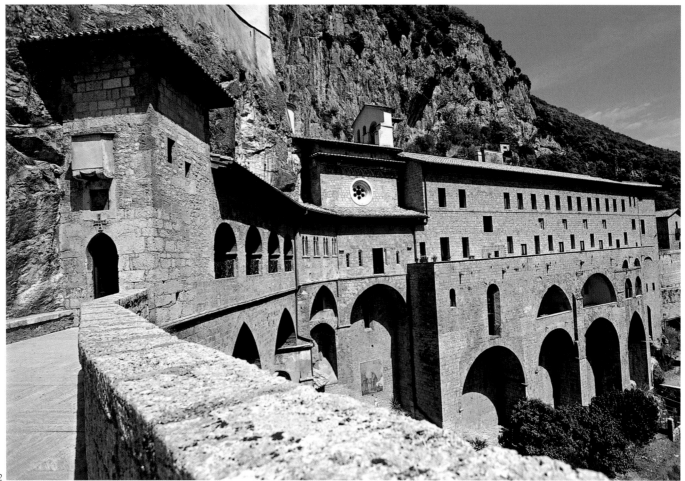

12

13

him as an unquestionably pious man, a thaumaturge capable of astonishing miracles, but above all a loving father of his flock of monks and an energetic, caring organizer.

It has been correctly argued that Benedict's monasticism was typically "Roman," since, unlike oriental monasticism, it did not exalt mysticism but rather achieving a balance among the life of the spirit, daily existence, and serene, firm engagement in resolving concrete problems. As the Roman spirit is characterized by realism, so, too, Benedictine monasticism represents a stern, disciplined, almost militaristic response to the needs of a time of crisis and a society in the process of disintegration.

Central to the *Regula Benedictii* (the Rule of St Benedict), written in Monte Cassino around 540, is the *opus Dei* (Godly work): it includes communal celebration of the Divine Office as well as communal celebration of the Mass and Holy Reading, particularly the Bible but also hagiographic texts, and praying privately. In addition, in order to defeat the "enemy of the soul," namely, idleness, which is the father of arrogance and sloth, Benedict prescribes manual labour: farming, artisanal labour, transcription of manuscripts and codices, and study, understood as the application of one's intellectual energies. Some basic precepts govern life in the Benedictine monastery, particularly the *stabilitas loci* (stability of place), i.e., the obligation to spend

14

15

one's entire life in the same monastery, as opposed to the nomadism that was wide-spread in those days among strange types of monks of questionable vocation. Other precepts included *conversation morum* or good moral conduct, mutual compassion, and the vow of obedience to the abbot, considered the *abba* or "father" of the family of the community.

Isolated in a rural environment, although subordinate to the bishop of the diocese on whose land it was erected, the Benedictine monastery, in those times of turmoil and insecurity, was to become an oasis of peace around which neighbouring peoples gathered in an effort to re-establish civilized living. Fields were ploughed and specialized plants, such as the vine and the olive tree, were re-introduced, and new settlements arose. Ancient texts were preserved in the libraries, while in adjoining scriptoria manuscripts were copied for distribution to sister abbeys and throughout Europe. Christian monasticism thus deserves credit for, among many other things, having safeguarded classical culture and handed it down to us.

From the ninth century onward, monasticism grew in importance in all the territories annexed by the Carolingian monarchs. Credit for this revival of the monastic phenomenon should go to Emperor Ludwig the Pious, who understood the

12. View of the monastery at Subiaco, where St Benedict lived as a hermit, prior to the establishment of the abbey of Monte Cassino.

13. Gregory the Great collects accounts of the life of St Benedict, detail of a miniature from 1437. Conde Museum, Chantilly.

14. Harvest scene from a miniature of the *Dialogues* of Gregory the Great, Abbey of St Lawrence, Liège, twelfth century. Royal Library, Brussels.

15. Piero della Francesca, *St Benedict*, detail of the polyptych of Our Lady of Mercy, 1450–60. Civic Museum, Sansepolcro.

16. Portrait of Ludwig the Pious in a miniature from 1175 originally in Anchin Abbey. Public Library, Douai, France.

17. King Edgar, Archbishop Dunstan and Bishop Aethelwold, founding fathers of the tenth-century Benedictine reform movement in England, miniature from an eleventh-century copy of the *Regularis Concordia* (Monastic Agreement) of 973. British Library, London.

16

17

importance of systematizing the rules that governed monastic life in his day. He recognized the unifying element in the Benedictine Rule as modified by Benedict of Anian and so sought to have it accepted by all the monasteries in his empire. At the Council of Aachen of 816, the idea of an "imperial monasticism" seemed to triumph and the reformed Benedictine Rule was on its way to becoming the unifying element of European monasticism.

POPES AND BISHOPS

As the bishops increasingly became the cornerstones of life in their cities, between the fourth and the fifth centuries the idea of the supremacy of Rome over the other Episcopal Sees, reaffirmed between 441 and 462 during the years of Pope Leo the Great, took root. The bishop of Rome sought to be considered as the vicar of the apostle Peter and therefore the supreme authority in the Church: this idea, which led to the emergence of a power that was parallel, but often opposed, to that of the emperor, was accepted only gradually and only after numerous conflicts with local sees.

The establishment of the Lombards in Italy and the Franks in Gaul were factors in the effective separation of the western part of the empire, which was, by now, centered on Byzantium. The only universal authority, though it had limited resources for enforcement, was the Roman patriarchate, the "papacy," which had inherited the symbolic city of Rome from the emperors. This inheritance was to be reinvented in religious terms; at the time, the city was partly abandoned and falling into ruin, although its architecture continued to serve as a powerful reminder of the past. Though in decline, ancient temples and palaces continued to dominate the urban landscape. The desire to preserve the memories of ancient Rome began to fade early in the sixth century. By that time, the papacy's aim was to convert the city to Christianity, even in terms of its architectural monuments; the imperial epoch no longer exerted genuine cultural appeal for either the elites or the other social classes, who now faced entirely different realities.

During the pontificate of Stephen II (752–57), Rome strengthened its relations with the Franks against the Lombards with the aim of assuring the sovereignty of the throne of St Peter over that of the Duchy of Rome and neutralizing the threat posed by the Lombards and Byzantines. It was probably in this context that the Roman Curia came up with the expedient of the Donation of Constantine, the famous document exposed as a forgery in the mid-fifteenth century by the humanist philologist Lorenzo Valla. This document claims that Emperor Constantine had transferred authority over the Western Empire to Pope Sylvester I, as symbolized by the emblems of imperial dignity. Although it is clear that the stipulations of the Donation were never fully put into effect, for many centuries popes used the decree as a pretext for ruling over terrestrial matters, especially in several regions of central Italy.

19

18

18. Stephen II and Pippin welcome the Lombard king Aistulf, who is penitent after his defeat, detail of Giovanni Villani's *Nuova Cronaca* (New chronicle), fourteenth century. Vatican Apostolic Library, Rome.

19. St Peter's chair, a gift from Charles the Bald to Pope John VIII in 875, symbolic of support for the papacy in the West.

Between the tenth and eleventh centuries, the situation of the Christian Church in the West was complex and problematic. In several areas of Europe, it was subject to strong pressures from the secular world. Since they traditionally held public administrative positions, bishops and abbots were tied to aristocratic families; as well, great feudal lords established churches called *ecclesiae propriae* or *Eigenkirchen* (private churches), which were entirely dependent on them. The political importance of the episcopal and abbatial function gave rise to practices such as simony (the sale of offices; the term derives from Simon Magus, the Samaritan who offered money to St Peter in exchange for the gifts of the Holy Spirit (Acts of the Apostles 8, 18) and Nicholaism (the passage of offices to one's next of kin; the Nicholaists were a first-century Christian sect accused of making compromises with paganism).

Rome was unable to exert its authority over these matters. The papacy itself, far from being a truly elected office, was in reality a privilege claimed by powerful Roman families, from the Crescenzi to the Counts of Tusculum. The rivalries among the nobles of Rome often required the direct intervention of the emperors of the House of Saxony, who swiftly stepped in, replacing the nobility and extending to the papal throne the *privilegium othonis* (Diploma Ottonianum), a form of "protection" of the Church already implemented in the Germanic kingdom. But this control of aristocratic interference in the life of the Church, which operated on many levels and throughout the Christian world, can be seen as a stimulus for ecclesiastical renewal as the emperors' interventions often served to raise the level of authority of the pontiffs and the clergy.

20. Portico of Lorsch Abbey, *Eigenkirche* (proprietary church) of Cancor, count of the Franks, and his mother, founded in 764 and entrusted by the proprietors to Chrodegang, Bishop of Metz, who became the city's first abbot.

21. In this miniature, Otto III, holding the imperial insignias, is in the centre, between prelates and soldiers. Otto III's Evangelion (Book of Gospels). Bavarian State Library, Munich.

22. View of Cluny.

23. The map shows some of the principal monasteries that adhered to the Cluniac reforms.

20

21

TOWARD THE CHURCH OF THE SECOND MILLENNIUM

Initiated originally in a small part of the Christian world, there was now increasing concern over the question of the *libertas ecclesiae* (freedom of the Church), understood as the liberation of Church institutions from interference on the part of the laity. The impetus for the renewal of the Church from within came largely from the Abbey of Cluny, founded in 910 by William, Duke of Aquitaine, and entrusted to the abbot Berno of Baume (c.850–917) who proposed an original program of reform. In fact, Berno advocated following the Benedictine Rule, but only with regard to the first of its two cardinal tenets, prayer and work, emphasizing prayer and liturgical service while leaving work to be carried out mainly by the laity. In addition, the rich abbey set out to create an organizational model that would exempt it from the power of both the laity and the bishops by placing itself directly under the protection of the Holy See. Monasteries modelled on Cluny sprang up throughout Europe.

Emperor Henry III, who succeeded Conrad II in 1039, followed the policy toward the influence of the nobility on the Church established by his predecessors. Given that bishops were also servants of the empire and invested with benefices by the sovereign, the sovereign expected behaviour appropriate to their rank in return. Henry III began to select bishops not from the ranks of the nobility but from the monasteries and the emerging middle class. And he did not hesitate to listen to the most intransigent voices, such as that of the monk Peter Damian (c.1007–1072)

22

23

24

25

who, from his hermitage at Fonte Avellana near Gubbio, used fiery rhetoric to castigate unworthy prelates and single them out for censure and condemnation by the emperor. In line with this ecclesiastical policy, in 1046 Henry insisted on the election of his candidate to the papal throne, the bishop of Bamberg, over three other candidates; the bishop took the name Clement II.

Imperial reform, however, was not well received by traditionalists. Henry III died in 1056, leaving his widow as regent for their young son. Reformers took advantage of this power vacuum and at the Lateran Synod of 1059, Pope Nicholas II could be said to have dictated the law of the reformed Church. From that point forward, the pope (as bishop of Rome) would be chosen only by the priests of Rome and the bishops of the dioceses of Suburbicarian Italy (Italy under the City), and "cardinals" appointed to these Roman titular churches and dioceses; churchmen could no longer receive offices from the laity (including the emperor), and celibacy would be strictly obligatory.

Traditionalist bishops, however, had no wish to see themselves deprived of the principle of simoniacal elections and opposed the papacy, which was increasingly in the hands of extremist reformers. When he was called to the papal throne in 1061, Anselmo da Baggio, head of the Milanese reformers called "patarini," took the name of Alexander II. The regent empress Agnes then convened a council at Basel, which elected Cadalo, the bishop of Parma, pope. This action set off a schism. Though he did not disavow it, Alexander II did not insist on the hard line previously taken against the simoniacal Church. If anything, he was concerned about creating a new image of the pope, one consistent with the reformist precepts: the papal throne was to become the centre of all power. The military campaigns of conquest that received Alexander II's blessing served this purpose as he offered the Banner of the Holy Roman Church (a symbol that made each of them a vassal of the pope) to the conquerors. William, Duke of Normandy, for conquering England in 1066, the Normans for invading Sicily in the last third of the eleventh century, and Sancho of Aragon, for fighting the Muslims in Spain, were all given the banner that made the pope ruler over the monarchies of Europe.

When Alexander II died in 1073, the reform program was taken up and improved upon by someone who had contributed to laying the groundwork for it: Hildebrand of Sovana, who ascended the papal throne, taking the name of Gregory VII. Gregory VII understood that the moment had come for a frontal attack. In 1074, he forbade all laics, under penalty of excommunication, to invest ecclesiastics. In 1078, he wrote the twenty-seven axiomatic statements of the *Dictatus Papae* (dictates of the pope), which affirmed that the pontiff has absolute power on earth, including the power to depose lay sovereigns. But the young Emperor Henry IV, who had assumed direct power in 1066, convened a synod of the Church loyal to the emperor in the city of Worms and had Gregory VII excommunicated and deposed. The pope, in his turn, excommunicated and deposed the emperor, thereby releasing his subjects from the duty of loyalty to him.

The conflict lasted for decades, until the Concordat of Worms of 1122 stipulated a "moderate" political solution to the investiture dispute. It was recognized that bishops performed both a spiritual and a temporal function. In the Germanic empire, the emperor would preside over the election (which meant that he would have to give his approval to the newly elected pope) and he would invest the new bishop with the temporal benefice before he was consecrated. In Italy and Burgundy, the election would be held without the presence, i.e., the supervision, of the emperor, and the temporal benefice would be granted only upon consecration. In 1123, Lateran Council I was held in Rome, the first ecumenical council of the Western Church. During its deliberations, the basic lines of the new concept of a hierarchically organized Church guided by the pope, to whom all the bishops owed their subservience, were reaffirmed.

28

26

27

24. Scene from the Bayeux tapestry showing preparations for the battle of Hastings: the meal and the blessing from Bishop Guillaume. William the Conqueror Centre, Bayeux.

25. The main pulpit and the paschal candle erected probably by William II (1154–89) at the far end of the nave of the Palatine Chapel in Palermo.

26. In this watercolour image of Alfonso Ciacconio from 1590, which pertains to the lost decoration of the oratory of St Nicholas in the Patriarchio Lateranese, we can see some papal reformers, including Gregory VII. Vatican Apostolic Library, Rome.

27. Onofrio Panvinio, *Concordat of Worms*, c.1570. Vatican Apostolic Library Rome.

28. The Worms Cathedral, built in 1181 over a pre-existing Ottonian structure.

1

2

1. Queen Radegonda is presented to her future husband Clothair, detail of a sixth-century manuscript. Municipal Library, Poitiers.

2. Detail of a capital in the west wing of the cloister of Santa Maria de l'Estany, Catalonia.

3. Processing wool and linen: from the top: combing, heaping, and carding, detail of the small vault to the left of the north portal of the left flank of Chartres Cathedral.

6

WOMEN IN THE CHURCH AND IN SOCIETY

3

THE "HISTORY OF WOMEN"

In recent decades, first in America and later in Europe, the issue of the "history of women" has become quite popular, as part of the larger movement of "gender studies." Studies on "gender," (understood as a specification of sex), however, run the risk of overlooking or omitting reference to the spatial, chronological, social, political, and economic factors that are the foundation of all historical research. It would then no longer be an analysis of the condition of women in history so much as a study of woman as "gender" in and of itself as though there existed a universal feminine outside the historical context. During the Middle Ages – but the same is true for all periods, including the twentieth century – societies, which are the subject of the present volume, did not see women as separate from society as a whole. For cultures that considered the person not simply as an individual but rather in terms of the role he or she played in the family and in society at large, it is not possible to theorize a "feminine condition" as such. The most typical example comes to us from the practice of marriage, which, especially in cases involving the upper classes, was always considered as a political instrument used to forge alliances between families and institutions. In the same way that it is not possible to speak of a bourgeoisie before the urban middle class begins to see itself as a social group or a self-aware class, during this period women did not represent a "gender" but were a part of society with its infinite articulations, from simple peasants to powerful and influential figures, some of whom are the focus of the paragraphs that follow.

MATRIMONY AND FAMILY LIFE

Matrimony and family life change with the passing of time as well as with location, circumstance, and social conditions. Sources of information on the subject are not exhaustive and the great variety of information that one finds does not lend itself easily to syntheses and generalizations. In the Italic-Lombard world described in the decrees of the sovereigns, for example, we find that the status of the free woman was held in high regard. Attention to issues of kinship is evident in the large number of paragraphs that the Edict of Rothari dedicates to systematization of the matter; indeed, there are more than twenty paragraphs devoted to questions of patrimony and inheritance, particularly as they pertain to legitimate children. The same can be said for questions relating to marriage and the position of women in the family and in society at large. The community vigorously protected the dignity of a free woman who was not able to defend herself. For instance, a violent crime committed against a woman called for a more eloquent prose than did a similar crime against a man, probably because he was considered better able to defend himself and therefore did not need protection.

4. A baker sells her bread, detail of a thirteenth-century stained glass window in the Cathedral of Saint-Étienne de Bourges.

5. A host with his wife holding the pouch, detail of a thirteenth-century Life of St Lubin, stained glass window, left aisle of Chartres Cathedral.

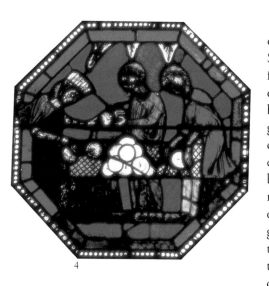

If a married woman observed the rules imposed by society – for example, that of not committing adultery – her husband did not have unlimited power over her. Situations where the husband could exercise his full authority were fairly specific, for instance, in cases of lack of interest or incompatibility with the woman's *Sippe*, or kin. What is more, a wife was not denied a part in her husband's patrimony, first because she brought to the marriage the *Faderfium*, i.e., the gifts her father freely gave her as a dowry, which she could take back with her if she became widowed and decided to return to her family. The institutions of the *meta* and the *morgingab* were even more important. The first consisted of the part of the patrimony that the husband promised to the woman on their wedding day; the second was the gift that the man was obligated to give as a public expression of his intention to confer full legality on the matrimonial bond (the term literally means "the gift of the morning," and the groom gave it to the bride on the morning following the wedding night to signify the consummation of the marriage). It appears that, originally, it was transferred to the *Sippe* of the bride, but as time passed, it became customary to give the gift directly to the woman as hers to keep. Indeed, a widow took this portion of her husband's estate back to her paternal home as her personal possession. If her father and brothers died, she was under no obligation to share the inheritance with her sisters, which was not the case with the *Faderfium*. Finally, the marriage of a free woman and a *haldus* (a semi-free man) was permitted under certain conditions, while the union of a servant and a free woman was absolutely prohibited; this rule was common to all the legal systems in the Germanic kingdoms.

It is probable that, in the centuries that followed, marriages based on the free will of the spouses, and therefore not obligatory for the woman, were fairly common among the peasant class, where fewer economic-patrimonial interests were involved. Conversely (and despite the fact that from the twelfth century on there would be new developments concerning the idea of love), arranged marriages based on family interests were the norm among the ruling classes, both feudal and urban.

MATILDA OF CANOSSA (1046–1115)

"*Mathilda, Dei gratia si quid est*" (Matilda, by the grace of God, if she is anything). The signature on the seal of Matilda of Canossa, Countess of Tuscany, seems to invoke the same aura of humility that a few years earlier had led a pope to define himself as "*servus servorum Dei*" (servant of the servants of God). Such mottos were inspired in part by the austere and passionate climate of Church reform in the eleventh century. At the same time, however, there is a subtle but stern political warning in those words. By declaring herself to be "something only by the grace of god," the grand lady, ruler of an "empire" that stretched from the Tyrrhenian Sea almost to the mouth of the Po River in the Adriatic and from Umbria to Lombardy, emphasized the fact that she owed her authority to God alone, "omitting" the emperor who legitimated her sovereignty.

In effect, a good portion of northern Italy had fallen into the hands of this inflexible woman and she ruled it despite the confusing assortment of rights that

6. The best-preserved sections of the castle at Canossa, destroyed in 1255 and again in 1557, are located in the collegial church and the crypt within it.

7. Map showing the extent of the estate of the Countess of Canossa.

6

7

8. Portrait of Matilda of Canossa from the *Vita di Matilda* (Life of Matilda) written by the monk Donizone at the start of the twelfth century. Vatican Apostolic Library, Rome.

authorized her to do so. She was born in 1046 to Boniface, Marquis (or "duke," as the Tuscans preferred, in keeping with a Lombard tradition) of Tuscany, and Beatrice of Lorraine. After the death of her three brothers, Matilda inherited not only the lands over which her father, by proxy, had exercised official authority, that is, "feudal," land (the March of Tuscany) but also a quantity of "allodial" (that is, private) lands, which, combined with the feudal holdings, included the counties of Bergamo, Brescia, Mantua, as well as the Middle Po Valley and southern Tuscany. To these were added her mother's vast land holdings in the Lorraine region.

Following the death of the Marquis Boniface in 1052, Beatrice remarried, to Godfrey the Bearded, Duke of Upper and Lower Lorraine, whose brother, upon being elected Pope Stephen IX, had transferred to him the Duchy of Spoleto. Since Matilda had inherited a vast estate, her stepfather attempted to arrange an irrevocable union between Tuscany and the Lorraine dynastic families through the marriage of his stepdaughter and Godfrey the Hunchback, his son by a previous marriage. But the union of Godfrey and Matilda did not last, and the duke returned to his homeland across the Alps.

In 1076, Matilda found herself without mother or consort, both having died, while the dispute between Pope Gregory VII and Henry IV intensified. Matilda boldly took the reins of power over her empire, siding with the pope, who sent her an astute advisor, Anselmo, the bishop of Lucca. It was in her family castle at Canossa that, in January of 1077, the meeting – traditionally attributed to Matilda's mediation – between Pope Gregory and Henry IV of Franconia took place. Recognizing that he had been defeated, Henry knelt in the snow and begged for the pope's forgiveness. The controversy resumed almost immediately after, however, and in 1081 the emperor settled in Lucca, the principal city of the March of Tuscany. From there he declared Matilda deposed and banished her from the empire, charging her with the crime of lese-majesty.

The tide had turned and everything seemed lost. Gregory VII, under siege in Rome, was freed through the intervention of his rowdy Norman vassals from southern Italy, but he spent his final embittered years in exile, although remaining pope until his death in 1085. Matilda, who had continued to resist, managed to defeat the emperor's supporters at Sorbaia near Modena on 12 July 1085. After this victory, the balance of power was restored, allowing the Great Countess (as she was known) to become the principal supporter of the reform movement, which gained strength under Pope Urban II, who came to power in 1088.

In 1089, on the advice of the pope, the now forty-year-old countess married Guelfo V, heir to the ducal crown of Bavaria and some twenty-five years younger than she. This was a solid anti-imperial alliance but an unhappy union for Matilda because she gave birth to only one son, who died at a very young age. Having now become the primary and implacable enemy of the emperor, Matilda instigated and supported revolts against him and his sons. The death of Henry IV and the accession to the throne by his son, Henry V, in 1111 did not significantly change the attitude of the countess toward the dynastic house of Franconia and when she died heirless on 24 July 1115 she left the Pontifical See all her holdings, both feudal and allodial, although there was a patrimonial obligation on some of these lands by which the property reverted back to the emperor. This produced a knotty problem, called a "matildina" in Italian, which troubled relations between the Church and the empire for centuries. Apart from this, hers was a courageous and forward-looking effort to construct an organic feudal principality like the ones that were

9. Matilda of Canossa meets the Church authorities of Modena in 1106 and, accompanied by the architect Lanfranco, the bishop of Reggio Emilia, and the entire population, proceeds to recognize the relics of St Geminiano, miniature from the *Relatio de innovatione ecclesie sancti Geminiani* (Report on the renovation of the Church of San Geminiano). Archivio Capitolare, Modena.

10. Pope Gregory VII and Matilda of Canossa welcome Emperor Henry IV, miniature from Giovanni Villani's *Nuova Cronaca* (New chronicle), fourteenth century. Vatican Apostolic Library, Rome.

being created in the same period in France and Germany on the basis of lands acquired from different ancestral lines.

HILDEGARD OF BINGEN (1098–1179)

Hildegard of Bingen was educated in the convent in Disibodenberg, becoming abbess in 1136. A very cultured person, she wrote mystical works, moral treatises, about seventy poems, and a great quantity of letters. Although she is remembered primarily as a mystic and prophetess, Hildegard was not unaware of the realities of her times. Her letters testify to her active involvement in the reform of the Church and the clergy. Her mysticism and prophesying did not prevent her from dedicating herself to the natural sciences and medicine, fields in which her theoretical knowledge appears to have gone hand in hand with practical interests related to popular traditions.

Her treatises dedicated to medicine and other natural sciences, collected in *Causes and Cures*, reveal knowledge that grew out of the Germanic experience and tradition, which was scarcely touched by Christianity. Hildegard claimed that natural substances possess magical powers linked to the area from which they come: oriental substances are potent and rich in medicinal powers; western substances are important for the art of magic but do not contribute much to maintaining or restoring the health of the body, which, in this context, mirrors the health of the soul. Many plants, especially trees, achieve their highest degree of magical potency in the spring, when they flower. This is when – in the "pure time," considered sacred to the ancient gods – the spirits of the air are most active. There are, however, ways of "neutralizing" the magical power of plants while preserving their medicinal properties. Hildegard claimed, for example, that the mandrake root is warm and hot, and that it was made of the same earth from which Adam was created; because it so closely resembles a human being, it is subject to the same assaults by the devil. For this reason, it is very useful in magic but its negative powers can be made to vanish if it is soaked in a spring of pure water for a day and a night immediately after it is removed from the ground. This soaking of the anthropomorphic root in pure, clear water may well be a symbol for baptism, the plant losing its negative properties in a way analogous to the way baptism cleans away original sin.

A remedy for male incontinence, both natural and induced by magic, consisted of the following: take the root of a female mandrake purified in a spring and keep it tied between the chest and stomach for three nights; then divide it in two and keep the two parts tied on the thigh for three days and three nights. The pulverized left part of the anthropomorphic root should then be mixed with camphor and eaten. If a woman was affected by the same disorder, she was required to repeat the same procedure using the male mandrake root and pulverizing the right side of the plant.

The mandrake is also useful in treating all kinds of pain. One merely needs to eat the part of the anthropomorphic root that corresponds to the part of the body where the pain is felt. A person who was agitated or suffered mood swings was advised to eat the mandrake, after purification in the usual spring for a day and taken it to bed with him/her and warmed by his/her sweat, and to pray to the Lord. If one could not find a mandrake plant, a leafy tuft of beech would do; the procedure was the same. It is obvious that, despite the prayers to the Lord, such instructions are part of a therapeutic magic ritual rather than actual medicine.

Hildegard was an original thinker and prominent figure of her age, and her writings reveal a twelfth-century world of magic to which had been added novel elements

11. Hildegard of Bingen writing on a wax tablet, detail of a miniature in the *Scivias* (Know the ways of the Lord). State Library, Wiesbaden.

12. Thirteenth-century miniature preserved in the Lucca Library, inspired by the mystical vision of Hildegard of Bingen. The cosmos is embraced by Christ Himself, mediator between the Father and the whole of Creation, of which mankind is the microcosm moved by waves of energy emitted by the fiery spheres: health and salvation converge.

13. *Fructus mandragora* (Fruit of the mandragora), from the *Remedium Sanitatis* (Health remedies). Casanatense Library, Rome.

newly arrived from the Orient or Spain. However, much of what she describes seem to be magic practices that had long been repudiated or kept secret in treatises on medicine or botany that Celtic and Germanic missionaries had sought to eliminate.

ELEANOR OF AQUITAINE (C.1122–1204)

When he died around 1137, during a pilgrimage to Santiago de Compostela, William X, Duke of Aquitaine, left Aquitaine and Gascony to his daughter Eleanor as her inheritance. That same year, as arranged with Louis VI, the French king, Eleanor married the heir to the throne, Louis VII. Her entry into court life was not particularly happy. Aquitaine was home to troubadours and the idea of courtly love, and, as she had been raised in this culture, the French court considered her behaviour scandalous. The troubadour Bernard de Ventadour, for example, had no qualms about declaring his love for Eleanor, comparing himself to Tristan. As well, when the king died, his heir undertook a series of bizarre political and military actions, which were attributed to Eleanor's influence on him and led to a papal interdiction on the couple. Eleanor then visited Bernard of Clairvaux, a prominent figure on the political scene, who advised her to resolve the dispute peacefully. She and Louis took his advice and the excommunication was rescinded. In 1145, the royal couple had a daughter, Marie, who would be an important literary patron of her age. (Chrétien de Troyes says that he is indebted to Marie de Champagne for the subject of his *Lancelot, the Knight of the Cart.*) In order to atone for her sins, Eleanor decided to accompany her husband on the crusade of 1147.

During the expedition, however, bitter misunderstandings drove the couple apart. The most serious episode occurred in 1148 when the vanguard, which included the queen and was led by one of her vassals from Aquitaine, disobeyed orders, failing to wait for the rearguard, which contained the king and pilgrims. The rearguard was attacked by the Turks and massacred, although Louis himself miraculously escaped. Upon their return home it was apparent that the marriage was at an end. It was, in fact, declared null and void in 1152, during the Beaugency synod, on the grounds of consanguinity (obviously an excuse). A few weeks later, Eleanor asked Henry, Count of Anjou and Duke of Normandy, who was eleven days younger than she, to come at once and marry her. When Henry was crowned King of England in 1154, Eleanor became queen for the second time.

Until the early part of the eleventh century, the Capetian kings actually ruled only crown lands, that is to say, a limited area in north-central France (the so-called Île-de-France, between the rivers Seine and the Loire). The rest of the kingdom was divided into powerful duchies (Normandy, Brittany, and Aquitaine) and large counties (Flanders, Lorraine, Champagne, Burgundy, and Toulouse), some of which were larger and richer than the royal lands. In 1066, a vassal of the king, William, Duke of Normandy, had become the king of England. This created a paradoxical situation:

14. The seal of Eleanor of Aquitaine.

15. The tomb of Eleanor of Aquitaine and Henry II of England in Fontevrault Abbey.

16. Louis VII, Conrad III, and Baldwin III in the 1147 crusade, detail of a miniature from the *Histoire de Guillaume de Tyr* (History of William of Tyre), 1097. Public Library, Lyons.

17. Henry II, detail of a miniature. British Library, London.

14

15

16

17

he was subject to the king of France because of his lands on the European side of the English Channel, while the territory on the English side of the channel belonged to him as well.

With the union of Henry and Eleanor, Normandy, Aquitaine, Anjou, and other important territories of the Kingdom of France were now also under the control of the king of England who, however, ruled these lands as a vassal of the French king. A long war ensued, one that did not come to an end until the middle of the fifteenth century and would establish a traditional rivalry between France and England.

1

7

THE EMPEROR

CHARLEMAGNE AND LEO III

After the deposition of Romulus Augustulus, the last Western Roman Emperor, in 476, the Eastern Roman Empire remained as the only recognized source of authority, law, and right. In the West, both the pope and the Romanized barbarians knew and accepted this undisputed reality. Only with the creation of a new imperial crown under Charlemagne (c.742–814) would the situation change. But the path that led to this new state of affairs was far from straight. In fact, when he arrived on the Italian peninsula, Charlemagne was taking a giant step toward the Orient. Italy included Ravenna, which had been the capital of the exarchate – the seat of the Byzantine governor of Italy – and Rome, a city still allied with the Eastern Empire. As well, the whole of southern Italy was a subject of Byzantium and its culture had been greatly influenced by Greece. For Charlemagne, as for the Lombards, occupying Italy meant coming into contact with Byzantium and becoming its neighbour.

1. Interior of the Basilica of San Vitale, Ravenna.

2. Empress Irene depicted in the south tribune mosaic of Sancta Sophia, Istanbul.

On the other hand, the Byzantine Empire was in crisis. The Iconoclastic schism had created serious internal conflicts and, at the end of the eighth century, only Empress Irene had attempted to deal with the crisis. However, serious accusations weighed heavily on her private life and her behaviour in the political sphere. Charlemagne was interested in establishing diplomatic relations and becoming interlocutor of the court of Constantinople. He was so successful in this that he began to negotiate a marriage between one of his sons and a daughter of the empress. The Frankish ruler understood, however, that he needed to avoid creating excessively close ties between the imperial court and the papal court; to this end, he even agreed to put his theological knowledge to the test by writing the *Libri Carolini* (Charles' books), which were meant to lead to a re-interpretation of the question of the veneration of images or icons that differed from the way the issue was viewed in Constantinople and Rome.

These actions contained a threat directed toward the pontiff: powerful Constantinople was far away, whereas Charlemagne was nearby and would be a trusted ally but, if necessary, an implacable enemy. Pope Leo III understood this message. He ascended the papal throne in 795 and immediately asked for Charlemagne's protection against the Roman nobles who challenged his authority. When the Romans continued their hostility towards him, he journeyed to France in 799 to make a personal plea for support. Charlemagne went to Rome, ostensibly as a mediator, but, on Christmas night of the year 800, he took an ambiguous imperial title. The pope crowned him as the crowd that had gathered at St Peter's acclaimed him (popular acclamation had been an important legal element in the imperial coronation from the time of the ancient Romans).

The gesture performed that Christmas remains an enigma. Perhaps Leo III meant to repay the man who had supported him; the gesture may also have been a way of proclaiming himself free from the Byzantine emperor. Or perhaps he wished

2

3–5. Meeting of Emperor Charlemagne
and Pope Leo III, who moves to greet
him at the city gates (3). Charlemagne
is crowned by the Roman people (4),
and by Pope Leo III (5), *Gothae
Weltenbronik*, 1270. MS. Memb, I90,
fol. 76r, 76v, 78v. Forschungs-und
Landesbibliothek Gotha.

to demonstrate his right to crown the emperor and, when necessary, to depose him. From their perspective, the Roman nobles were asserting the ancient right of acclamation, whereby the Roman people determined who would be emperor. According to some sources, Charlemagne was surprised by the situation and immediately showed his displeasure because he was being placed in direct confrontation with Byzantium; however, he had been given moral authority over his people and over the West, which no previous Germanic king had enjoyed.

THE HOLY ROMAN EMPIRE

To understand the evolution of the imperial and royal crowns in post-Carolingian Europe, it is essential to distinguish between *auctoritas* and *potestas*, as the Romans had done: that is, the right to exercise power (*auctoritas*) and the exercise of power in and of itself (*potestas*). This distinction is needed because in the West, even when public authority waned, the idea that a sovereign authority was necessary to legitimate power that could be exercised by the simple application of force never disappeared. The feudal lords ruled, at least formally, because they had been invested with power; however, they and their families had acquired positions in public administration – in the absence of state institutions capable of exercising control over such matters – and used them almost as "allodial" or private possessions.

In 962, the imperial crown ended up in the hands of a Saxon prince, Otto I, who asserted his authority as king of Germany and Italy. From that moment on, the future of the empire and of the three kingdoms – the Germanic, the Italic, and the Burgundian (the latter would pass to the king of Germany at the start of the eleventh century) – would remain entwined, in medieval as well as modern Europe, forming a sort of "sphere of sovereign powers" that would experience a number of vicissitudes. Nevertheless, Otto's political dream and obsession would remain important and far-reaching aspects of the legal and political culture of Europe for a long time.

3

4

5

6

7

6. Ninth-century iron crown of the Italic kingdom, with which the designate king of Italy was crowned. Museum and Treasury of the Monza Cathedral.

7. Map of the Carolingian Empire at the point of its greatest extent.

8. Emperor Charlemagne's "jewel box" reliquary, 1215. On the front panel of the box, Charlemagne, Pope Leo III, and Turpin, the bishop of Reims; on the side panel, other emperors. Chorhalle des Doms St Maria, Aachen.

9. Miniature showing the Luthar Evangelar (Gospel book): Luthar offers the Evangelar to Otto III *christomimetes* (representative of Christ). Domschatz, Aachen.

10. King Narsete is invested by the goddess Anahita, c.300 A.D. Naqsh-i Rustam, Iran.

This "sphere of sovereign powers" is what we have come to know as the "Holy Roman Empire of the German Nation": "holy" and "Roman" (two terms used as a way of emulating Byzantium) because it was considered in some sense the heir and continuation of the Roman Empire, which in the minds of people of those times had never actually fallen but, instead, while the institutions of the West deteriorated, had remained vibrant in the eastern part of the "Kingdom of the Germans," a name used because at its core were those Germanic tribes that saw themselves as part of the kingdom of the "eastern Franks" – increasingly called the "Kingdom of Germany."

In the centuries that followed, the position of emperor would remain primarily an elected one in that it was linked to the determination of the Germanic crown, which was conferred on the basis of an election with an electoral body consisting of the Germanic nobles. With the passage of time, some great families were tempted to make the right to the throne hereditary, as was occurring in other countries. Finally, towards the end of the Middle Ages, the Habsburg family ascended the throne of the Holy Roman Empire, which they would retain until 1806.

But in what way could the new empire really call itself "Roman"? The Roman-Germanic emperors used various means – diplomatic relationships, threats, and the establishment of various family ties – in a series of attempts to be recognized by the

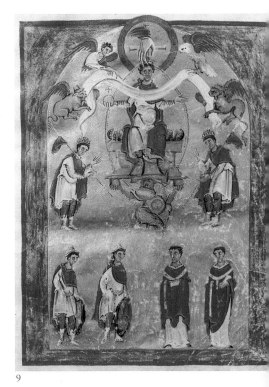

Byzantine emperors as their equal. But the rulers of Constantinople continued to call them by the title "King of the Germans."

The Holy Roman Empire of the Germanic Nation developed out of a series of misunderstandings and political actions. However, it soon became a fundamental concept without which not only is it not possible to understand the history of medieval, modern, and contemporary Europe, but it is not possible to see Europe in terms of the culturally, historically, and politically unified image that has become a necessity for a great number of European countries today.

THE SACREDNESS OF POWER

According to the studies of Georges Dumézil, the regal function is "contested" by two spheres, the magical-priestly sphere and the heroic-warrior sphere, because both participate in the delicate task of establishing the concept of right and the administration of justice. Mircea Eliade places divine kingship at the centre of his complex reflection on the equilibrium of the cosmos: in many civilizations, the ruler appears to be the guarantor of that balance, that is to say, the relationship between the sky and the earth for which the sovereign is a "bridge" or mediator. Eliade's conclusions have been confirmed by anthropologist Gilbert Durand, who has studied the monarchy in the context of symbols of ascent, underscoring the connection between celestial divinity, royalty, and paternity from which is derived the strong relationship we find in many different traditions between the concepts of the celestial God-Father and the King-Father.

9

10

The point here is to establish whether the King-Father is an aspect of the God-Father or his vicar, representative, or image. The two archetypes of divine monarchy, the Egyptian and the Babylonian, provide us with two *Urgestalten* (prototypes) of the King-God and the King-Priest. Eliade's reflections are of fundamental importance for historians in terms of understanding the Christian concept of royalty, especially the imperial theology developed in both the Byzantine Empire and the Western Empire from the time of the Ottonian rulers. It is clear that Christian *basileus* (king or sovereign) and *imperatores* (emperor) develop their concept of divine kingship in light of the model of the royalty of Christ, but the sources of the Christian notion of emperor, which is assured by Christ the cosmic ruler, ruler of time and space, *Kosmokrator* and *Kronokrator*, were essentially part of the Egyptian and Persian traditions, as redefined by Alexander the Great but initially paired by Caesar and then by Augustus, Ptolemaic Egypt, and the *Soldatenkaiser* of the third century, who developed the concept of the Syrian King-Priests devoted to the cult of the sun, as well as the great Arsacidian kings.

To the Christianization of the empire developed in conformity with these models was added the Davidic-Solomonic model derived from the Old Testament, providing a strong Messianic component. From that point on, the Christian emperor presented himself as the vicar, an image of the True King, the Christ. Earthly rulers were a *typus Christi* (sacrament of Christ), but the sacramental nature of their coronation, especially after the adoption of the Old Testament ritual of unction, made them "Christs of the Lord." This complex dynamic is reflected in rituals, both those of

11. Emperor Charlemagne between Cato and Seneca, fourteenth-century tapestry. Domschatz, Halberstadt.

the pagan Roman Empire and those of the Christian Empire, which represented a continuation as well as a profound reform of the pagan world.

In the Incarnation, and therefore in the Christian justification of divine kingship as a symbol of and substitute for the royalty of Christ, the rituals could converge. By being present in the Incarnation – in accordance with the three functions foretold in the story of the gifts of the Magi – as True God, True King, and True Man, Christ presents Himself as ruler and guarantor of an order that comes from above and a cosmic order that regulates the things of creation and organizes them.

The crown is the symbol par excellence of this power. After Christianity was decreed to be the state religion at the end of the fourth century, Roman emperors retained the diadem, which had entered imperial custom, especially from the third century A.D. on, as part of a progressive and unopposed assimilation of the imperial function of sacred royalty derived from Greece and developed further by Alexander and his successors from Egyptian and Persian models. But if, in the pagan tradition, the crown of branches and leaves (either natural or metallic but always including some form of branches and leaves) was awarded to the winners in a contest and in the Christian tradition to the *athletae Christi* (champions of Christ) martyrs, the crown of thorns of Christ *rex unius diei* (king for a day) was analogous to the crown of roses that was worn to signify joy. The Christian emperors did not dare to adopt the Christ-imitative symbol of the crown of thorns; in fact, when the Crusaders conquered Jerusalem in 1099, it was said that it was not legitimate to establish a Christian kingdom there and that no one should dare to wear the crown of gold where Christ had been crowned with thorns. Medieval crowns represented a development of the imperial diadem, which consisted of a continuous band of precious metal encrusted with jewels, or, later, a band with a crown of hinged plates, as we see in the crown of the Imperial Treasury of Vienna, which apparently dates from the tenth century and is surmounted by a golden bridge; this style suggests the image of the ruler as mediator or "bridge" between the divine will and the people. Later, other forms of the crown would be reintroduced, for example, the "radial" crowns, which were originally associated with the imperial cult of *Sol comes invictus* (Invincible Sun). The crown surmounted by a cross remains traditional for all the monarchies of Europe despite the process of secularization. It alludes to the divine origin of power, which may be rejected on the conceptual level but recurs repeatedly on the symbolic level.

SYMBOLS OF HOMAGE

The concept of kingship as sacred in the West, especially in its imperial Roman and Germanic form but also in the Frankish, Franco-Norman, Italic-Norman, and Iberian monarchies, continued to be loyal to the Christian or Christ-imitative aspect of the ruler. We can see this clearly both in affirmations that reveal the ruler's

12. *Reichskrone*, the imperial crown used for centuries to crown the Germanic emperors. Kuntshistorisches Museum, Hofsburg, Vienna.

13. The crown of golden oak leaves placed on the bones of the king in the tomb of Philip of Macedon in Vergina, Greece.

12

self-conscious awareness of his mission – homiletic and propagandist statements, the writings of the apologists of the empire, the coronation ritual – and in the symbols of royalty, the first of which is the crown.

The founder of the concept of the empire as sacred in terms that accommodate both the Carolingian and Ottonian legacy and the imperial office seen in terms of the Roman law recently brought back to the West, while adding a new awareness of this aspect, is Frederick I of Swabia. The new ruler, who was still called "King of the Romans" and therefore was a candidate for the imperial crown that only the pope could confer, differed from his predecessors, not only Carolingian but also Saxon and Franconian. This can be seen in the meeting between Frederick, who had come to Italy to assume the Italic and imperial crown, and Pope Hadrian IV. Their encounter, "the meeting at Sutri," took place on the eighth or ninth of June 1155 in the emperor's encampment, not far from the forbidding city of Sutri and its tufa ramparts. As often happens in circumstances where formal diplomacy and political tension clash, the meeting was so dramatic that it was almost ridiculous.

14

14. The empire and the priesthood, tapestry from c.1200. Collegiate Church of St Servatius, Quedlinburg, Saxony-Anhalt.

15. Emperor Frederick Barbarossa, depicted as a court dignitary prior to 1205, on the portal of the façade of the Freising Cathedral.

15

Frederick stood waiting for the pope to dismount from his horse and sit on the throne prepared for him; after this, like a good Christian and son of the Church, he was prepared to kiss the pontiff's foot. The ritual called for the pope, at a certain point, to place his hands on the shoulders of the ruler, raise him up, and give him the *osculum pacis* (kiss of peace). But the pope refused to perform that gesture because the king had not performed the service of the *strator* (an officer of the staff of a legate). According to a tradition that seems to date back to the middle of the ninth century, to the coronation of Ludwig II, and based on the "Donation of Constantine," during an encounter with the pope, the Germanic king would take the reins of the pontiff's horse, lead the horse for a short distance, and come to a stop; then, holding the stirrup in his left hand, he would help the pope dismount. This service was normally provided by a page to his knight and Frederick had refused to perform it because he saw the act as the gesture of a vassal: performing the ritual would have meant that he was acknowledging that he was a *fidelis* (loyal subject) of the pope and was thus recognizing him as his lord.

The entire situation was extremely ambiguous. The pope declared that the behaviour of the ruler indicated a lack of respect for the vicar of Peter and was thus a sign that he did not attribute any real legal value to the custom of "service of the *strator*." The stalemate was finally overcome and the imperial army continued toward Rome, arriving there around the eighteenth of June, the day on which Frederick was crowned in St Peter's. This took place on a Saturday rather than a Sunday, as custom dictated, proving that the coronation ceremony was conducted in haste, perhaps because the participants were preoccupied. The evening before the ceremony, Cardinal Ottaviano Monticelli had secretly entered through the city walls with a small army and surrounded the basilica. The next day, the pope and the cardinals entered through the same walls; then Frederick arrived, dismounted, and, before entering the great basilica, in the small church of Santa Maria in Turri (which his troops would burn to the ground twelve years later), he swore to be a loyal defender of the Church of Rome. The king and his entourage then proceeded in solemn procession towards St Peter's, where Frederick received the sacrament of Holy Unction. During the Mass, he took the symbols of imperial power from the hands of the pope: the ring *signaculum sanctae fidei* (seal of holy faith), the sword, the crown *signum gloriae* (sign of glory), the sceptre *virgam virtutis* (rod of power), and the globe.

Later, in 1158, Frederick sent a version of an encyclical letter to the prelates and the Christian princes. In it he maintained that he had received the crown directly from God through his election by the princes. He proclaimed that he would rather die than suffer an offence to his *honor imperii*. He cited the doctrine of the "two swords" in his letter, but interpreted it in the sense that both belonged to God, who gave one to the pontiff and the other to the ruler. God is one and the Church is one; the empire was created by divine providence to protect the Church from the evils of this world.

Furthermore the *plenitudo potestatis* (fullness of power) of "Justinian's successor," i.e., his theoretical right to *dominium mundi* (universal dominion) was established. From that point forward, Christianity no longer identified itself with the *Sancta Romana Res Publica* (Holy Roman Republic) but with the *Sacrum Romanum Imperium* (Holy Roman Empire), where the substitution of *Sancta* with *Sacrum* is not simply a linguistic or stylistic gesture; rather, it constitutes a precise reference to the *ius in sacris* (right in sacred matters) in which the powers of the emperor included the right to intervene

16. Map showing the Roman-Germanic Empire during the Hohenstaufen dynasty (1136–1254), ruled by Frederick Barbarossa and Frederick II.

17

17. Portrait of Emperor Charles IV in the triforium of San Vito Cathedral, which the emperor constructed after moving his capital city to Prague.

18. The Golden Door of San Vito Cathedral, Prague.

in ecclesiastical matters. The Carolingian legacy was not rejected or overlooked but was inserted into a continuum extending from Roman antiquity to the present, something no one in the West had ever dared to proclaim.

TOWARDS EMPIRE

In the first half of the thirteenth century, Frederick II, a nephew of Barbarossa and heir to the Norman kingdom of southern Italy through his mother, appears to represent the apex of the imperial ideology. His defeat at the hands of the papacy and the Italian communes, as well as his unexpected death in 1250, resulted in a fifty-year period in which the empire found itself in difficulty. During the fourteenth century, the empire underwent structural changes and became more rooted in Germanic territory.

In the 1300s, Germany was divided into a number of feudal states, ruled by secular or ecclesiastical princes, and a great number of mercantile cities, which tended to form leagues. Since the emperor was primarily the king of Germany, the empire was a sort of symbol and guarantor of German "unity," which was more cultural and spiritual than political. However, the emperor did not exercise real power over the territory; he was elected, although in the past there had been attempts to make the throne hereditary. From the second half of the 1200s onward there had been a tendency to select the emperor from only two dynastic families: the Habsburgs who, in the first half of the century, had managed to create the Duchy of Austria, and the House of Luxembourg, who had intermarried with the rulers of Bohemia.

In 1322, Ludwig IV of Bavaria was crowned king of Germany without seeking papal confirmation. He immediately marched into Italy in support of his loyal imperial vicars, the Visconti, lords of Milan. Pope John XXII excommunicated the emperor, who responded by accusing the pope not only of abusing his power, because he was usurping temporal functions that did not pertain to him, but of heresy. Finally, in January 1327, Ludwig was crowned in Rome, not by a bishop sent by the pope but by the senator of the city, Sciarra Colonna.

Ludwig's decision was made largely due to the influence of two great thinkers who were close to him: Marsilius of Padua and William of Ockham. Marsilius of Padua (1275–1342) was a thinker and scholar from Padua as well as a scholar at the Sorbonne. In 1324, he composed a treatise on political theory, the *Defensor Pacis* (Defender of peace) on the origin of law, in which the concept of political authority as completely autonomous from religious authority and supported by the "people," or, better, by the *sanior* (healthier) and *melior pars* (best part) of the people, was formulated. Furthermore, Marsilius argued that bishops should be elected by popular assemblies and the highest ecclesiastical authority should no longer reside in the papacy but in the council.

William of Ockham (1280–1349), English by birth, entered the Franciscan order at a young age and from 1307 to 1318 studied at Oxford, where he subsequently taught. According to him, there must be a clear distinction between religious and civil authority because each has its own objectives. The work that provided the most support for the theses of Ludwig IV was *Dialogus* (The dialogue), in which Ockham contends that the authority of the emperor derives from God not through the pope, but through mankind. He goes on to say that the emperor is above the law but subject to natural justice. He must not issue orders that are harmful to his people and, if he does, it is lawful to disobey them. In the writings of Marsilius of Padua

18

19

and William of Ockham, we have the foundations of the powers of the state as we understand them in modern times.

When Ludwig IV died in 1346, Charles IV became king of Germany; he was the son of John of Luxembourg who, after marrying Elizabeth, heiress to the throne of Bohemia, had become king of Bohemia. In 1355 Charles IV (1316–1378) travelled to Italy to take the imperial crown, but he generally resided north of the Alps. He was very clear about two things: that the destiny of the Roman-Germanic emperor, if he truly wanted power, was to perform the role of king of the Germans, and that this role could be performed better if the territorial power base was directly and actually ruled by the emperor. To this end, he set out to reinforce his territories in Bohemia. He made Prague the splendid capital of his empire, providing it with a great university, among other things, and he encouraged the use of German rather than Latin in his chancellery.

Charles IV knew very well that one of the reasons for the chronic weakness of the German crown was the relative uncertainty as to who had the right to elect the king. This right was generally granted to the nobles of Germany but no particular hierarchy was specified. Once he was crowned emperor, Charles IV issued an edict called the "Golden Bull" (1356), which specified that henceforth the "prince-electors" of the empire would consist of four laymen (the king of Bohemia, the margrave of Brandenburg, the Duke of Saxony, and the Count of the Palatinate) and three prelates (the archbishops of Mainz, Cologne, and Trier). The election was to take place in Frankfurt, and the coronation of the king of Germany in Aachen. Since the base of dynastic powers was power over territory, Charles acquired "Upper Palatinate" in 1353, and in 1373 he acquired Brandenburg. The German kingdom was founded on three "Orders" (*Stände*): the great imperial princes, the lay and ecclesiastical nobility, and the manufacturing and entrepreneurial classes.

19. Choir and triforium of San Vito Cathedral, Prague.

20. Map showing the location of the prince-electors after the Golden Bull of 1356.

20

KARRVLꝫ MAG

1

8

KINGS

THE IBERIAN PENINSULA

Following the breakup of the Carolingian Empire, a process of reorganization around monarchical powers began in various countries of Western Europe. Initially, this process did not entail the elimination of the network of vassalage and benefice, in the sense that some dynastic families placed themselves at the head of a complex seigneurial system that, for good or bad, governed post-Carolingian Europe. As a result, monarchies arose that integrated, with mixed results, the feudal system into the logic of government in an attempt to force the aristocracy to act in a coherent fashion consonant with the policies of the monarch. The most typical examples of a "feudal" monarchy are found on the Iberian Peninsula and in England and France.

2

	Kingdom of the Franks
	Conquests of Pippin the Short
	Conquests of Charlemagne
	Areas of Carolingian influence
	Maximum expansion of Carolingian Empire
	Western boundary of the Kingdom of Ludwig
	Boundary of the Kingdom of Lothair
	Eastern Boundary of the Kingdom at Charles the Bald

1. Emperor Charlemagne enthroned, fresco in the cloister of the Bressanone Cathedral, c.1410–20.

2. Map of Carolingian and post-Carolingian Europe, eighth and ninth centuries.

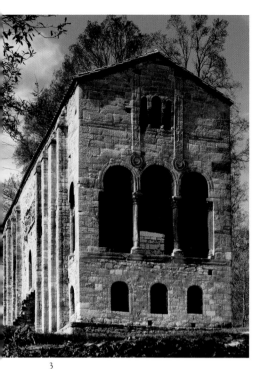

3

It was probably towards the end of July 711 that a large Muslim fleet, commanded by the Berber Tariq Ibn Ziyàd, arrived at the Bay of Algeciras in Spain. The Berber forces numbered approximately 10,000. The swiftness of the conquest of what the Arabs called *al-Andalus* (they had learned to call it by this name in Africa, where it was still known as the "land of the Vandals") was such that, in order to explain it, historians have attributed it to the complicity of the Jews, heretics who remained Arian after the Visigoths had been converted to "Roman" Christianity, and a faction of Goths hostile to Archbishop Rodrigo. However the Saracen conquest of the Iberian Peninsula was not total because "pockets" of Christian resistance survived in the harsh Pyrenees and Cantabrian mountains. In 720, the Goth Pelagius established in Asturias the principality that would become a kingdom some twenty years later, with its capital the new city of Oviedo, founded in 760. The Basque and Navarre peoples, who had resisted the Visigoths, managed to retain their independence and in the third or fourth decade of the ninth century, surrounded by Galicians, Cantabrians, and Asturians, organized themselves as an independent state with the help of a small group of Visigoth warriors who had taken refuge in the small principality of Navarre, which was to become a kingdom about a century later. From Asturias to Navarre and northern Aragon, the movement that would come to be known as the *Reconquista* would soon be underway. At the end of the tenth century, the border between Muslim and Christian Spain, which ran along the Duero River, was rather fluid. On the northeast portion of that border, the Catalans, after repelling a series of Muslim attacks on Barcelona between 985 and 1003, sought to extend the territory under their control at least to Tarragona, halfway between their capital and the Muslim city of Tortosa at the mouth of the Ebro River.

The situation began to change significantly only toward the end of the twelfth century. On 16 July 1195, Almohad Caliph al-Mansur (Almohadism was an

3. View of the Naranco Palace, Asturia, which was originally designed for ceremonial functions.

4. The phases of the *Reconquista*.

5. Gormaz Castle, in the Duero Valley, served to defend against attacks by the Christian kingdoms in the North.

6, 7. Miniature with battle scenes from the *Cantigas de Santa Maria* (Songs of Holy Mary), Real Biblioteca de El Escorial.

8. The Almohad banner called "de Las Navas de Tolosa," c.1212–50, from the site of the decisive battle of 1212. Museo de Telas Medievales, Real Monasterio de las Huelgas, Burgos.

4

5

6

7

8

extremist doctrine that had been imposed on the entire Maghreb region) had defeated the Castilian King Alfonso VII in the great battle of Alarcos. Only eight years had passed since the Muslim conquest of Jerusalem and the new pope, Innocent III, was determined to keep the situation on the Iberian Peninsula under control. King Alfonso of Castile and Peter of Aragon, the knights of Santiago and those of Alcontara and Calatrava, who were in Spain to fight against the Muslims, along with many Spanish, Portuguese, and Frankish knights, and later Sancho of Navarre, all participated in the resulting campaign. The forces on the battlefield were overwhelming and the expedition concluded on 17 July 1212 with the great victory at Navar Tolosa, located between Castile and Andalusia.

The victory opened up the rich and beautiful region of Andalusia to the Christians and was a prelude to the fall of Cordoba, the capital of the caliphate, which was

9

10

11

conquered in 1236. By 1260, the *Reconquista* could be said to be complete, while the Kingdom of Portugal (recognized by the pope in 1179) colonized the southwest portion of the Iberian Peninsula, the zone called Algarve, and, as a result, came into conflict with Castile, which was taking possession of the area south of Guadalquivir, with the exception of the civilized but small emirate of Granada, which remained in Muslim hands until 1492. The long-lasting conflict with the Muslims profoundly affected the culture of Castile, introducing into that culture an austere and warrior-influenced religiosity. From the standpoint of "quality of life," the Christian *Reconquista* did not mark the beginning of a positive period. In the almost five centuries of their control of the Iberian lands, the Muslims had transformed deserts, such as the arid highlands of Meseta, into fertile land by bringing water into the areas with impressive irrigation systems and had begun to grow cereal crops, sugar cane, and citrus fruits. In the highly populated cities ruled by the Muslims, Christian communities called "mozarabic" (that is, those who used Arabic in their liturgy) and Jewish communities lived in peace and harmony. In addition, an urban class of merchants and artisans had developed. Supported by a feudal aristocracy of knights whose economic interests were tied to the more primitive pastoral economy, the rulers of Castile were not interested in maintaining these levels of civilized living. Therefore, they did not encourage agriculture, craftsmanship, and commerce. Indeed, they obstructed developments in these areas by persecuting Muslims and Jews, who were the nerve centre of these activities. Castile began to become a desolate land of poor shepherds and wretched peasants, with an aristocracy that had no financial means, a lifestyle inspired by warrior values, and a religiosity that consisted solely of waging war against the infidels.

The destiny of the Kingdom of Aragon, which from 1137 had been united with the County of Catalonia, whose origins went back to Charlemagne's campaign on the Iberian Peninsula and corresponded to the historic territory of Catalonia, located between the northeastern end of the Pyrenees Mountains and the sea, was quite different. Catalonia had brought to the rigid Aragonese structure – in many respects similar to the Castilian – the gift of fresh forces in the form of coastal cities. The Catalan culture and language were very similar to those of Provence, the area in France south of the Loire River. Catalonia, therefore, was distinct from the Hispanic-Christian world dominated by the Castilian language and the French world that lay beyond the Pyrenees. Furthermore, Barcelona was one of the more flourishing Mediterranean ports – a beautiful city inhabited by merchants and enterprising sailors. The Catalan economy was based on the sea and commerce, a feature that continued to predominate during the thirteenth century. Between 1239 and 1255, the Balearic Islands were conquered, representing a first step in the creation of the future "Mediterranean Empire" of the Aragon dynasty, which incorporated Sicily in 1302 and Sardinia in 1328.

ENGLAND FROM THE NORMANS TO THE PLANTAGENET KINGS

Early medieval England consisted of a number of small kingdoms. English rulers, with varying degrees of success, had attempted to stem the advances of the Danes. However, in 1055 the Danish King Cnut launched a decisive attack. Cnut the Great, king of England, Denmark, and Norway, lord of lands in Slavia (located in the area between the Oder and Vistula Rivers), found himself ruler of a vast territory that was difficult to govern. He implemented a prudent political policy, acquiring the fealty of the kings of Scotland and Ireland. He also promoted the union of the Danish and Anglo-Saxon inhabitants of the island, while reserving positions of authority for his loyal Vikings. Finally, he maintained good relations with the English Church. However, when Cnut died in 1035, a war of succession broke out among his sons, a conflict that opened the way for the imperialist ambitions of the Normans. A new king, Harold, ascended the throne for a brief period of time, but the Duke of Normandy, William the Bastard, defeated the English king at Hastings and, on 25 December 1066, William the Conqueror was crowned king of England at Westminster. During his reign, which lasted until 1089, he subjugated the old Anglo-Saxon nobility and, though he did not take all their possessions, he confiscated a substantial portion of them, giving them as fiefs to his followers. However, he made certain that the fiefs were small so that the English nobility would never again influence the crown, as was happening in France. In addition, he carefully organized the regions into shires governed by officials called sheriffs. Following the organization of the territories, in 1086 he ordered the execution of the survey that created what is known as the *Domesday Book,* which enabled the sovereign to know who owned what in his kingdom.

9. The Barcelona arsenal, one of the flourishing ports in the Mediterranean.

10, 11. Two examples of Catalan-style architecture, a product of Aragon expansion that was not merely commercial: the sanctuary of Santa Maria di Bonaria in Cagliari and the bell-tower of the Alghero Cathedral.

12. Troops under the command of William the Conqueror headed for England, detail from a twelfth-century manuscript. National Library of France, Paris.

13. England and Normandy after 1066.

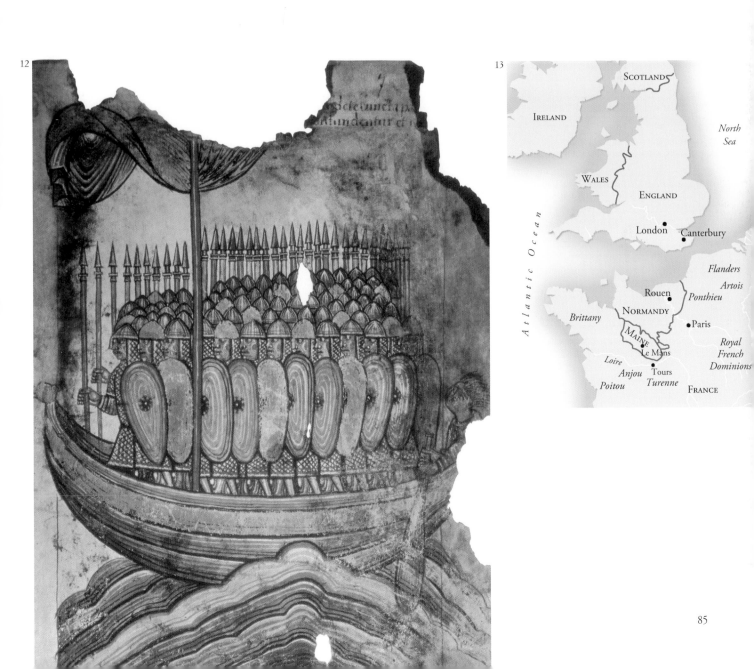

85

14
15
16

14. The troops of William the Conqueror disembarking in Gascony, fourteenth-century miniature. British Library, London.

15, 16. Scenes from the life of Thomas Becket, miniature preserved in the British Library, London. Above, Thomas's return to Canterbury; below, deposition of his body.

The balance William had achieved was upset by his successors. The early twelfth century was characterized by the restlessness of the Norman aristocracy, which led to a civil war in 1135, from which emerged a new dynasty, the Plantagenet, led by Henry II, the Count of Anjou. Henry instituted a domestic policy of reorganization and restoration of the authority of the crown, as well as an important foreign policy. In this regard, he established significant diplomatic and political relations with the Spanish, Sicilian-Norman, and Germanic monarchs, which allowed him to take advantage of a vast network of confederates in his conflict with the king of France.

Henry II had two important adversaries in the Kingdom of England: a group of barons, who were especially unhappy with his tendency to centralize control of the kingdom, and the high-ranking clergy, who were unhappy with his desire to take upon himself ecclesiastical jurisdiction, which went against the traditions that called for respect for its independence of royal power. A fierce adversary of the ruler was his former friend and collaborator Thomas Beckett, who had become archbishop of Canterbury and bravely defended the rights of the Church. Thomas died in his cathedral, victim of a violent act perpetrated by Norman barons. The king himself was suspected of having ordered the murder and the Roman Church responded to the provocation by proclaiming Thomas Beckett a saint. The serious situation caused by the murder of the archbishop turned into a civil war (1173–74) fomented by the king's sons. Henry II, however, triumphed over the opposition of the nobles and his own family and was able to institute a permanent court of justice.

The situation deteriorated under Henry's sons and successors, Richard the Lion-Heart (1189–99) and John Lackland (1199–1216). They had repeatedly rebelled against their father during his reign, but there was also an intense rivalry between them. In addition, both were weak characters who lacked the political ability that had been the trademark of their predecessors. A courageous knight but a cruel and mediocre military leader, Richard had participated in the Third Crusade (1187–89). Upon returning from that campaign, he found himself king due to his father's death, but he had to put down a feudal rebellion led by his brother. The latter, however, succeeded him in 1199 and implemented an imprudent policy that made enemies of both the lay nobility and the ecclesiastical hierarchies. He went so far as to confiscate the possessions of the Church and was excommunicated by Pope Innocent III, after which, intimidated by such a response, he took measures to pay homage to the pontiff.

18

17. The kingdom and French lands of Henry II.

18. Innocent III, painted by Giotto in the Upper Basilica of St Francis, Assisi.

During the ninth century, the French crown was contested by the descendants of Charlemagne and those of Eudes, the count of Paris (who had ruled at the end of the previous century), until Hugh Capet, from the dynasty of Eudes, managed to wrest power from the hands of his adversaries in 987, thereby establishing that dynasty that would be called "Capetian."

However, during the twelfth century the King of France, Louis VII (1137–1180), who had to deal with a number of crises (the failure of the Second Crusade, which greatly reduced his prestige, and his divorce from Eleanor of Aquitaine), reorganized the royal bureaucracy by creating a network of "provosts" and "bailiffs" charged with the administration of justice and tax collection in the name of the ruler. Rather than the great feudal lords, Louis VII supported the petty nobility and the urban middle classes, who were anxious to engage in free trade and were therefore ready to accept a strong monarch who could protect them from the abuses of the high nobility.

His work was continued by his son Philip II (Philip Augustus) (1180–1223) who reorganized the chancellery and the court. He also contributed to the administrative reorganization of the crown and its relationship with the merchant classes, who felt privileged and protected. One of his priorities was to resolve the problem created by the fact that the king of England – who had been Duke of Normandy since the eleventh century and was Count of Anjou and of Maine as a member of the Plantagenet feudal lords of those lands, as well as Count of Poitou and Duke of Aquitaine and Gascony as an heir of Eleanor of Aquitaine – was the effective ruler of most of the Frankish territory. All the French aristocrats who, in one way or another, intended to exercise political autonomy from their king looked to him for leadership.

Philip Augustus exploited John Lackland's weaknesses and, following his excommunication, in 1202 declared him guilty of "felony" (the crime committed by a disloyal vassal) and formally removed from him his Frankish fiefs, excluding Aquitaine. Initially, John did not surrender, but with the fall of Rouen in 1204 he accepted

19. The Louvre and the centre of Paris were first expanded by Philip II, who assembled his counsellors either in the palace or in the adjacent buildings.

20. The Battle of Bouvines, from Giovanni Villani's *Nuova Cronaca* (New chronicle), fourteenth century. Vatican Apostolic Library, Rome.

the forfeiture of all feudal rights to his Frankish territory north of the Loire River. In practice, however, the English king had no intention of abandoning those rich lands. A few years later he intervened in the civil war over the imperial crown that had once again broken out in Germany between the heirs of the House of Swabia and the heirs of Henry the Lion. This led to the decisive battle on Sunday, 27 July 1214, at Bouvines, a town in the north of France, not far from Lilles, between the supporters of the young King of Germany, Frederick II of Swabia, whose principal ally was the Frankish ruler, and his adversary, Otto IV of Braunschweig, supported by his relative John of England as well as some Frankish feudal lords. Although the Battle of Bouvines decided the fate of the Germanic throne, in reality what was at stake was the throne of France. For Philip Augustus, his victory meant that he was able to think in terms of unity by finally subordinating the Frankish feudal lords to the crown and preventing them from looking beyond the frontiers of the kingdom in search of external support for their decentralist policies.

NATIONAL MONARCHIES

John Lackland continued to rule until his death in 1216, but his policies displeased virtually everyone: the prelates, whose possessions he had confiscated, for which he was excommunicated; the feudal lords, to whom he had promised much when he encouraged them to rebel against his brother, but whom he then tried to subjugate with an oppressive policy; and the cities, whose growing importance he had not understood. His ill-advised policies on the continent, particularly the defeat at Bouvines, followed by the loss of the territories north of Loire, were a signal for the English nobles to rebel. John was forced to swear respect for the ancient customs that concerned the barons, which meant, among other things, that he was obliged to consult them before imposing any new taxes. In addition, no nobleman was to be punished except on the basis of a sentence pronounced by his peers. Finally, protection of the rights of the Church and the feudal lords was codified.

22

21

21. Detail of the Magna Carta. British Library, London.

22. The seal of Frederick II, from 1215. Hessisches Staatsarchiv, Darmstadt.

23. Bronze statue of Pope Boniface VIII. Medieval Civic Museum, Bologna.

24. Philip the Fair, the king of France, receives the book of good governance as a gift, miniature from 1440. Royal Library, Brussels.

25. Map showing the political situation in Europe prior to the discovery of America.

23

This is the meaning of the Magna Carta, issued in June 1215; it was a document that stipulated fundamental agreement between the crown and the nobility and would shape life in the kingdom from that point on by limiting the powers of the king while at the same time asserting their traditional stability. Among other things, a *Magnum Concilium* (Great Council) of nobles was instituted, which assisted the king in performing the functions of government and had the special right of controlling his fiscal policy. In 1242, this administrative organ took the name "Parliament," which, as we know, was destined to have a long history in modern civilization. It is important, however, to emphasize that, initially, the Magna Carta was not understood to be an instrument of "modernization" – a concept that would not have had any meaning at that time. On the contrary, it was the Frankish crown, with its strong tendency toward centralizing its powers, that established the foundations of the modern state; the English barons merely reaffirmed the traditional rights that the feudal system had always conceded to the crown.

In France, Philip IV, called the Fair, can be considered to be the ruler who, between the 1200s and 1300s, best understood the consequences of the fact that the king's universal powers were in decline. He connected this reality with another, namely the disintegration of the feudal system at the hands of the new urban middle classes, with their liquid capital. In the first years of the fourteenth century, Philip came into conflict with Pope Boniface VIII by challenging his right to rule the Church of France directly and emerged victorious from the dispute.

Although the actions of the French sovereign appeared to be somewhat unusual, they were supported by royal political doctrine as formulated by famous legists and politicians who, not accidentally, were in the circle of his closest collaborators. Among these, Pierre Dubois and Guillaume de Nogaret are worthy of mention. Dubois was the author of a number of treatises on a variety of topics, from the liberation of the Holy Land to ways of shortening wars. In particular, he is credited with a text, anonymous at the time, in which he accused Pope Boniface VIII of heresy for having dared to claim not only supreme spiritual power but temporal power as well. Considered an extremist, even among William IV's advisors, Dubois is nonetheless thought to be one of the true founders of the modern concept of politics and the state.

Guillaume de Nogaret, an advisor and minister of Philip IV, as well as a protagonist in the dispute with Boniface VIII, was also author of theoretical writings that argue the autonomy of the king's powers in relation to all other powers, including the king's traditional universal ones. The essence of regalism or the doctrine of royal prerogative – which would be further developed in the political philosophy in the age of the communes, the Europe of the 1500s and 1600s – is captured in the famous motto "*Rex superior non recognoscit et imperitorum est rex in territorio suo*" (The king does not recognize a superior and the king is emperor in his lands). Regalism, which constituted a clear break with Christian tradition as corroborated by Roman law, which intended Christianity to be united in one socio-political body, affirms that the king does not recognize any superior, not even the Roman-Germanic emperor. It follows that the powers of the emperor, i.e., the prerogatives that made the emperor the sole source of right and attributed to him *plenitudo potestades* (fullness of power) effectively belonged to the king within the territory of his kingdom. The universalism of medieval thought was formulated and the modern concept of the absolute state established.

Although the so-called Hundred Years' War between France and England, waged in the years straddling the fourteenth and fifteenth centuries, represented a setback for the French monarchy, the foundations for the modern state were already established and, in the second half of the fourteenth century, France emerged as the most organized and cohesive nation in Europe. This was a path that England was able to take (although differently) only at the end of that century, at the end of the so-called Wars of the Roses, from which the Tudor dynasty emerged. At the same time, on the Iberian Peninsula, the marriage between the two heirs to the thrones of Castile and Aragon, Isabella and Ferdinand, celebrated in 1469, created modern Spain.

26. The Catholic monarchs Ferdinand of Aragon and Isabella of Castile, roundel on the façade of the University of Salamanca, c.1520.

26

25

9

THE ARISTOCRACY

CAVALRYMEN

Among the various terms used from the end of the tenth century on to define feudal dependence and the profession of arms, one gradually emerged as dominant. This is the term *miles*, which refers to a warrior on horseback who uses heavy armour and can be translated as "knight." During the middle centuries of the medieval age, the knight was not necessarily a high-ranking person: he could be a free man who owned land, and he could also be a free man (perhaps a *ministerialis* or agent) who was not free originally. However, his livelihood depended on his speciality, fighting wars, and he usually received what he needed from a *senior* in order to acquire his costly weapons. In the European feudal system of the late Middle Ages, the expression "fief of the knight" was used to indicate a feudal benefice, the income from which was sufficient to keep a knight in armour. In reality, the knight was not

1. The ninth-century Metz *Psalterium Aureum* (Golden psalter) illustrating the siege and destruction of a city. Stiftsbibliothek, St Gall.

2. Knights in combat, from an eleventh-century miniature. Monte Cassino Abbey.

3. Knights in battle at Capua during a campaign conducted in Italy by the Germanic Emperor Henry IV. Coloured-ink drawing from before the middle of the thirteenth century. Bürgherbibliothek, Berne.

4

4. A fierce pitched battle described in Vincent de Beauvais' *Speculum Historiale* (Mirror of history), thirteenth century. Condé Museum, Chantilly.

5. A scene from Chrétien de Troyes' *Lancelot.*

6. A priest administers communion to a knight, counter-façade of the Reims Cathedral.

merely an isolated individual; he was also part of a combat unit. In fact, he needed a group of acolytes, assistants, and apprentices.

The tenth to eleventh-century *miles* (soldier) was a violent, lawless warrior who did battle against antagonists belonging to his own socio-political class. As such, he was quite different from the *chevalier* – an *idealtypus* or ideal type – who would eventually be defined in moral and behavioural terms. This raises the question of the historical definition of the knightly code of ethical conduct. Even before the code was formulated in positive terms, during the eleventh and twelfth centuries it was defined in negative terms, that is, in terms of what the knight was not supposed to do. If the first and clearest expressions of the knightly code of conduct can be found in the canons of the twelfth-century Church, which are the patterns for knightly ideals, it follows that the *latro* (thief), *raptor* (robber), *praedo* (pirate), and the *effractor pacis* (breaker of the peace) – in other words the violator of the *Pax* (Peace) and the *Tregua Dei* (Truce of God), which had been established by the Church to provide relief for a Europe torn apart by conflicts – are the precedent and model for the *Raubritter* (robber baron) or the knight-predator, who would become the "anti-knight" who challenges the Christian warrior.

We should not underestimate the importance of the propaganda used by the Church to create this ethical revolution, out of which emerges a conceptually new *miles*, a figure that can be described with the expression – which up to that time had been used only in monastic and mystical literature – *miles Christi* (soldier of Christ). To demonize the *Raubritter*, a host of values and resources was mobilized, including the re-reading of legends whose roots were in Celtic-Germanic mythology and constituted part of the folklore of early medieval Europe. Between the eleventh and thirteenth centuries, the chronicles and epic literature often relate, with many variations, the story of a knight who, though he shares with his brothers-in-arms the dignity of knighthood acquired through initiation (or at least some sort of ceremony) as well as knowledge of the rituals and professional skills, does not respect ethical norms. These norms do not yet correspond to anything professed firmly, but they are still part of the ethical behaviour from which the "system of chivalric values" emerges. The complex figure of the transgressor casts its shadow on the whole of medieval chivalrous literature, to the point of becoming fixed in certain characters and dynasties.

RITUALS AND CUSTOMS

Aware that they belonged to an elite group or body that was to some extent separate from the rest of the society, medieval knights also developed their own culture, which led to the creation of an ethics and a specific literature (chansons de geste and chivalrous romances). With the formalization of feudal rights, entry into the order of knights also began to be regulated by a series of rules. At first, these were presumably expressed in various forms of initiation and later (at least from the eleventh century on) more formal ceremonies, although they were still simple. This ritual, which was called "dubbing," from the Germanic *dubban* (to strike), has remained in the English language and involves two things: the giving of weapons and the mark, a light, ritual wound (which could be simply a slap or a tap on the nape of the neck or on the shoulder of the newly knighted candidate; in Italian it is "accolta" or welcome). Similar to the *alapa militaris*, the slap given to a Roman soldier, which became the Christian ritual of confirmation (making one a "soldier of Christ"), it was

5

6

7

8

transformed into a type of caress that the officiant administers with his right hand to the cheek of the person being confirmed. It was probably a test of strength, courage, and the capacity to withstand pain. It may be that originally it was an actual wound, which the knight was expected to accept in a manly fashion; later it became merely symbolic.

When the knight was not fighting, his basic activity was hunting. The hunt, which took place among the aristocracy on the great reserves of the feudal lands, involved large wild animals, such as bears and boars, as well as deer, which are also powerful and can be dangerous; hunting was a prerogative that became both a noble activity and practical training for warfare. During the late Middle Ages, a noble class began to form within the feudal system and the ranks of the *milites*, whose status was made legally transmissible from generation to generation. Historians have long debated the origins of this phenomenon; today, the prevailing tendency, especially among French and Italian scholars, is to consider the range of ruling feudal classes as "aristocracy" and to reserve the term "nobility" for the succeeding period, at least until the eleventh century. (This usage is preferred, despite the fact that the sources of the period are unaware of the term "aristocracy" but use the term "*nobiles*" indiscriminately.) At this time the privileges associated with kinship were codified and the noble class was transformed into lineages as a result of the decision to privilege patrilineal descent, particularly through the first-born son. This system was developed to avoid the dispersal of land holdings once these became inheritable. In theory, noble lineage was independent of a family's wealth and titles; in reality, things remained fluid, and for a long time it was possible to acquire noble titles by purchasing them, as well as through politically arranged marriages.

9

10

ORDERS OF KNIGHTS

With the development of the Latin settlements in the East, a new image of the knight was created. The forces that supported the Latin kingdom of Jerusalem – immediately threatened by the surrounding Islamic states, which launched a counter-attack after recovering from the surprise invasion – consisted largely of the aristocrats who had participated in the crusades and who quickly married into Syrian-Christian or Armenian noble families, the inhabitants of Italian cities that had participated in the capture of many coastal cities where they established prosperous commercial colonies, and the religious-military orders established to protect pilgrims. These militias, which we incorrectly refer to as "religious-military orders," were an original creation of the crusades to the Holy Lands. They are religious orders whose code of conduct was based on the canonical Rule of St Augustine but adapted to the cenobitic Rule of St Benedict. In addition to relatively few priests, the orders included a large group of "lay brothers" – that is to say, those who were not ordained and are therefore distinct from the clergy – some of whom were engaged in various activities in accordance with the tradition established by Benedict in Nursia, while others (either *milites* or *servientes*, depending on whether or not they were knighted prior to entering the order) had the task of defending pilgrims and keeping the roads safe. During the second decade of the twelfth century, in two different parts of the city of Jerusalem – around the al-Aqsa mosque on the courtyard of the temple that the crusaders called the *Templum Salomonis* (Temple of Solomon), originally used as a court of the king, and around the Hospital of Saint John near the Basilica of the Resurrection – two *fraternitates* (brotherhoods) were established and, with papal approval, transformed into

7. Hunting scene, c.1160, mosaic on the west wall of the "salon" of King Roger II, Royal Palace, Palermo.

8. Return from the hunt with falcon, detail of the frescoes in the Deer Room, Italian-French workshop, 1343. Papal Palace, Avignon.

9. Image of a knight with the crossed shield, thirteenth-century fresco. Cressae, France.

10. The temple-fortress of San Juan of Portomarin, erected by the Order of St John on the road to Santiago de Compostela.

religious orders. This is how the *Pauperes Commilitones Christi Templique Solomonici* (The Poor Fellow-Soldiers of Christ and of the Temple of Solomon), the Templars, and the Knights of St John (subsequently Knights of Cyprus and today Knights of Malta) came into existence. Later, the Knights of St Mary were added, who came exclusively from the Germanic nation and were therefore called Teutonic. The idea of religious orders containing fighters, which was justified in a world in a constant state of war where free fighters were scarce and a large territory had to be continually defended, naturally created many problems for the Church. Dealing with these problems required the full authority of the greatest mystic of the twelfth century, the Cistercian Bernard, Abbot of Clairvaux (1090–1153, canonized in 1104). Bernard was interested in the Templar *fraternitas*, supported the Church's recognition of the fraternity as a militia and, for the Templars, wrote the *Liber de laude novae militiae* (Book in Praise of the New Militia), in which he contrasts the vices of the worldly knights with the virtues of those who converted to the religious life; he also describes the Holy Land as a spiritual and allegorical landscape. The military orders were also builders. The Templar fortresses and hostels, which were constructed one behind the other in a double cordon running from the Syrian north to the Palestinian south to guard the coastline, as well as the roads in the interior and on the shores of the Jordan River remain impressive reminders of a great project of defence and territorial organization. The new religious-military institutions soon attracted many knights; in addition, they received donations of property and other goods to the point where, in an institution that practised an austere form of personal poverty, they became very wealthy and built their "mansions" throughout the Christian world. They were also entrusted with large sums of money, the management of which enabled them to invent new and more effective ways of conducting banking transactions, for example, by depositing sums of money in the various Templar houses from which merchants, in any location where the order was established, were able to access money without physically transferring it by using letters authenticated by means of seals issued by the order.

CASTLES

Between the fifth and eighth centuries, Europe was repeatedly invaded by tribes originating in the eastern steppes, tribes we customarily call barbarians, but in the

11

12

13

early part of the ninth century, a more serious phenomenon got underway. Already impoverished by the contraction of trade and a return to life in the countryside, Europe was the site of incursions by groups that were not large in terms of numbers but were violent and predacious. These incursions came not only from the east (Hungarians or Magyars, whose language and culture were originally similar to those of the Huns, Bulgars, and Avars), but also from the north (the "Normans") as well as from the south (the "Agarens" or "Saracens," that is the Arab-Berbers of northern Africa, who were Muslims). Exposed to these continuous and bloody attacks, the Carolingian Empire began to falter; many rich monasteries were sacked and many coastal cities evacuated or at least "re-established" in the interior, far from the risk of attacks from the sea. Up to that time, only the Vandal assault in the fifth century had been such a phenomenon, that is to say, an attack from the sea, but the conversion of the coastal cities of Asia and Africa to Islam had changed the cultural balance in the Mediterranean. From the first decades of the ninth century, a wave of Scandinavian people was added to the mix; these were people who explored the European continent, perhaps following an improvement in the climate, which had partly melted the glaciers and made navigation in the northern seas more feasible.

Danger and the constant need for defence characterized the ninth and tenth centuries and not only caused power vacuums throughout Europe but also led

11. Two Templars, detail of a fourteenth-century miniature. National Library of France, Paris.

12. The city of Segovia. In the foreground, the Church of the Holy Sepulchre, consecrated in 1208 with the participation of the Knights of the Holy Sepulchre and Knights Templar.

13. View of the Loarre Castle, Aragon, built in the eleventh century.

14

15

to new social organs that "spontaneously" filled these voids. New centres of aristo-cratic power arose in many places almost out of nothing, often maintained through the sheer force of their weapons and subsequently legitimated by the fact that they had assumed the responsibility of defending the inhabitants of a city or a region in the absence of others capable of doing so. The lack of security and the need to defend oneself against the barbarian invasions caused the emergence of new power structures "from below": local "signoria" based on landed property and character-ized by mutual dependence. The abstract idea of the state, which had survived the collapse of the Roman Empire and was still alive during the time of Charlemagne, disappeared in the following period in the face of immediate realities, which con-sisted of meeting primary needs: defence, food, and the production of goods for immediate consumption.

Europe became dotted with "castles," which the order of the *milites* defended. These were fortified settlements within whose protective walls the tower, keep, and forecastle were located – the dwelling of the local lord with storehouses for grain and the implements of work and war, along with more modest buildings for his household staff and the peasants who were his subjects. Around the castle there were various structures and areas of production administered by figures of different

ranks – some were fighters on horseback, while others were workers on the land, but all were bound to the "lord of the manor" by a precise relationship of dependence.

Building castles was a fundamental feature of the organization of territory between the ninth and eleventh centuries, occurring in varying degrees at different times throughout the period, and the process involved all of Western Europe. The various "castellanies," which included the area surrounding the castle, were part of larger parcels of land arranged in a system of hierarchical dependence, which, at least in theory, had at its apex the lords, who were also public officials: these were dukes, marquis, and counts who depended directly on the king. However, this dependence was purely formal, at least beyond a certain point. The feudal system was based on the delegation of powers from the apex to the base and from the centre to the periphery. In theory, no one was exempt from these ties; in practice, personal liberty and the free ownership of goods and lands continued to survive.

14. Beseno Castle in Rovereto. Mentioned in references dating from 1151, it is one of the oldest castles in the Trentino region of Italy.

15. Colour drawing that shows the destructive incursions of Hungarians in 925. University Library, Leiden.

1. A farm, third-century mosaic from
    Uthina. Bardo Museum, Tunis.

2. Bronze boar from the Gallo-Roman
    period, from Neuvy-en-Sullias.

1

3. Adam Elsheimer (1578–1609),
    Flight into Egypt, 1609, detail.
    Depicted here is a forest on the edge
    of a bog.

10

PEASANTS

We imagine the medieval peasant to be poor, frail, haggard, and almost savage; perhaps, if we compare him to the peasant of recent times, he might well appear to be so. In absolute terms, however, even if his rural life was bleak, we are once again victims of a strange prejudice by which we attribute to the Middle Ages a series of negative features that "anticipate" the history of Europe, whereas these features actually developed later. The panorama of medieval Europe was quite different from what it is today. Villages and cultivated areas were located in woodlands, marshes, and pasturelands in the high hills and mountains. The medieval peasant, that is the inhabitant of areas other than the urban centres, was thus not a farmer, although the two terms are synonymous for us – at least not strictly a farmer. He was also a shepherd, hunter, pig-farmer, fisherman, and wild fruit gatherer. But his narrative underwent substantial changes over the one-thousand-year span of the Middle Ages.

2

From a political and institutional standpoint, fifth-century Western Europe underwent a difficult reorganization that led to the so-called "Roman-barbarian monarchies," which were always formally recognized by the Roman emperor (by this time the only one in existence was in Constantinople), while the old municipal organizations continued to function for a long time. The economy and social structure, however, suffered serious problems that were aggravated in the next century – at least in the Mediterranean regions and especially in Italy – by the effects of the Greco-Gothic war. One of the principal changes involved the depopulation of the cities. Another was the progressive disappearance of *servitus* or classical slavery, because the slave workforce on the large landed estates was replaced by settlers. The figure of the settler was already known in previous centuries, but at that time his legal status was clearly superior. Between Late Antiquity and the early Middle Ages, despite his personal freedom (which by now was only an empty legal and formal status), the settler began to be increasingly bound to the land on which he worked. He did obligatory tasks without receiving payment and the quantity of work was often determined unilaterally by the landowner. The settler was obliged to acquire products from or use the infrastructures in the owner's estate and was legally dependent on the landowner. But this "flight from freedom" increased his chances of living a secure life because the estates had their own vigilantes.

The subdivision of large landed estates among several families of settlers also altered the type of crop produced. Previously, monoculture was the norm on large estates: wheat, grapes, olives, etc. The division of the estate into lots assigned to families, as opposed to slaves, brought about a diversification of agricultural products that subsequently circulated, particularly within the estate. It would be a mistake to think that this was a completely self-sufficient system of production: if the harvest was more abundant than was required within the estate itself, the surplus could be traded. In addition, it was difficult for a manor to produce enough variety of goods to satisfy all its needs and so trading of valuable merchandise and hand-made goods occurred.

3

THE MANORIAL SYSTEM

4

5

By this time, forests had become the dominant feature of the early medieval European landscape, despite the great diversity in the Mediterranean region relative to that of the Germanic part of the continent. In the sparsely urbanized regions of the north and in the heart of the continent, the relationship between humans and the environment remained largely unchanged with respect to the preceding centuries. Northern France, that is north of the Loire, and the areas where there had been the most intensive settlement by the Germanic tribes, from the Rhine basin to the Elbe River basin, had remained mostly untouched by Roman civilization and its social system. Meanwhile, in the coastal south, the culture of the Late Empire had survived in spite of depopulation and recession, and despite the fact that the culture had come into contact with another city-based civilization: Islam. The great forests of the North also remained unchanged because of the characteristics of Germanic settlement and its relationship with the environment, in which the primary source of food was hunting and animal-rearing in open ranges.

With regard to agricultural practices in these areas, there was a limited use of the soil, which was primarily ploughed or used as pastureland but did not produce sufficient food. The very low yield (the relationship between the planting and the harvest) caused by the use of agricultural implements inappropriate for the harsh northern terrain – use of the great wheel-plough, with its mouldboard and coulter, spread slowly only after the eighth century – meant that the production of cereal crops was secondary to animal-rearing, in particular pig-farming. Northern peoples were thus less vulnerable to climatic conditions, on which the harvest depended, and therefore also less exposed to the famines that made survival problematic in the Mediterranean where, despite the spread of woodlands and uncultivated areas, agriculture thrived because the soil was lighter and easier to work. As an integral part of obtaining food from the environment, woodlands and scrubland became essential reserves that ensured survival by providing the protein needed for a varied diet. However, important ethnic differences in eating habits persisted: the Germanic peoples introduced their custom of consuming the meat from large animals, whereas the Roman-Byzantine world continued to prefer mutton and lamb, alongside the Mediterranean consumption of flours and cereals.

The spread of uncultivated land had some positive aspects that explain the importance of vast scrublands and woodlands in the manorial system. It has long been believed that the economic effect of this system of organization of production was a move toward self-sufficiency and especially toward immobility and closure. It cannot be denied that the *curtis* or manorial court tended to produce all that it needed within its own boundaries, particularly in light of the reduced quantities of artisanal goods coming from the cities. However, the management of resources brought about the circulation of surplus goods, which often, as was the case with some important monasteries in northern Italy, led to the construction of warehouses in major urban areas or along the important rivers in order to ensure the marketing of the excess agricultural products. The concentration of land in the hands of a few, for instance in ecclesiastical property, also promoted, to some extent, the circulation of agricultural products among distant courts, thereby stimulating trade, which was also stimulated by an increased variety of products, especially in places where mining activity and a residual capacity in iron production were maintained.

6

7

The manorial system was probably the only possible answer to the environmental and social situation of Europe during this time. It is important to remember, however, that this type of organization was not the only agricultural model that existed in Europe: it coexisted with other forms of production related to the survival of small tracts of land, whose structures – which were not very rigid – remained unchanged. In addition to the lord's properties, there were also lands that did not belong to him and were held and worked by the peasants as their own. In the Mediterranean areas, and therefore in Italy, they had full ownership. In north-central Europe, the small tract of land was less common and the peasants worked lands that they did not necessarily own and that were not owned by a lord but instead by other members of the lay nobility or by ecclesiastical bodies that exercised feudal dominion over those lands. This did not, however, prevent the lord of the castle from exercising rights, not necessarily over these properties but over the peasants themselves, as residents on his lands.

IMPROVEMENTS, FOR WHOM?

The traditional theory of a sudden expansion of European society around the year 1000 is now declining in favour of the idea of a long period of growth in the

8.

8. The labours of farmers in the fields, miniature from a thirteenth-century Flemish manuscript. Royal Library, Brussels.

9. San Zeno, Verona, detail of one of the bronze doors, early twelfth century. In the foreground is a wheeled plough.

economy and the population between the eighth and thirteenth centuries. Many factors played a role in this process, such as the dynamic character of the manorial system and seigneurial society. In the traditional image of this period, as well as in the modern collective imagination, these elements have been seen as indicators of backwardness rather than progress. More definitely needs to be said about the idea of progress. If the general state of the economy in the tenth and eleventh centuries improved, it is probable that this positive trend did not correspond to improvement in the per capita income and the living conditions of the rural populations. In the 1960s, some historians emphasized the innovative and "technological" character of the Middle Ages – in particular the eleventh century – in contrast to the traditional notion of an immobile or static medieval Europe. Today the debate on these issues is less heated and historians tend to focus on the idea of a Middle Ages in which people made better use of techniques that were already known, rather than inventing new ones.

Let us look briefly at the changes brought about by techniques used to work the land. The introduction of new ploughing methods was of great importance in the cultivation of cereals. In the first centuries of the early Middle Ages, rural populations continued to use the traditional Mediterranean plough; it was light, wooden, and had only one blade reinforced with metal. Beginning in the eighth century, but especially in the tenth, a heavier plough was introduced in many areas of central and northern Europe (including the Po Valley), one made of metal, with wheels and a coulter that could till the soil. Horses and oxen were used to pull the plough, and metal shoes and a new yoke were introduced; these items gave ploughing a new power and provided a better method of preparing the soil that made it more productive. We should also recall the introduction of so-called "triennial crop rotation," which meant that every year only a third of the land was left fallow, as opposed to the traditional half, thereby increasing the yield. In addition, this new rotation system allowed the farmers to plant grass seeds during the spring in the portion of the field that was used for cereals during the winter. The other innovation of this period was the introduction of the watermill, which was known in theory prior to the tenth and eleventh centuries but was introduced on a massive scale in regions of Europe where the growth of agricultural products made it necessary. But it is clear that these technical innovations alone cannot convincingly explain the level of increased economic growth. Unless we combine these factors with the changes in the system of administering the agricultural lands, described in the first chapter of the present volume, we are destined not to understand the deeper reasons for the change that got underway around the year 1000.

We need to include climactic phenomena among the causes of the general increase in production during this time. It seems that the end of the tenth century saw a significant heating of the earth's atmosphere and an improved climate, at least in the northern regions. This change coincided with other phenomena, especially a reduction in the amount of rainfall and, naturally, the melting of the polar icecaps. These events had extraordinarily important consequences. Meanwhile, the retraction of the polar ice and the melting of the glaciers opened the North Sea, enabling the Vikings to explore and to settle in Iceland. In addition, the more favourable climate had a positive impact on several important infantile illnesses, such as those affecting the respiratory tract, thereby creating conditions conducive to population growth. At the same time, in some cases the reduced amount of precipitation created conditions for improved agriculture.

Combined with a positive trend in agricultural production, technical innovation and the end of epidemics – as far as we know they are nonexistent between in seventh and eighth centuries – promoted demographic growth and an increase in cultivated lands. The effects, however, were not all positive. In a period in which the macro-economy was growing, the situation in which peasants found themselves often worsened. It is during this period that the rural masses began to eat primarily grains and legumes, supplemented with a few proteins. Not only was agricultural space being reclaimed from the woodlands and forests for the production of cereals, but, it must be pointed out, in the context of a general deterioration of their social status, the peasants lost their traditional right to hunt and forage in woodlands and marshlands. In this sense, peasants undoubtedly experienced a regression in the quality of their nutrition after the ninth century. In the early Middle Ages, peasants ate better because, by exploiting the woods and the underbrush, they had a broader range of foods at their disposal. In the eleventh century, with the increase in population, it was necessary to plan the gathering of food in a different way. In the meantime – and this is the most important fact – the importance of feudal-seigneurial ties and values grew. Probably between the eleventh and thirteenth centuries, the physical conditions of the peasants deteriorated to the extent that, when the plague struck Europe in the mid-1300s, a large portion of the rural population fell victim – some say 60 percent of the population in certain areas. The cause was not only the unforgiving nature of the disease but also the lack of resistance caused by poor nutrition.

TOWARDS MARGINALITY

The peasant, this "marginal" creature living between cultivated fields and scrublands where wild animals live and where hermits and outlaws took refuge – like the shepherd who is even more "marginalized" – is a liminal figure in the anthropological sense as well. He is a link in the chain, since he is often portrayed in chivalrous romances as something between human and bestial-demonic, between the civilized man of the agrarian world with his eyes on the city and the savage who inhabits the forests and terrorizes wayfarers. He is a sort of contorted Caliban who speaks an incomprehensible language; the hunched back and other ailments that afflict him, products of the hard labour he must endure in order to eke out a living, are reflected in the literature as well as in the plastic and figurative arts of the time – which give us an image wherein satire approaches disdain, and in some cases a vague sense of fear. During the age of the communes, the "satire of the boor" was a product of this long, chivalrous, goliardic, ecclesiastical, and intellectual tradition.

In a certain sense, we could say that in a society, such as that of thirteenth-century Italy, which was on its triumphant path to becoming predominantly urbanized – since by this time the city was the centre of political decision-making, economic policy, and cultural production – the peasant was becoming increasingly marginalized. It is no surprise that he tried to escape this marginalization by moving into the city. This trend toward moving to the city was far from being limited to peasants and "fugitive slaves." It was also possible to be marginalized in the city. Poverty, a constant presence throughout the Middle Ages, was perhaps no less harsh in the feudal and pre-communal era. However, it was less obvious because the hostels established by the Church lessened its effects and because the poverty was less tragic, less "present" since the population was more widely dispersed over

10

10. The Month of October, east wall of the Aula Greca (Greek Room), fifth decade of the thirteenth century. Basilica of the Four Crowned Saints, Rome.

11. Ambrogio Lorenzetti (1317–1348), *The Effects of Good Government*, detail, the orderly life in the countryside outside the city walls. Palazzo Pubblico, Siena.

12. Hieronymus Bosch, *The Prodigal Son* (detail). This beautiful image depicts the liberty enjoyed in the country and in the city. Boymans van Beuningen Museum, Rotterdam.

11

12

the territory; injustices and inequities were therefore less conspicuous. As well, the generally accepted concept of social stratification made it more "natural" and less scandalous that there was extensive socio-economic stratification. This was especially true since, during the feudal and pre-communal age, prestige and power were not as tightly connected to the money economy and, therefore, to the possession of money, property, and goods, as they would soon become.

1

2

11

ROADS

THE NETWORK OF ROADS

Ancient cities arose mainly along the coastline of the Mediterranean Sea or on the banks of the great navigable rivers. In antiquity, the construction of carriageable roads was always an enormous problem and crossing the mountains or tunnelling through them was a difficult technical hurdle. Only the Romans, with their slave-based economy and military organization, had a comprehensive policy of road construction. But during the early Middle Ages many of the Roman roads in the west were either completely or partly abandoned or damaged (we need only think of the Via Aurelia, which was interrupted by marshes in many sections along the coast of Tuscany and Lazio) or reduced to being used as stone quarries for the construction of buildings, especially churches.

Unlike the Roman road, the medieval road (at least up to the 1200s) was not paved but dirt; it was not straight but winding and followed the contours of the terrain in which it was located; it was a mule path rather than a carriageable road. Despite these poor conditions, the Middle Ages were a time of travel. Everyone travelled: rulers and lords for the responsibilities of government, prelates for pastoral duties, and merchants for trade. People travelled in groups, on foot, or on the backs of animals; carts or carriages were rare, uncomfortable, and used primarily to transport merchandise. The poor state of the roads made it easier to transport goods on pack animals than on wheels.

1. Travel scene from a psalter datable from 1320–40. British Library, London.

2. During the Middle Ages, people continued to use the old paved Roman roads, such as the Via Cassia.

The maintenance of roads and bridges – typically a public responsibility – had become the responsibility of various regional rulers, often with disastrous results. Both roads and bridges were neglected and travelling on them ended up costing a great deal as a result of the many tariffs levied along the way. The revival of commerce – which in the twelfth century was centred on fairs in Champagne, located between the rivers Seine and Marne – was thus essentially tied to traffic along waterways, which in the interior of the continent meant rivers. Transporting goods on large flat-bottom boats along rivers was less costly than taking them via overland routes: merchandise could be transported more securely and in greater quantities on water. As a result, chains of towns and villages developed along the European rivers. The watercourses for the entire system were the Rhine, Rhône, Danube, and Po. In addition to these great rivers there were other important rivers, including the Garonne in France, the Elbe in Germany, and the Drava and Sava in the Balkans; in Italy there were the Adige and the Arno, which were either fully or partly navigable. Hybrid systems of communication emerged in which goods were passed along waterways where possible – but also on roads that often ran alongside the rivers – and were unloaded and transferred onto mules, usually in order to negotiate the mountain passes. A route running parallel to the Rhine connected the cities of Cologne, Mainz, Worms, and Spier to the Po Valley, which could be reached through the Splügen Pass. From Milan, it was possible to reach both the port of Genoa on the Tyrrhenian Sea and the port of Venice on the Adriatic as well as the road junction at Piacenza. There, the great Italian road of the Middle Ages, the Via Francigena (so called because it was used by those who travelled from France), after traversing the St Bernard Pass, reached the cities of Ivrea, Vercelli, and Pavia and crossed the Po at Piacenza. It continued through the Cisa Pass in Tuscany to link with the route traced by the ancient consular road, the Via Cassia, and extend on to Rome. From there, following the trail of another consular road, the Via Traiana, it was possible to reach the ports in the region of Puglia, where one could (by crossing the Otranto Channel) easily reach Constantinople by taking yet another Roman road, the Via Egnazia, and even continue on to the Near East.

3. The *Camino de la Plata* (The Silver Way), the dirt road on which the pilgrims travelled to Santiago de Compostela, which passes through the Arch at Caparra, which stands as a symbol of this route.

4. One of the first maps containing the pilgrimage routes, by the English monk, Matthew Paris, first half of the thirteenth century. British Library, London.

5. Map showing medieval land and water routes, as well as the most important cities for trade in the twelfth century.

6

7

8

FAIRS AND MARKETS

The states that emerged from the ruins of the Roman world in the west maintained relatively intensive trade and commerce for a long time. The Greeks and Syrians, who were able to occupy vast areas in the Mediterranean ports, remained the commercial protagonists of many cities in southern Gaul and Visigoth Spain, areas where the fairs (*nundinae*) and markets cited in the decrees of Late Antiquity were held. Throughout the seventh century, those port cities where Roman law and its precise provisions regarding customs and warehouses survived longest preserved traces of the existence of *thelonarii* (local merchants). This indicates the persistence of a practice wherein both foreigners and natives co-operated in trade; these individuals then distributed the merchandise into the interior of the continent. The commercial sectors that typified the principal trading centres of the Roman-Byzantine world may have survived longer than we usually think, and Gregory of Tours informs us that a similar area of specialization existed in Merovingian Paris. It is in this context that we find not only the first fairs but also the new function that fairs performed in the economy of the time. The purpose of the great fair at Saint-Denis, established by Dagobert I,

6. The bishop of Paris blesses the annual fair at Saint-Denis, detail of a miniature preserved in the National Library of France, Paris.

7. Façade of the Gothic abbey church of Saint-Denis.

8. Detail of a miniature from the mid-fifteenth century, which shows a table at a fair with pieces of armour. Germanisches Nationalmuseum, Nuremburg.

9. Ampulla containing soil from the Holy Land, with the image of the Church of the Holy Sepulchre.

10. Relief on the tombstone of the Danish pilgrim Jonas, who holds a palm, a symbol of the pilgrimage to Jerusalem, while the shell identifies him as a pilgrim to Santiago de Compostela.

9

10

was to provide an important source of income for the Saint-Denis Abbey, which was permitted to make use of all the taxes and tariffs collected by royal consent. In the eighth century, Childebert III described the international importance of the fair, with merchants coming from Saxony and other nations. This type of royal protection afforded to the great abbeys near the commercial centres on the feast day of the patron saint or the liturgical commemoration of their founding, although more evident in the next epoch, shows that commercial activities adjusted to suit the new centres of power and confirms the existence of several economic levels: from the local – connected to the sale of surplus goods from the lands of the feudal lord or the village – to those created by the demand for goods in major urban centres, which stimulated trade. Whether occasional or periodic, as in the case of fairs, the mobility of merchants continued right up to the urban renewal of the eleventh century. From the eleventh and twelfth centuries on, in order to promote trade seasonal markets were set up in cities throughout Europe, usually on days devoted to the celebration of the feast of local patron saints. The most famous of these markets were held in six cities in the eastern region of France called Champagne, where every centre organized a market that lasted for three months. This meant there was at least one great fair open every day of the year.

PILGRIMAGE ROUTES

The medieval traveller par excellence was the pilgrim. The main destinations for medieval pilgrimage were Santiago de Compostela in Galicia (Spain), Rome, and Jerusalem. There were also secondary destinations for less important or "minor" pilgrimages, especially those associated with devotion to the Archangel Michael (Mont-Saint Michel in Normandy, the Sacra di San Michele in Val di Susa, and Monte Gargano in Puglia) or the Madonna (Le Puy, Chartres, and Rocamadour). Pilgrims were protected by the Church, which excommunicated anyone who harmed them. They were often penitents who could be identified by their bags and walking staffs; as a sign of their penance and the holiness of their destination, they wore special badges on their clothing or caps.

It is also important to emphasize that, during the early Middle Ages, the idea of pilgrimage did not remain static. There were two different, although interconnected, forms of pilgrimage: one was strictly religious and the other penitential. Practice of the first was widespread from early Christianity on and was essentially a form of conversion or complete change of life, undertaken when one wanted to free oneself from the anxieties and temptations of the world. In this case, individuals travelled as far as Jerusalem, where they lived as pilgrims, that is, as "foreigners" or "exiles," for the rest of their lives. The most famous example is that of Emperor Constantine's mother, St Helena, who visited the Holy Land in order to find religious relics. The penitential or expiatory pilgrimage had a different origin and emerged later since it was associated with Christianity among the Anglo-Saxon, especially the Irish, populations of the British Isles; it was subsequently brought to the continent in the sixth and seventh centuries.

From the examples recorded in the *Liber Poenitentialis* (penitential), we can conclude that for the most part it was the clergy who incurred this kind of punishment, possibly because they were exempt from the sort of punishment meted out to the laity. Originally, the penitential pilgrimage was a form of harsh punishment for serious crimes (from homicide to incest). Until the eighth century, there is no reference to penitential pilgrimages to holy sites so the pilgrim was, like a vagabond, forced to

11

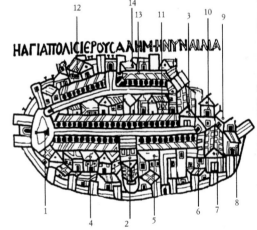

move continually through unfamiliar and dangerous lands, and to live on alms; he was someone who could not work, settle in any location, or rebuild his life in another place. Like Cain after the murder of Abel (Genesis 4:12–14), he was obliged to display the signs of his sin: he travelled almost nude and shoeless and wore shackles on his wrists and legs. It is not by accident that in early medieval hagiographies chains that broke spontaneously were a common miracle, a sign of the compassion of God and that the penance could be considered expiated. Other symbols that were not defamatory but that identified individuals as pilgrims were the walking staff, bag, and badges with holy effigies.

On several occasions, Carolingian rulers issued decrees discouraging this type of pilgrimage, citing concern for public order as the reason for their disapproval. At the same time, many bishops began to send this particular type of criminal directly to the pope so that he might impose the penance in person. However, not all the Episcopal Sees observed this custom; in fact, we know that the tradition was followed inconsistently for a long time and many bishops considered pilgrims' penances received from the pope to be null and void without the ratification of their bishop. This practice gave rise to a jurisdictional dispute and penitents sometimes took advantage of the situation: for example, if they were unhappy with the sentence of their bishop, they travelled to Rome to seek a less severe punishment. This was one of the many jurisdictional disputes that the bishops created with the successor of Peter during the centuries when there was no universally accepted delineation of respective roles and when dioceses often found it difficult to accept the supremacy of the pope, except as purely symbolic.

11. The city of Jerusalem in a detail of the sixth-century Madaba Mosaic Map in Jordan, in which it is possible to make out the principal monuments: 1. Damascus Gate; 2. Church of the Holy Sepulchre; 3. Church of the Theotokos; 4. Area of the Patriarchate; 5. Byzantine Forum; 6. Church of the House of Caiaphas; 7. Holy Zion Church or Church of the Dormition; 8. Church of the Last Supper(?); 9–10. Siloam Pool and Siloam Church; 11. Church of Holy Wisdom (S. Sophia and Praetorium (?); 12. Church of the Probatic Pool; 13. Courtyard of the Temple; 14. The Antonia Fortress (?).

12

13

14

12. Map showing the course of the
Via Francigena in Italy.

13. 1575 print by A. Lafréry depicting the
seven pilgrim churches in Rome.

14. Pilgrims on the road to Rome,
fourteenth-century depiction in Madonna
del Parto, a cave church in Sutri,
near Rome.

In any case, using Rome as a point of reference prompted a fundamental change in the older practice of penitential pilgrimage: the person guilty of serious crimes now travelled to the same destinations as common pilgrims, and the two practices were often confused as the two forms of pilgrimage became increasingly conflated. If the criminal was a pilgrim, then every pilgrim was a sinner who sought expiation.

Pilgrims – including old men, children, and women – were accompanied by wanderers, travelling merchants, and, between the tenth and eleventh centuries, peasants in search of new lands, and they travelled more frequently. In addition, during the eleventh century the great Cluny Abbey encouraged pilgrims to make their way to Santiago del Compostela in Galicia, located in the northwest corner of Iberian Peninsula. It was believed that their encouragement would help support the war being conducted by Christians to re-conquer Spain from the Muslims. Finally, there was Jerusalem, which was controlled by the Abbasid Empire, but visited by a growing number of western pilgrims.

In the strictly ecclesiastical context, there was a certain amount of scepticism with respect to pilgrimages, in part because the organization of the Church was rigorously territorial and the regular orders were established on the basis of *stabilitas loci* (stability of place), which prevented a monk from changing monasteries after he entered the order. However, the pilgrimage experience was accepted as a central fact in the life of the Church, consecrated by taking a vow and receiving the pertinent spiritual indulgences. In this way, the Church, by providing some discipline, inserted itself into the vast movement on the roads of the eleventh century.

COASTAL ROADS

Then there were the great maritime trading emporia, which were more important than those found in the interior of the continent. Constantinople was the great

16

17

15. Pilgrims, wearing the symbolic cross and shell, journey to salvation with the souls of the resurrected. Detail of the architrave of the façade of Saint-Lazare Cathedral, Autun.

16. An astrolabe from the Carolingian age, evidence of the Muslim influence in the development of science. Arab World Institute, Paris.

17. Medieval compass and solar clock. Museo Naval, Madrid.

clearinghouse for all the merchandise that came from the Black Sea, the north (furs, honey, wood, and amber travelled along the Russian rivers, especially the Don), and in particular from the south and the Far East, where the most valuable commodities originated. Other important emporia were Antioch, Alexandria of Egypt, Damietta, at the mouth of the Nile, and Beirut, the "natural" port of Damascus. In turn, Damascus was the great emporium where valuable merchandise, especially spices, arrived from central Asia and the Far East. But spices could also come from Asia by sea – across the Indian Ocean during the favourable monsoon season – which promoted a rapid increase in the production of sailing vessels. The monsoons are constant winds that, though dangerous, make it possible to travel great distances in a relatively short time. Chinese, Indian, and Arabian fleets transported spices from Java, Sumatra, and Malaysia all the way to the Horn of Africa across the Indian Ocean; from the Horn of Africa, they travelled to Egypt along the Nile or into the Red Sea, arriving once again in Egypt or Syria, Palestine, etc.

At the turn of the millennium, the great Mediterranean trade was firmly in the hands of Byzantine, especially Arabian, traders. Even though the most valuable goods originated in the continent of Asia, there was significant trade activity in the western portion of the Mediterranean Sea, forming an imperfect triangle that connected Sicily, Maghreb, and al-Andalus. The Genizah repository in Cairo contains documents that attest to the early presence of western merchants, who travelled between these ports and beyond. Merchants from the cities of Bari, Venice, Amalfi, Pisa, and Genoa were present in many ports in the Byzantine and Arab Mediterranean from the tenth century. From the next century onward, some of these cities became more enterprising, combining short-lived military expeditions with the normal traffic of goods.

18. Detail of the *Cantigas de Santa Maria* (Songs of Holy Mary), with Muslim ships, thirteenth century. Royal Library, El Escorial.

12

THE CITY

URBAN REVIVAL

During the early Middle Ages, society underwent an intensive "ruralization" that corresponded with the depopulation of cities, which were increasingly affected by social insecurity, a lack of strong rulers who could provide support to the residents, and runaway inflation that brought the middle classes to their knees. The process of "ruralization" was not felt to the same degree everywhere: the urban network declined less dramatically in Italy and parts of Gaul than in other western regions, but the general tendency was felt on the entire continent.

Cities were governed primarily by a council of officials called *decuriones* (drawn from the wealthy middle class), who made decisions on a number of issues, including the collection of tariffs, public activities, and general maintenance. The accumulation of large fortunes permitted the formation of small clienteles of the indigent, who relied on public welfare in all the cities of the empire. The more fortunate of the mid-level administrators, the *curiales*, were able to enter the Senate, which in the fifth century loosened its election criteria, basing eligibility more on wealth than on the social and geographical origin of the candidate. Larger clienteles formed around the old senatorial families; these no longer consisted of the indigent and the needy but anyone who needed to turn to a senator to intervene with a public official or to grant some sort of privilege.

4

4. Master of the Register. In the background, presumably, are the city and the Porta Nigra. Codex Egberti, c.985, *Annunciation*. Staadbibliothek, Trier.

A reversal of this tendency is clearly recorded at least from the tenth century: the insecurity of that period – marked by Viking, Magyar, and Saracen incursions – was one of the factors in the revitalization of the cities and towns. The need to organize security led to the repopulation and fortification of the urban centres, some of which had long been abandoned or almost abandoned. The bishops, who traditionally had the centres of their dioceses in the cities, were the first champions of this rebirth. An aristocracy of *boni homines* (good men) coalesced around them, bringing with them property and other assets, as well as experience and military skills. By collaborating with the urban prelates, this group contributed to the emergence of a communal government in ways that varied from city to city: government involved all the inhabitants in the sense that they were all responsible for decision-making, but they were also affected by decisions made by the more powerful oligarchy.

THE MEDIEVAL COMMUNE

Unlike the ancient city, which also developed forms of self-government but which was usually first and foremost a centre of consumers, the medieval city was also a

5

centre of producers who were determined to establish an intricate relationship of integration of, and in some cases hegemony over, the surrounding lands ("county," "district," "territory"). In general, we can say that the "medieval commune" was a social and institutional phenomenon throughout western and central Europe from the eleventh to the fourteenth centuries that reached a level of civic development and political self-awareness particularly in central and western Italy, most specifically in western part of the Veneto region, i.e., in the Po Valley and Tuscany. This development occurred in the context of the *Regnum Italicum* (The Kingdom of Italy) in the eighth to ninth century, which meant that Italy would remain institutionally tied to the Kingdom of Germany and the Holy Roman Empire from the tenth century to the early nineteenth century, although this link became largely a *fictio juris* (a fiction of the law) in the modern era.

Coinciding with the investiture controversy that, in the second half of the eleventh century, often called into question the legitimacy of the rights of bishops, the ruling classes, which increasingly included the petty nobility that was moving into the city without, however, abandoning its possessions in the countryside or its warrior mentality (which meant that they lived in fortified structures in the city, the

6

6. Cimabue, detail of the fresco of St Mark the Evangelist with Italy ("Ytaly" in the fresco) depicted as a walled city, late thirteenth century. Upper Basilica of St Francis, Assisi.

7. The famous monumental secular and religious centre of Cremona with buildings from the age of the communes lining the square: the brickwork Torrazzo civic tower, almost 111 metres high, and bell-tower; the baptistery; the Gothic Loggia dei Militi; the Palazzo del Comune (1206–46); and the Romanesque Cathedral of Santa Maria Assunta.

house-towers), acquired a growing self-awareness and an awareness of their role in the city. This occurred sometimes with the concurrence of the bishop but more often despite or against his authority. This system of urban government developed between the eleventh and twelfth centuries – coinciding significantly with the maturation of the new economic and commercial activity in the cities of the West, especially those facing the sea – and it began to define itself in terms of public law as a result of involvement in the nascent "communal" movement as well as in terms of a powerful, ambitious class of legists or jurists The urban oligarchy of *possessores* of landed property and *milites*, who engaged in trade and shipbuilding in port cities, gave rise to the formation of collegial judiciaries of *consules* (consuls).

Consuls were elected in varying numbers and for a length of term that varied from city to city and they generally came from the richest and most powerful families. Only on the peninsula did the communal civilization – though in decline as the autonomous cities began to grow and evolve into the "regional state" while the wider institutions evolved into the type called seigneurial and later princely – acquire full awareness of its autonomy. In the thirteenth century, Florentine humanist Coluccio Salutati argued for the dignity of the commune of Florence using the expression "*superium non recognosciens*" (it does not recognize a superior), thereby rejecting what was by that time the city's virtually insignificant, but legally undeniable, dependence on the Holy Roman Empire.

"BOURGEOIS" CULTURE

The Italian communes were also centres of culture. Many of them boasted famous universities, but especially noteworthy was the creation of new professions related to the development of the city and the middle classes: judges, notaries, and physicians. The culture of the commune was not limited to knowledge of the Latin language and theology, although this kind of knowledge was never disavowed. On the contrary, theological colleges were common in the cities and some mendicant orders established colleges with vast libraries next to their monasteries. Discussions on ethics and politics typically took place in these sites. The communal mind, open to everything that was practical and concrete, rejected abstractions and demanded that theology come down to earth in order to deal with social, political, and even economic issues.

The world of the commune was profoundly secular, although this fact did not lead to the abandonment of faith. The ruling classes in the city, tied in part to the countryside by their landed property and often by their kinship with feudal families, enjoyed displaying a kind of "aristocratic" lifestyle. This led them to appreciate so-called "courtly" culture, which consisted of epic poems, erotic lyrical compositions, and chivalrous romances. Bankers, merchants, and entrepreneurs also wanted to acquire more precise scientific knowledge, but they were hampered in achieving this goal, particularly by the fact that the language of the scientific treatises of the time was Latin. As a result, summaries, translations, or more often vernacular versions of scientific works, such as Brunetto Latini's *Trésor* (Treasure) and *Tesoretto* (The little treasure) and Ristoro D'Arezzo's *Della composizione del mondo* (On the composition of the world), appeared; Dante also composed a treatise of type called the *Convivium* (Banquet)

Finally, the communes needed to have their own historical "memory." Political factions and families also increasingly needed to make their historical situation and rights permanently available in some way. Old medieval chronicles, which were general and written in Latin, were no longer adequate. In the twelfth century, and even

8

10

9

more so in the thirteenth, the urban chronicle came to the fore, typically using vernacular language and paying close attention to current and immediate matters, with an emphasis on politics.

Despite the importance of culture, the communes never organized an actual system of "public education." In the 1200s, there were private teachers who ran a kind of school – usually in their own homes – where they taught children the rudiments of reading, writing, and Latin; these teachers were often subsidized by the commune. For those children who passed the first level of learning, there were "grammar" schools (this term generally indicated the Latin language) where the disciplines of the *trivium* and *quadrivium* were taught. The "abacus" schools, where mathematics and calculation for commerce were taught, were especially important. Because merchants were the emerging class in the communes, it was obvious that the school system would adapt to their requirements. It was precisely because of these mercantile interests in Italy between the 1200s and the 1400s that a middle class developed that was, for the most part, literate and capable of writing and, in some cases, composing works of literature.

THE CITIES OF EUROPE

In contrast, across the Alps, the Frankish and German feudal aristocracy generally distrusted the urban centres and criticized them, refusing to establish relations with them

11

12

that were not based on conflict and distrust. In those areas, the city became established as and remained a phenomenon essentially tied to the entrepreneurial and mercantile classes. Stratification quickly developed consisting of *maiores* (the greatest), *mediocres* (ordinary people), and *minores* (lesser clans), with power concentrated in the hands of the richest commercial corporations (*ghilde*), which extracted certificates of autonomy from the sovereign or the feudal lord within whose jurisdiction their city was located, often after paying a steep price and at other times only after acts of sedition.

In Flanders, the city acquired political autonomy by means of pacts between "caravans" of merchants (*Hanse*), i.e., the guilds of local producers, and the seigneurial authority (ecclesiastical or laic) that was officially responsible for the governance of the city. There was a dichotomy created by the fact that the city had two nuclei: the fortress of the "signoria" or government and the commercial district. This configuration began quite early, around 1060, without, however, being institutionalized. Institutionalization would come later. In a similar fashion, some communes developed in northern France in the second half of the eleventh century. Rather than having consuls in charge of the city government, as was the case in Italy, they had "scabini," or aldermen, who were often legists from the entourage of the aristocracy. A feature of the area between Flanders and central-north France was the coexistence of communes in a *coniuratio*, a sworn association recognized by the authorities – a king or a lord – by means of certificates that are referred to in the sources as "chartes de commune" (communal charters). A larger number of cities had instead "chartes de franchises" that

8. A grammar class, miniature from a tenth-century edition of Marziano Capella's *The Marriage of Philology and Mercury*. National Library of France, Paris.

9. A teacher and pupils in a grammar school, detail of a mid-thirteenth-century manuscript, Rein monastery, Styria. Austrian National Library, Vienna.

10. Gossuin de Metz, *Imago mundi* (Mirror of the world), 1246, miniature depicting a teacher with raised finger.

11. Gossuin de Metz, *Imago Mundi* (Image of the world), 1246: in the foreground, the sea with fishes, the land furrowed by a stream; on the left, the castle; on the right, the city and cathedral.

12. Commune charter granted to the city of Péronne by King Philip Augustus in 1209.

13

14

15

is to say, charters or franchises, a term that in the ancient Franconian dialect derived from the word "frank," meaning "free." In the south of France, the so-called "villes de consulat" experienced an initial phase similar to that in Italy but because of different development in their ability to control the monarchy and competition from Italian ships in the Tyrrhenian Sea, cities of the Midi did not evolve in the same way.

The case of the German cities is also different, as they developed an intermediate level between cities governed by bishops and communes. During the preceding centuries, in many German cities, the bishops had assumed a central role; however, the local secular powers had profited during the dispute between the pope and the emperor, as the ducal dynasties and the powerful groups of merchants found a common interest in commercial and territorial expansion to the north and the east. As a result, the cities attained forms of autonomy that promoted these developments, but they always remained within the framework of superior powers of different kinds: in Germany, cities governed by bishops coexisted with regional cities subject to princes or lords, as well as with urban centres directly under royal protection.

CENTRES OF PRODUCTION

In addition to being trade centres, the cities of the West were also important places of production. However, the precise moment when working raw materials and the production of goods changed from an artisanal to what can more properly be called a manufacturing system is not easy to identify. It varies from place to place and from product to product. As well, from the eleventh to the thirteenth centuries there was change everywhere within the urban economy, based on greater availability of raw materials, money, the ability to accept the risks associated with trade, and sensitivity to the demands of the market, as well as the ability to anticipate these demands and, to some extent, even determine them.

An area in which great quantitative and qualitative progress took place was terracotta pottery. With the introduction of the foot-wheel, the artisan could work on the shape of the vase with both hands, which allowed a better quality of product and greater speed in production. In the early part of the 1300s, ceramics glazed with a lead-base mixture began to circulate in the west; they were meant to imitate Chinese porcelain. This procedure had been acquired from the Arabs and the new ceramics developed into what would be known as "maiolica." (The most famous centre of production of these ceramics was the city of Faenza.)

At the end of the twelfth century, in the west – especially in Normandy, England, and Italy – we see the spread of the art of glass-making, up that time a closely guarded secret of the Orient. The manufacture of coloured glass, which was so important for the cathedrals in the north, began to spread in 1170: greens and reds were produced by adding copper to the glass paste, brown and yellow by adding iron, blue by adding a mixture called "zaffera," from the Greek *sáppheiros* (lapis lazuli).

Fabrics and leather were the two great resources in the areas of clothing and armaments. Since the manufacture of both was long and complicated, the process was usually concentrated in specific locations, which provided certain resources (for instance, abundant water), and which became somewhat unhealthy as a result of the process. In terms of textile manufacturing, the three basic medieval innovations were the spinning wheel, the handloom (which was often owned or rented by tailors) and the "fulling" mill, that is a mill that "fulls" the fabric (thickens it by pounding the fibres). In the cities, a system of "decentralized manufacturing" soon developed: the

16

13. The mantle of Emperor Henry II, detail. German manufacture, c.1020. Diocesan Museum, Bamberg.

14. Cut velvet fabric with silver plaques, detail. Florentine manufacture, c.1540. Bargello National Museum, Florence.

15. Dyers at work, detail of a miniature from Bartholomeus Anglicus's *De proprietatibus rerum* (On the order of things) dating from end of the fifteenth century. St John's College, Cambridge.

16. *Monks Witnessing St Benedict's Ascension to Heaven*, c.1145. National Museum of the Middle Ages, Paris.

17. Veit Hirschvogel's workshop, *Mary at the Loom*, 1505, Parochial Church of Grossgründlach in Bavaria.

17

phases of fabric-working were entrusted to specialized workers, which soon included the "dyers," who used complicated implements and expensive raw materials.

Metalworking and the manufacture of weapons developed rapidly in the Rhine region of Germany and in Lombardy; so much so that even the Muslims became accustomed to fighting with "Frankish swords" (that is, western). They imported raw materials, which they worked, especially in Spain and Syria, as well as finished

18

products. The mining area par excellence was Saxony, where the most famous min-iaturists originated. Important improvements in the construction of metal-casting kilns allowed for increasingly faster working of metals.

THE "GENTE NOVA"

During the twelfth century, factional disputes were a constant feature of life in the commune. New classes were being created and, toward the end of that century and the beginning of the thirteenth, the major representatives of these groups, who had stayed out of the commune because they did not belong to the urban consular no-bility, asked to be allowed to participate in the government. Who were these people, whom Dante would disparagingly call the "gente nova" (new people)? Often, they were members of the rural class who had moved to the city with substantial means, encouraged by the flow of people, which increased the demand for food in the marketplace to the benefit of those who owned arable land. This flow corresponded to a tendency on the part of the city to control the countryside. There was also an opposite movement, control of the city itself by an emerging rural class that considered it useful and convenient to move to the city and to invest its assets in new land, houses, and warehouses, as well as in banking and commercial specula-tion. In the coastal cities, builders and merchants became wealthy, particularly as a result of the crusades and income from the trade in spices and luxury goods. In all the centres, the increasing need for cash was advantageous for moneylenders, who quickly became speculators and entrepreneurs (bankers). Finally, the demand for products in European markets encouraged manufacturing.

19

20

18. Biadaiolo Master, *The Sale of Grain*. The two images depict the weighing and the selling of grain. Laurentian Library, Florence.

19. Three Venetian cloth merchants in a miniature from the end of the fourteenth century. Correr Museum, Venice.

20. A commercial transaction from the *Libro degli Statuti e delle Corporazioni* (Statutes of the Guilds and Corporations), fourteenth century.

21. Camel caravan of the Patriarch of Constantinople, detail of the frescoes of Benozzo Gozzoli (1420–98). Chapel of the Magi, Medici-Riccardi Palace, Florence.

22. Italian bankers depicted in a miniature from the end of the fourteenth century. British Library, London.

Throughout central and northern Italy, a well-organized class emerged, consisting of bankers, entrepreneurs, merchants, and artisans, to which practitioners of the "liberal" professions, like law and medicine, were added. These citizens joined together in professional associations (guilds) that exercised control over their specialized skills, the quality and prices of products, and the right of new members of the professional organization to exercise their trade. The citizens were originally called *mediocres* (ordinary) or *minores* (lesser) or simply *populares* (commoners); because they did not belong to the families of the *potentes* (powerful), *milites* (equestrian class), or "magnati" (great men), they did not have the right to participate in the administration of the commune or in the governance of the system. However, from the first decades of the thirteenth century, they began to constitute their own legal association (the "people"), parallel to the commune, and began to challenge the "magnati" for power. The conflict between the "*magnati*" and the "*populari*" during the 1300s accompanied an internal struggle within the class of magnates.

1

13

THE DISCOVERY OF THE OTHER

THE JEWS

In the Christian world, both Byzantine and Western, the legal and civic conditions for Jews were characterized by a powerful view of the group as inferior. The relationships between Christians and Jews had been tense from the second century, and the laws of the Roman Christian Empire imposed various forms of discrimination on the sons of Israel. Jews were better off under Islam, since the Muslims had not developed any kind of anti-Semitic philosophy in contrast to what was happening in the Christian regions, where a stubborn anti-Semitism had developed. However, up to the eleventh century, Jewish communities were able to live essentially undisturbed in the Latin world; in fact, the Roman-Germanic emperors afforded them protection.

In the spring of 1096, the Jewish communities in many cities in the basins of the rivers Rhône and Danube were attacked and almost destroyed by hordes of pilgrims, enflamed by the apocalyptic sermons of travelling preachers and led by the sinister figures of robber-knights and adventurers belonging to the petty nobility. Pope Urban II of Clermont's call for a crusade had had a strong and immediate effect on what could be defined as the "popular level" and the event that we are accustomed to call the "First Crusade" became for the Jews the sorrowful and terrible time of the first great "pogrom" recorded in European history.

1. Burchard of Mount Zion, *Jerusalem and the Holy Places*. National Library of France, Paris.

2. Map showing the route of the so-called People's Crusade.

3. Pope Urban II preaches in support of the First Crusade during the Council of Clermont in 1095, miniature from the *Livre des Passages d'Outre-mer* (Expeditions to Outremer), c.1490. National Library of France, Paris.

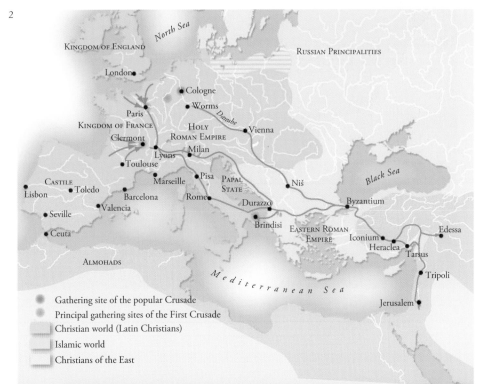

4

4. Frontispiece of the last book of the *Torah*, thirteenth-century biblical manuscript, Germany.

5. *The Conquered Temple*, miniature from the homiliary of the Venerable Bede, c.1180.

Hordes of pilgrims, convinced that the end of time had come and the Day of Judgment (prophesied to coincide with the conversion of the Jews) was at hand, attacked the prosperous and peaceful Jewish communities of the Rhône Valley – although it has been proposed that the persecutions of 1096 may have been "suggested" to the pilgrims by Christian inhabitants of the cities near the Rhone and Danube who were irritated by the flourishing economic, financial, and commercial activities of the Jews.

The horror began on Holy Saturday of 1096 in Cologne, where a famous fair was being held. In the valleys of the rivers Rhône, Main, Moselle, and Danube, the Jews were mercilessly slaughtered and not even women and children were spared; synagogues were attacked and profaned. Bishops of those cities were also frequently attacked as they remained faithful to the orders of Emperor Henry IV and attempted to defend the Jews, in several instances welcoming them into their own homes. Those responsible for the massacre were not only fanatical preachers who eluded ecclesiastical discipline; the chronicles also blame predator-knights, such as the disreputable William the Carpenter (who reportedly distinguished himself in the crusade, between 1097 and 1098, by committing horrible deeds), or Emicho of Leiningen, who for a long time was the protagonist of a dark German folktale.

For all these reasons, between the eleventh and twelfth centuries the Jews supported the Muslims during the crusades as well as in other military clashes between them and the Christians. The Jews fought to defend the city of Jerusalem against the crusaders, who conquered the city in 1099, and were expelled by the victors but returned in 1187 when Saladin conquered the city. There is no doubt that, in the four centuries between the massacres of the Jewish communities in central Europe perpetrated by "crusader pilgrims" in the spring of 1096 and the expulsion of Jews from Christian Spain on the excuse of "limpiza de sangre" (purity of blood), through the expulsion of the Jewish communities from France and England and

5

6

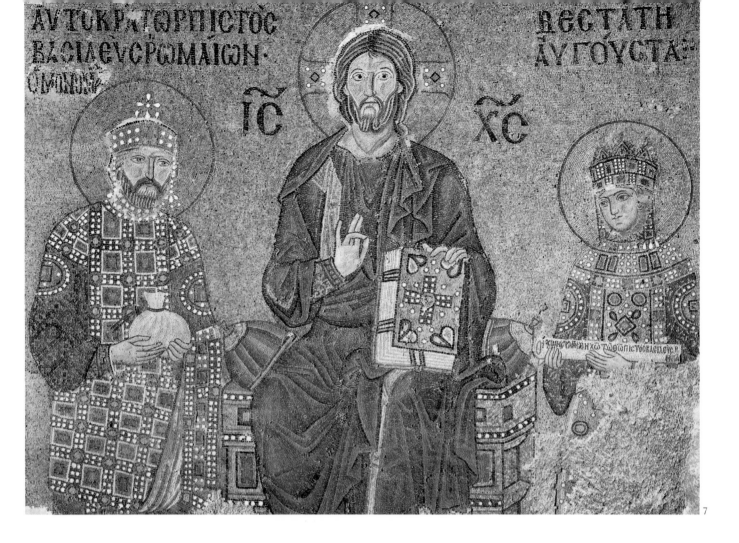

ΑΥΤΟΚΡΑΤωΡΠΙΟΤΟΟ
ΒΑΟΙΛΕΥΟΡωΜΑΙωΝ·
ΟΜΟΝΟΝ

ΙC ΧC

ΘΕΟΤΑΤΗ
ΑΥΓΟΥΟΤΑ

7

the emergence of slanderous legends relating to accusations of ritual infanticide, something that went beyond the anti-Semitism of apologetics and scholasticism developed in Europe.

BYZANTIUM

The word "Byzantine" is somewhat ambiguous and its meaning fluctuates between condemnation of something abstruse, complicated, decadent, and corrupt, on the one hand, and subtle, aesthetic fascination for something refined, magical, and sensual on the other. The culture that we define as Byzantine, which is actually the culture of the Greek-speaking world that developed in the Eastern Roman Empire between the seventh and the fifteenth centuries, fully justifies the use we make of both the noun and the adjective with their connotations of refinement and complexity. Byzantium was the Greek city on the Bosphorus that, in 330, was chosen by Emperor Constantine as the site of his new capital, so the words Constantinople and Byzantium can be considered synonyms for the capital, whose official name was "New Rome." In the late Middle Ages, however, the term "Byzantium" referred to many other things as well: the Eastern Roman Empire as a whole, its territory, and its civilization (for which one normally uses the expression "Byzantine civilization").

6. Santa Maria la Blanca synagogue in Toledo, c.1200.

7. Emperor Constantine IX Monomachus who, despite the fact that he participated in the division of Eastern and Western Christendom, is portrayed with his wife, Zoe, to the right of Christ, detail of the eleventh-century mosaic in the south tribune of Sancta Sophia, Constantinople.

135

8

8. *Jesus Crowns Roger II*, the first king of the Normans of Sicily (1130), mosaic in the Church of Santa Maria della Martorana, Palermo.

9. *The Siege of Constantinople by the Crusaders in 1204*, fifteenth-century miniature. Library of the Arsenal, Paris.

10. A porphyry sculptural group of Tetrarchs (end of the third century–early fourth century), brought from Constantinople to Venice and placed on the exterior corner of the St Mark's Treasury, Venice.

As for the *Romaioi* (Greek for "Romans"), from that point forward they would all be the inhabitants of lands subject to the Byzantine Empire, the name used by western Europeans and Arabs. (It was *Romania* in medieval Latin, from which the Italian terms "Romania" and "Romagna" derive, and "Rum" in Arabic). During the early Middle Ages, the relationship between Byzantium and Latin-Germanic Europe was unstable. A serious break occurred towards the middle of the eleventh century when Rome reneged on its alliance with the Byzantines in their war against the Normans in southern Italy, who were threatening Constantinople militarily, and switched to the side of the Normans. Against this political backdrop, a schism occurred in 1054 between the two Churches, officially over a theological question (the controversy over the *filioque* [and (from) the Son] term) and especially over the fact that in the West the doctrine of the "primacy of Peter," that is to say, the primacy of the bishop of Rome over other patriarchal sees (Constantinople, Antioch, Alexandria, and Jerusalem), had emerged and with it the idea of its hegemony over the entire Church, while the Byzantines remained faithful to the idea of a Church guided by bishops and under the strict control of their emperor.

Another serious crisis came at the end of the twelfth century, when the Angelos Dynasty lost Serbia, Croatia, and Dalmatia and proved to be incapable of dealing with the rise and expansionism of the Bulgar monarchy. The government of Isaac Angelos was discredited, to the point that his brother, Alexius III, assumed power after having Isaac blinded and imprisoned with his son, Alexius. The latter managed to

9

escape and turned to Venice for help – a decision destined to set off a chain of serious consequences. In 1202, the crusader forces were concentrated in Venice, which had offered them a powerful fleet of fifty galleys to transport them overseas. The Venetian contribution, however, was not gratis, and the crusader army did not have sufficient funds to pay for the fleet. The elderly but energetic doge Enrico Dandolo suggested that the crusaders could repay their debt by helping Venice subdue the Dalmatian city of Zara.

In Zara, the Byzantine prince Alexius, son of the deposed Isaac, presented himself to the crusaders and asked for help to defeat the usurper, promising money as well as an end to the schism between the two Churches. In July of 1203, Venetians and crusaders reached Constantinople, defeated Alexius III, and restored Isaac and his son Alexius IV to the imperial throne. Their actions provoked a rebellion on the part of the Byzantine public, which was tired of the West's interference in the politics of the empire and the life of the capital. The Venetians and crusaders responded by savagely sacking the city, overthrowing the Byzantine Empire, and establishing a new "Latin empire of Constantinople."

Pope Innocent III was unable to approve this "betrayed crusade" (the Fourth Crusade). It offered him reunification of the two Churches but at the cost of seeing a Venetian elected Latin patriarch of Constantinople. What we normally call the "Fourth Crusade" actually only deepened the gulf of incomprehension between Catholics and orthodox Christians. The Latin empire continued in crisis for several

10

11

12

13

14

decades until Michael VIII Paleologus, allied with Genoa, brought it to an end after 1261. Although the new dynasty would devote itself entirely to efforts aimed at re-establishing diplomatic relationships with both the East and the West, Byzantium had been seriously tested during the years of Latin domination.

ISLAM

The Arabs had inherited a number of rituals and cults, especially astrological ones, along with a number of mythological figures, in particular female figures similar to Babylonian and Phoenician deities from the ancient Moabite, Edomite, and Nabatite kingdoms. But they – and in a special way the Bedouins who rapidly assimilated the customs and traditions of the people with whom they came into contact as they moved from place to place – were profoundly affected by the people who were closest to them (in terms of ethnic origins, language, and traditions): the Jewish people. Thus in the sixth century the majority of Arabs practised a kind of imperfect monotheism: they believed in the one God of the Bible, but they were also familiar with and observed the practices of various idolatrous cults, including those devoted to the god Bethel, which were of fundamental importance and involved the worship of stones of celestial origin (usually meteorites, which were believed to be the "god's source of power" – the meaning of the word "bethel"). The most famous bethel was the black stone preserved in Mecca. A number of Bedouin tribes periodically assembled in the sanctuary of Kaaba, where the stone was housed. This made Mecca a rich trade centre as well. But the Arabian Peninsula also had Christians; the Abbasids had spread Monophysitism, while there had been a substantial spread of Nestorianism under the aegis of the Persians.

THE DISCOVERY OF THE OTHER

Around 610, life in the city of Mecca was turned upside down by the preaching of Mohammed, a forty-year-old member of the most important family of the city, the Banu Quraysh. About fifteen years after his marriage, he began to manifest the first signs of his vocation: long spiritual retreats, then visions (the archangel Gabriel), and voices that spoke to him. At first Mohammed disclosed these experiences only to his close friends, who would subsequently become his vicars and successors (caliphs). He did not preach in public until the end of the second decade of the seventh century. His were essentially sermons on monotheistic revelation. He proclaimed his faith in one God (Allah), from whom he claimed to have been sent as an emissary (*rasule*) to follow and bring to fulfillment the message of the prophets of the Bible. His sermons, which were initially characterized by an austere apocalyptic tone and a stern opposition to idolatrous practices – which were, as we have seen, one of the sources of Mecca's prosperity – were violently opposed by the merchant nobility of Mecca, who were becoming wealthy from pilgrimages to the Kaaba stone. Mohammed therefore took refuge in 622 in the city of Yatrib (this is the Hegira migration), where his message was accepted. From there, his true preaching as both prophet and conqueror began. In 622, the city became the site of the opening of a new era for all Muslim lands. Yatrib became Medina (in Arabic "the city" par excellence) in that it was favoured by the prophet. In January of 630, Mohammed's authority could no longer be resisted. Even the Meccans submitted to it, as did many Bedouin tribes, and the prophet was able to re-enter his city in triumph; but not without accepting the compromise of preserving the Kaaba sanctuary, which had become the sacred centre of Islam. The prophet died in Medina in June 632. Mohammed's great achievement was his positive encounter with the Bedouin tribes, who embraced the new faith. Thanks to the Bedouins and their ethic of personal and family loyalty and honour, extraordinary combative bravery, and extreme frugality, the prophet was able to establish a true empire in just a few years.

The Islamic tide changed the face of the African-Asian-Mediterranean world. In the course of about twenty-five years, from the Hegira to the middle of the seventh century, the Persian Empire was destroyed and assimilated. The Byzantine Empire was forced to revise its entire territorial defensive policies, while the sea power of Islam obliged the empire to abandon the African coast and to share its thalassocracy with the Islamic world, which until that point had been undisputed.

11. Funerary stele found in the north-western region of pre-Islamic Arabia, originally in the al-'Ula oasis or Teima.

12. Fragment of a relief sculpture from the time of Alexander the Great. Petra.

13. First-second-century bronze statuette of the god Ilmuqah, Marib. The robe draped over his shoulder is obligatory clothing for Islamic faithful on their pilgrimage to Mecca.

14. A city is offered to the prophet Mohammed, Topkapi Sarayi, Istanbul.

15. Map showing the expansion of Islam to 750.

16. Mohammed before the Kaaba in an ancient miniature.

17. In this sixteenth-century miniature the Kaaba and Mecca are shown as the centre of the world. From W. Trutman, *Il mondo del religioni* (The world of religions). Milnai: Jaca Book, 1998.

16

17

15

Conquests up to the death of Mohammed (632)
Conquests from the period 632–661
Umayyad period (661–750)

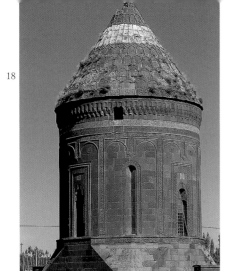

18. Sheyb Egirt Kumbeti, Ablat, in the Seljuk region of Lake Van.

19. Emperor Alexius I Comnenus (1048–1118), who was promised help in the form of the First Crusade when his empire was threatened by the Seljuks. Miniature preserved in the Vatican Apostolic Library.

The pilgrim movement was not only "popular." Many nobles, who sometimes offered to escort and defend vulnerable travellers, participated as well. For this more elevated social class, the pilgrimage was also the expression of a certain social anxiety. In much of Europe, the younger sons of noble families were not entitled to an inheritance and so the only choice they had was a career in the Church or as soldiers (knights). This helps us to understand the flood of knights from all parts of the Christian West, but especially France, who came to participate in the wars against the Muslims on the Iberian Peninsula, wars identified by the Spanish term *Reconquista*. In the eleventh century, the Church, which was engaged in a controversy with the Holy Roman Empire, defended the campaigns of the Spanish monarchs and encouraged the knights of Europe to intervene alongside them. In the meantime, beyond the Iberian Peninsula, several military expeditions were indications of a new level of aggressiveness on the part of the West. The increased mobility on the European continent found new outlets due to the activities of some cities along the Adriatic, Tyrrhenian, Provençal, and Catalan coasts. At the end of the century, these phenomena led to the beginning of a movement that no one was able to grasp at the time: the crusade. The name "crusade" appears late and is not found in its current form before the twelfth century. The movement seems to have originated by accident – only later did the Church think of proposing the crusade in some form. A crusade is not a "holy war" because the Christian religion, although it may in some instances (for example, in self-defence) consider wars just, does not attribute sacredness to them. The crusade perhaps represents an original fusion of war and pilgrimage (the crusaders were granted the same spiritual privileges that the Church granted to pilgrims), based on the model of the anti-Muslim campaigns in Spain, Sicily, and northern Africa, during which a process of sanctification of war against the infidel took shape. This is the atmosphere created in the "chansons de geste." In Spain, Sicily, and Africa, the pope gave the leaders of the Christian armies the banner of St Peter (symbolic of a feudal relationship but also of benediction) and the chroniclers of those campaigns refer to divine and miraculous interventions on behalf of the soldiers of faith. The war between the Christians and the "infidels" is presented as a symbol of the spiritual conflict between virtues and vices. At the end of the century, therefore, we have the concept of the war against the Muslims as something spiritually meritorious. This is what Pope Urban II emphasized in 1095 during a council convened at Clermont in the Auvergne, where he urged the French nobility, who had just emerged from the long crisis of the feudal wars, to go to the aid of the emperor in Constantinople, where he was being threatened by the Seljuk Turks.

This horde of armed warriors and semi-defenceless pilgrims, hardened by the long journey, angered by privations, and caught up in fanatical enthusiasm, was unleashed on Jerusalem toward the beginning of summer in 1099. The city was taken by assault on 15 July of that same year. In the years that followed, the crusaders succeeded in conquering the areas around the city and took control of a region corresponding to the lands between the eastern Mediterranean Sea and the Jordan River on an east-west axis and from Syria to the Red Sea on a north-south axis. However, if this and later crusades were armed conflicts between Christians and Muslims, they also offered an opportunity for the two civilizations to encounter each other. As chronicler Fulcher of Chartres writes: "We have already forgotten the places of our birth; many of us do not know them or have never heard anyone speak about them. Here, there

are people who already own a house and servants as though they had inherited them from their father; those who have taken as wives an Assyrian, an Armenian, or a baptized Saracen rather than a woman from the homeland; and those who have in-laws, descendants, and relatives here. One already has children and grandchildren, another already drinks wine from his vineyards, and still another eats the products of his own fields. We use the different languages of the country easily: the indigenous inhabitants as well as the western colonists have become polyglots and mutual trust brings even races that are foreign to one another closer together. What is written in Scripture is coming to pass: the lion and the ox will eat from the same manger (Isaiah 65:25). The settler has become like the native, the immigrant is being assimilated with the original inhabitants. Each day relatives and friends come from the west to join us and do not hesitate to abandon everything they own there because those who are poor there have achieved opulence here by the grace of God; those who had little money there, possess great treasures here; he who did not have even a small piece of property, is the ruler of a city here. Therefore, why return since we have found such an Orient?"

20. In twelfth-century Toledo, which had come under the control of a Christian government, the Andalusian tradition fuses with the Romanesque to produce a style called *mudéjar*. In the Church of San Román we find these elements as well as features such as horseshoe arches, which are reminiscent of the synagogue of Santa Maria la Blanca.

21. An example of Islamic art with Christian subject matter: polo players and the resurrection of Lazarus, in the d'Aremberg basin, 1290–1310. British Museum, London.

22. Syrian flask showing that Christian iconography became an integral part of Islamic decorative art, as, for example, this Mother of God and Child with scenes from the life of Jesus. Louvre Museum, Paris.

14

CATHEDRALS AND TOWERS

1. Construction of the Cistercian Abbey at Maulbronn, painting on wood, 1450. Evangelisches Seminar, Maulbronn.

2. South aisle of the abbey church of Pontigny.

3. View of Pontigny.

A "WHITE MANTLE OF CHURCHES"

The eleventh and twelfth centuries represent an important phase in the development of architecture. If for a long time some cities were able to maintain the capacity to grow and assume a hegemonic position with respect to other cities and in succeeding centuries developed a monumental architecture reflective of their role, most other cities did not experience such prosperity. However, a noteworthy artistic renewal generally accompanied the great progress made by European society beginning in the eleventh and especially the twelfth century.

During this time, the Cistercians spread the "white mantle of churches," a phrase used by the chronicler Raoul Glaber, over many areas of Europe. This was the spread

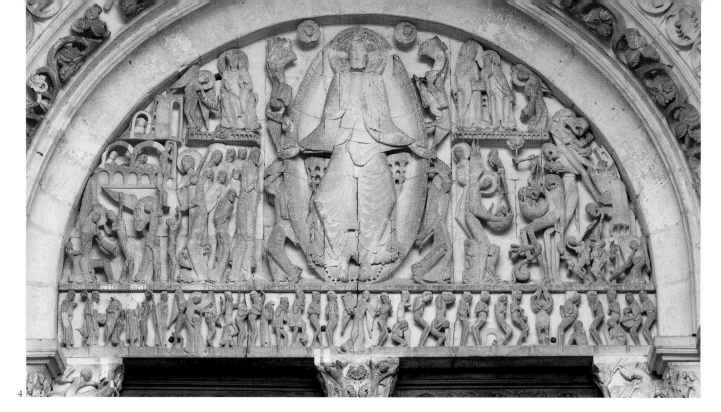

4

5

6

of a style that in the nineteenth century would be called "Romanesque." In practice, the forms of Romanesque architecture were extremely varied. They were influenced by the Islamic style in Norman southern Italy and in areas of Christian-Muslim Spain, as well as by the art of Late Antiquity, Early Christianity, and Byzantium in Italy. Generally speaking, these are buildings in which the wooden ceilings used up to that point were replaced by cross-vaults or barrel-vaults resting on solid, heavy supports. The sparsely decorated forms initially preferred by the Cistercians slowly gave way to relief sculpture on the façades and capitals. As well, the first names of the artists began to appear: Gislebertus, Antelami, and Niccolò. Cities were enhanced with new cathedrals, symbols of the new economic growth and the birth of communal institutions.

The "minor" guilds – ivory carvers, goldsmiths, and manuscript illuminators – participated in the renewal. The original eclecticism can be seen very well in Tuscany where the Pisa model, clearly influenced by Byzantine style, in turn influenced the rest of the region (but not only that region since the influence of artists from Pisa can also been in Puglia and particularly in Sardinia). Buscheto, the first cathedral builder, has a name of Greek origin and some of the craftsmen who worked on the baptistery in the next century were also Byzantine. The same models reappear in painting, especially in the work of Giunta Pisano. Interest in the ancient world and classical art is not an exclusive feature of the Renaissance – throughout the "middle centuries" of the medieval period, intellectuals reflected on the ties between their own culture and classical antiquity, and between their history and the history of ancient Rome. At certain times and in certain locations (the Carolingian age or the kingdom of Frederick I in southern Italy, for example), this interest was expressed in a particular way. In Tuscany, during the age of the communes, cities such as Pisa and Florence, which were at the height of their prosperity, did not contest the appeal of ancient Rome. In fact, they occasionally advanced the notion of a direct line of descent from the city that,

4, 5. Tympanum (4) of the west portal of the Saint-Lazare Cathedral in Autun, the work of the sculptor Giselbertus, who signs his name, as can be seen in the detail (5).

6. Detail of Benedetto Antelami's *Acts of Mercy*. Portal of the Last Judgment, Parma Baptistery.

7. Detail of Giunta Pisano's *Crucifixion*. Santa Maria degli Angeli, Assisi.

8. Prophets with scrolls in the portal of the Verona Cathedral, by the workshop of Niccolò.

more than any other, had succeeded in conquering vast areas. Materials taken from the ruins of ancient Roman monuments were important for the construction of the Pisa Cathedral. According to a fourteenth-century tradition attested to by chronicler Giovanni Villani, the legend that the Baptistery of St John, a Romanesque structure from the eleventh century, had been built during the time of Constantine over the ruins of a temple dedicated to Mars was well known in Florence. This was not an unusual story for the times and could be found in other cities, such as Mantua, in the case of the centrally planned church (in fact, it is called a Rotonda), also from the eleventh century, dedicated to the martyrdom of St Lawrence.

9

11

10

THE GOTHIC

Across the Alps, however, a new style emerged in the second half of the twelfth century. It, too, would become known by a label that did not exist at the time but was coined, with negative connotations, during the Renaissance: the Gothic, which would shape all aspects of the arts during the late Middle Ages with its revolutionary forms, the thrust of its pointed arches, which replaced the barrel-vaults, and the stunning height of the spires in the Île-de-France, where the most famous example is the Chartres Cathedral. After they abandoned the Romanesque, the Cistercians became the major propagators of this new style in Europe. Only Italy was initially sceptical when faced with Gothic forms, which slowly gained ground during the 1200s. The first buildings on the Italian peninsula to display this influence were those built by the Cistercians, for example, Fossanova Abbey and the Abbey of San Galgano.

The mendicant orders also contributed to introducing these new architectural forms into the cities. In fact, as noted some time ago by Jacques Le Goff, the number of monasteries and churches built by the mendicant orders in the city centres can be taken as an indicator of the degree of urbanization achieved. Between the 1200s and 1300s, cities and mendicant quarters constituted an indissoluble combination. The urban vocation of the Dominicans was evident from the time of the establishment of the order; in contrast, the first buildings of the Franciscans were

located at the edges of urban centres and the move to the centre occurred gradually. Both orders, however, needed large spaces suitable for preaching, which naturally pushed them to find sites on the edges of densely populated zones. In Florence, for example, Santa Croce for the Franciscans and Santa Maria Novella for the Dominicans, built by Arnolfo di Cambio, were constructed inside the city but outside the second ring of walls.

Franciscan and Dominican monasteries with ever-larger churches were built with enormous squares in front, which were used for preaching, of which Franciscans and Dominicans were masters. In addition to being preachers and organizers of institutions for the assistance of the poor and sick, Franciscans and Dominicans also served as confessors and spiritual advisors to the main aristocratic and mercantile families in the city, who built their family chapels in the churches of the mendicant orders and named the orders as beneficiaries in their wills. Increasingly, famous artists were commissioned to provide frescos for these chapels. The most interesting structure of thirteenth century Italy, the basilica in Assisi, consisting of two churches, was produced by the Franciscan order. The Rule of both orders prescribed the rejection of excessive forms of display in architecture, even though the basilica in Assisi provides an example of a different standard. The decoration of the basilica continued well into the 1300s and the best artists in Italy, including Cimabue, Duccio di Buoninsegna, and Giotto, worked on it; it contains some of the best examples of the revival of painting during the thirteenth and fourteenth centuries.

9. View of the façade of Chartres Cathedral.

10. Interior view of the nave elevation in the abbey church of Fossanova.

11, 12. Aerial view of the Florentine churches of Santa Croce (11) and Santa Maria Novella (12).

13. Upper Basilica of St Francis, Assisi.

14

15

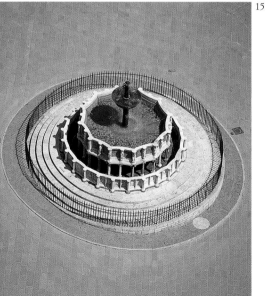

PUBLIC BUILDINGS

From the standpoint of urban planning and architecture, the age of the communes coincides with the construction of public buildings – which were meant to make explicit the role and importance of the commune. At the time of the so-called "consular" commune of the twelfth century, the administration of governmental affairs was often not discussed in public places and was conducted in rented facilities. Especially from the thirteenth century onward, however, cities undertook a program of public building that was particularly significant in central and northern Italy. The construction of parliament buildings did not respond to a practical need as much as to a desire to symbolize freedom from dependence on the class of "magnates." In fact, it is no coincidence that the construction of parliament buildings is often tied to the emergence of the commune governed by a "podestà" (mayor). During this period, the "palazzo pubblico" (town hall) was usually designed as a structure that was superior to other secular buildings in both decoration and size;

for instance, its towers had to surpass those built by families of the noble class and family towers risked being "decapitated" if they were taller than the parliament buildings. The location for the new structure was chosen because it was strategically important in the life of the city, even at the cost of incorporating pre-existing buildings, as already noted.

In short, from the standpoint of urban planning and architecture, the emergence of the commune corresponds to the emergence of public buildings, which complement the cathedrals. Up to the twelfth century, the cathedral was the only pivot around which the city rotated. Beginning in the thirteenth to fourteenth century, as noted above, secular authorities identified the parliament building as a second important centre in the life of the city; if we add to these buildings the omnipresent market square, which is both the site and the symbol of the economy, and the churches of the mendicant orders, we have the model of a polycentric city.

Furthermore, up to that time, we could say that urban centres had been designed in something of a haphazard fashion that accommodated the increase in the city population. This same growth, however, called for some kind of planning; we certainly cannot speak of a genuine urban plan, but rather of greater attention to the growth of the city, which, as has been mentioned, also contained important centres of production. The most significant project was the one proposed for the city of Florence in the second half of the 1200s and entrusted to architect Arnolfo di Cambio.

Between 1280 and 1300, Florence had a population of between 80,000 and 100,000. Its growth had been very rapid and it was therefore necessary to reorganize the city in a rational fashion. As well, the defeat at Montaperti in 1260 (in which the exiled Florentine Ghibelines and the Sienese defeated the Guelphs) had led to the destruction of the towers, houses, and palaces once owned by the Guelphs and the centre of Florence had been partly gutted. The primary interventions were concentrated in the northern section of the city with the opening of a series of parallel arteries. There were other projects designed to improve the roadways along and across the river Arno as well as the expansion and paving of some city squares. Finally, between 1284 and 1333, another perimeter wall was constructed, also designed by Arnolfo di Cambio.

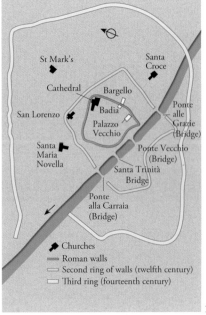

17

16

14. Piazza IV Novembre in Perugia. The piazza, with its late thirteenth-century fountain in the centre, is lined with important civic buildings, including the Palazzo dei Priori, built in the thirteenth-fourteenth century.

15. The Fontana Maggiore of Perugia, the work of the father-son team of Nicola and Giovanni Pisano following a design by Fra Bevignate from Perugia.

16. Palazzo della Ragione, Padua. A fourteenth-century work by Giovanni degli Eremitani, it is located between the Piazza delle Erbe and Piazza della Frutta.

17. Survey map showing the expansion of the city of Florence.

18

18. The stained glass windows of Beauvais, showing masons at work.

19. A fresco by Saint-Savin-sur-Gartempe depicting the construction of the Tower of Babel.

20. Construction scene, from a thirteenth-century manuscript showing tradesmen at work.

THE STONE MASON'S GUILDS

The protagonists of the flowering of the medieval cities were the masons guilds. Unlike other guilds , which were quick to produce charters, the masons guilds maintained the oral tradition for a long time, probably to protect the secrecy of the technical aspects of their profession. One of the first mentions of a masons guild occurs in 926 in the town of York and the guild appears to have been created by order of King Athelstan. For information on the inner workings of these guilds, however, we have to wait until the economic rebirth and expansion of Europe, when we begin to see such texts as the *Livre des métiers* (Book of professions), a collection of guild charters written in 1268 by Étienne Boileau, one of the first provosts of Paris under Louis IX, called the Saint. During the next century, the sources increase and many come from England. We have the charters of the masons of York for the years 1352, 1370, and 1409 and of those of London for 1356, written in Latin and French. (Since the cities were governed by the Plantagenet dynasty, which was of Angevin origin, French was a prestigious vernacular and would remain so for a long time.) These are the writings of the Old Charges, which the historic tradition on the subject identifies as possible ancestors (but it might be better to consider them as models since there appears to be no direct link) of the charters of modern Masonic societies.

Masons are sometimes called freemasons in the sources, where we find them mentioned for the first time in a document from 1376. The debate on the original meaning of the term has been lively, given the context of modern freemasonry, among the scholars who study this phenomenon. There are today two hypotheses: according to the first, proposed especially by English historians, the freemason was originally a worker who was more skilled than the others, a cutter of freestone (that is a freestone mason), which was a particular type of soft stone, which was sandy or chalky and therefore suitable for more delicate work, such as relief sculpture, while the hard stone was left to common stone carvers. The second hypothesis identifies the freemason as a free worker in that his abilities as a builder provide him with the esteem and protection of the civil and ecclesiastical authorities. The *Livres des métiers* speaks of "franc-mestier." At any rate, in the thirteenth century, the term freemason did not imply the worker's "freedom" from belonging to a guild, to which he was, instead, bound.

Among the various surviving texts, one is particularly important. This is the so-called *Regius Manuscript* (Royal Book) dated from around 1390 (but perhaps copied from an earlier document) and preserved in the Museum of London. The text is divided into six parts: a brief history of the masons guilds, the regulations of the guilds, set out in fifteen articles and five points, a commemoration of the four crowned saints, who were the patrons of the masons, the story of the Tower of Babel, a hymn of praise to the seven liberal arts, and a short code of good manners. Also, described in the form of precepts, are rules governing morality and behaviour that the master mason must follow. These are moral and professional rules regarding what must be done in order to become a member of the guild. There are also norms defending the members, for example, one that prohibits night work.

20

Such texts demonstrate that the guilds considered the training of apprentices to be important in as much as the standardization of rules for membership was the best way to protect the profession from counterfeiters. The master masons had special signs that enabled them to recognize one another (words or hand gestures) and that identified them as members of the guild, even among artisans from other masons guilds. In this way, they could show that they possessed the skills of the trade without necessarily having to demonstrate their knowledge each time. The apprentice began to work at the age of twelve and was bound to a master mason by a seven-year contract. After three years, he underwent an initiation ceremony. He learned the secret signs that he would use in order to identify himself as an apprentice mason and was authorized to have his own logo, a type of signature in the form of a small symbol that he would henceforth sculpt on the stone in order to identify his work. At the end of seven years, he became a full member of the guild and, after a time, a master mason himself, with the opportunity to teach other apprentices.

The patrons of the masons guilds were the so-called four crowned saints: Symphorian, Claudius, Nicostratus, and Castorius, four Christian sculptors martyred in Pannonia in 304 during the rule of Emperor Diocletian. The saints were celebrated at the end of the 1200s in the story of their martyrdom contained in the *Golden Legend*, written by Jacobus de Varagine. In addition to Christian martyrs, the guilds liked to identify as their predecessors the mythic figures who had created the great architecture of the past, including Solomon and Hyrum.

1. Raymond Lully, summoned to the University of Paris, presents his conception of the cosmos during the biennial 1297–99.

2. *Trivium*: grammar, dialectic, and rhetoric, miniature from a twelfth-century edition of Martianus Capella's *De nuptiis Philologiae et Mercurii* (On the marriage of Philology and Mercury). National Museum of France, Paris.

3. Interior view of the Palatine Chapel in Aachen, built by Charlemagne and inspired by the Church of San Vitale in Ravenna.

4. Interior view of San Vitale, Ravenna.

152

15

EDUCATION AND UNIVERSITIES

CULTURE IN THE EARLY MIDDLE AGES

Charlemagne chose the city of Aachen as his capital and gave it monuments that were splendid for the Germany of the time and a *sacrum palatium* (sacred palace) whose chapel was inspired by the Basilica of San Vitale in Ravenna. Charlemagne's kingdom coincided with a general revival of culture in the entire West. Instead of an increase in monastic libraries and centres where ancient manuscripts were copied and new works written, but always in the shadow of the abbeys, the first schools began to be established. These were administered by the clergy, which included young men from secular aristocratic families who were not necessarily destined for a career in the Church.

In fact, the emperor believed that culture was an excellent vehicle for improving the public service and, though he could hardly read or write, he studied philosophical, theological, and even scientific matters. We should not be surprised by the fact

5

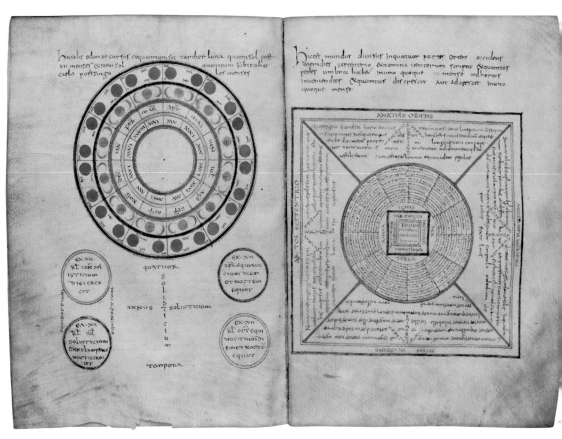

6

that a semi-literate man might be interested in such things. Reading and writing were not widespread in the west well into the twelfth century because they were considered activities unsuitable for the lay nobility and were delegated to specifically trained members of their staff, while culture was entrusted to the oral tradition and memory.

The *Schola Palatina* (Palace School) was established around the sovereign in Aachen. It was not an actual institution but rather a circle of learned men whose composition and number varied from time to time and was inspired and coordinated by a Saxon Benedictine monk named Alcuin of York, one of the great intellectuals of his day. This was not a "school" in the modern sense but rather a kind of academy where questions were debated, questions that in one way or another had to do with the administration of power. Similarly, many reforms sponsored by Charlemagne – from the standardization of the liturgy to the new writing script that spread throughout the west, making manuscripts clear and legible – had an immediate, concrete, and practical purpose. Subsequently, schools and cultural centres arose inside monasteries or in the vicinity of cathedrals and courts, but it was only after the millennium that study, education, and cultural production in the West underwent a significant change. The combined effect of renewed intense trade with the rich and cultured Orient and the upsurge in city life stimulated a rapid cultural revival. A connection with the past was, however, part of this new epoch. Between the eleventh and twelfth centuries, cathedral schools continued to play an important role in the

5. Alcuin of York, detail of a miniature from a late twelfth-century manuscript. Museum August Kestner, Hannover.

6. Illuminated Evangeliary of the Treasury of Aachen (early ninth century). Domkapittel, Aachen.

7. A page from a treatise, c.805, showing the phases of the moon and the sun as well as the four classical elements: fire, air, earth, and water. Dombibliothek, Cologne.

8. Vincent of Beauvais, *Speculum majus* (Great mirror), miniature from a fifteenth-century edition: *trivium* and *quadrivium*.

9. A geometry teacher who has on his desk rings and solid spheres, miniature from a twelfth-century edition of Martianus Capella's *De nuptiis Philologiae et Mercurii* (On the marriage of Philology and Mercury). National Library of France, Paris.

European schools. They were organized in conformity with the Roman educational system which consisted of a program of study that included the *Quadrivium*, i.e., the four mathematical disciplines of arithmetic, geometry, astronomy, and music, and the *Trivium*, i.e., the three philosophical-literary disciplines of "grammar," which is to say the Latin language, "rhetoric," which is the art of composing discourse and speaking in public, and "dialectic" or philosophy. The scientific bases consisted of the encyclopaedic books *Naturalis Historia* (Natural history) written by Pliny the Elder in the first century A.D.

FROM LOGIC TO SCHOLASTICISM

Scholars at the Chartres Cathedral school studied not only Scripture but also nature and the sciences, which up to that point had been considered profane and secondary, if not outright dangerous. They were very much inspired by the Neoplatonic tradition but were also interested in everything that was new. Their intellectual interests did not eliminate or replace respect for the ancient *auctoritates*; however, at Chartres there was the feeling that modern science could surpass that of the ancients, not because it was better but because it was not doomed to be repeated in the new commentaries; instead, ancient knowledge could be amplified and deepened through critique. "We are dwarves on the shoulders of giants" was the saying. What was meant was that the ancient masters were great but, by relying on them, it was possible to

c

d

e

f

b

10

g

a

see further than they did, within one's limitations. At Chartres, texts were studied not only for the purpose of commenting on them but also in order to interpret and master their content.

A new science emerged as the key to knowledge: logic. It taught the fundamentals not only of the knowable per se but also of the method with which to approach the knowable. Rather than the old method, which was based on literal commentary on the Bible and the writings of the ancients, scholars now sought new criteria for understanding what was just and what was not with the aid of human reason alone. At the base of the renewal was the work of Peter Abelard, a priest who taught in Paris. His *Sic et Non* (Yes and no) is a manual on logic in which he teaches the reader how to organize his intellectual choices rationally by opposing one argument with another. Abelard was rejected by traditionalists; however, Gratian compiled the collection of canonical laws

10. Nature and science as well as theology were studied in the Chartres Cathedral school. On the voussoirs of the right portal of the cathedral façade, with sculptures of Aristotle, Cicero, Euclid, Boethius, Ptolemy, Donatus, and Pythagoras, are sculptures of the arts: a. dialectic; b. rhetoric; c. geometry; d. arithmetic; e. astronomy; f. grammar; g. music.

11

13

11. A course on mineralogy, miniature from the twelfth-century edition of Martianus Capella's *De nuptiis Philologiae et Mercurii* (On the marriage of Philology and Mercury). National Library of France, Paris.

12. The Arab philosopher Averroes, detail of Raphael's fresco *The School of Athens*. Stanza della Segnatura, Palace of the Vatican.

12

14

called the *Decretum* (Canon law), using Abelard's method and logic, as the foundation for the scholastic system that renewed Christian theology and philosophy.

The principal exponents of Scholasticism were Albertus Magnus, Thomas Aquinas, and Duns Scotus. They applied the logical-scientific method to the study of revelation, affirming that theology is a part of science and therefore it can be investigated with the instrument of human intelligence. St Thomas (1221–1274) originally studied in the Faculty of Arts in Naples before deciding to enter the Dominican order. After a period of time in Cologne, he moved to Paris, where he began his university career, devoting himself to theological studies. In addition to the influence of Abelard's logical method, mediated through Thomas Aquinas's teacher Albertus Magnus, Latin translations of the writings of Aristotle and the Arab philosophers, especially Averroes, were very important in the development of Aquinas's philosophy.

13. Juste de Gand (1435–1480), *St Thomas Aquinas* counts his arguments off on his fingers. Louvre Museum, Paris.

14. Juste de Gand, *Duns Scotus*. National Gallery of Marche, Urbino.

15

16

17

15. Students at the University of Bologna, 1393. Museo Civico Medievale, Bologna.

16. A theology lecture at the Sorbonne, from Nicolas de Lyre's fourteenth-century manuscript *Postilles sur l'Ancien Testament* (Notes on the Old Testament). Municipal Library, Troyes.

17. Giovanni Pietro da Cemmo (1474?–1533), the blessed Egidio from Rome at the podium in the act of teaching, detail. Library of the former convent of San Barnaba, Brescia.

UNIVERSITIES BETWEEN LAW AND THEOLOGY

An innovation that affected the future of European culture was the establishment of the universities, which, for the first time, offered clearly defined programs of study, final examinations, and divisions into faculties. Universities arose in the twelfth century as private associations of students and teachers but soon sought official recognition from the authorities and concession of economic and legal privileges. A prototype university was established in Salerno between the tenth and eleventh centuries. This was not a true university with courses and examinations but rather a famed school of medicine where medicine and philosophy were studied and Greek and Arabic texts were translated into Latin. Frederick II transformed the school into a university in 1231, giving it a charter and instituting public final exams. Before that date, there is no certain information on how the Salerno institute operated.

Between the twelfth and thirteenth centuries the principal universities arose throughout Europe, sometimes in association with cathedral schools and at other times autonomously. Even though the centre of activity in the twelfth century was Paris (where many Italians taught, including the theologian who would later become a bishop, Peter Lombard), universities flourished in various Italian cities, where theology and law were studied and renewed. What is considered to be the first university, apart from the dubious case of Salerno, was established in Bologna with the institutionalization of law schools that already existed and was administered by the laity. In 1222, the University of Padua was founded and in 1224 that of Naples, also by order of Frederick II. The establishment of universities had important consequences for the cities in terms of general culture as well since they stimulated the production of books and the spread of texts and literacy.

Outside of France and Italy, universities developed slightly later. Cambridge and Oxford were founded during the first two decades of the thirteenth century; in 1218, the important Castilian centre of Salamanca was established. During the fourteenth century, many centres developed in central and eastern Europe: Prague in 1348, Cracow in 1364, Vienna in 1365, Heidelberg in 1382, and Cologne in 1388. Other countries, such as those in Scandinavia, had to wait until the fifteenth century: Uppsala in 1477 and Copenhagen in 1479.

The need for numerous copies of the same text for courses made the use of traditional codices unfeasible because they were too expensive and took copyists a long time to make. Therefore, an alternative system called the "*peciae* system" was invented: texts, which were approved by a university committee, were sent to book sellers (*stationarii*) who sold them to students in the form of pamphlets (*peciae*) at affordable prices. While expensive parchment was still the most commonly used writing material, paper, which was more economical, was increasingly adopted.

18. Pliny, *Naturalis historia* (Natural history) in Nicolò Moscardini's copy for Pico della Mirandola. Vatican Apostolic Library.

19. Map showing the growth of universities in the Middle Ages.

18

19

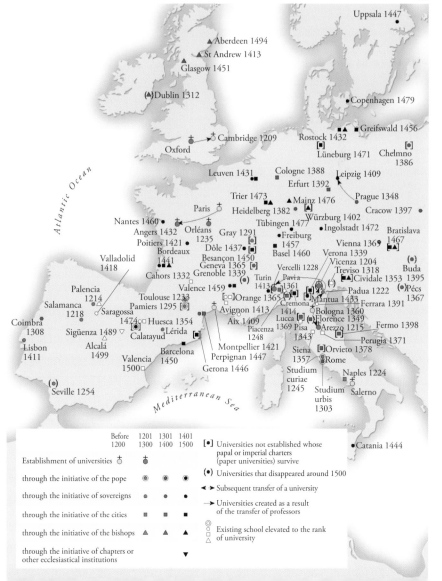

	Before 1200	1201 1300	1301 1400	1401 1500
Establishment of universities	☥	☥		
through the initiative of the pope	◉	◉	◉	
through the initiative of sovereigns	●	●	●	
through the initiative of the cities	■	■	■	
through the initiative of the bishops	▲	▲	▲	
through the initiative of chapters or other ecclesiastical institutions				▼

[■] Universities not established whose papal or imperial charters (paper universities) survive

(●) Universities that disappeared around 1500

◄► Subsequent transfer of a university

→ Universities created as a result of the transfer of professors

◎ Existing school elevated to the rank △ of university

21

22

20. In this fifteenth-century miniature, Constantinus Africanus, a Benedictine monk from the eleventh century, who had brought elements of Arabic medicine to Europe, makes a diagnosis by examining urine. Bodleian Library, Oxford.

21. A conversation between Hippocrates and Hunayn ibn Ishaq, his translator, detail of a Pisan edition from 1330–40 of Manfredus de Monte Imperiali's *De herbis* (On herbs). National Library of France, Paris.

22. Gerardo da Cremona, treatise on medicine translated from the Arabic, second half of the thirteenth century. National Museum of the Middle Ages, Paris.

23. Ptolemy, *Geography*, detail of the diagram of the son, mid-ninth century, Constantinople. Vatican Apostolic Library.

THE NEW SCIENCES

Arab philosophy and literature had inherited the great Greek, Syrian, Egyptian, Persian traditions and created a new culture, produced in the same way that Islamic art was produced – with many local variants. This was a culture with an exceptional capacity for synthesis. Though originally nomadic, Islamic culture was able to adapt to a sedentary society and urban life. The new demands, especially in agriculture, prompted it to develop extraordinary abilities in the area of hydraulics. The demand for writing material, created by a religion in which knowledge of the Koran was fundamental, stimulated the introduction of paper, which the Arabs borrowed from China in the middle of the eighth century, while Europe had stopped cultivating papyrus completely in the tenth century and shifted to the more costly parchment, i.e., sheepskin.

Revived contacts with both the Byzantine world and the great Arab-Islamic culture (in Spain, Sicily, and the Holy Land), as a result of commercial ties in the Mediterranean as well as the crusades, had as a consequence the bringing of texts and knowledge to the west. In the middle of the twelfth century a team of scholars, encouraged by Peter the Venerable, the Abbot of Cluny, undertook the translation of the Koran. Around 1187, the works of Aristotle began to circulate throughout Europe thanks to the singular figure of a nomadic scholar named Gerardo da Cremona, who had found a number of treatises on logic, optics, and geometry in Toledo and had learned the Arabic language in order to translate them. Most of these texts and this knowledge were the legacy of Greco-Roman antiquity; while this cultural legacy had been preserved in Byzantium and in the Islamic world, in the west it had been completely forgotten. Now it returned to Europe, enriched by knowledge originating in Persia and India (also mediated by China) through Islam.

These were very important texts, especially those pertaining to medicine (as already noted, it was originally studied in the school of Salerno and spread to the rest of Europe), astronomy, and mathematics. According to a legend, the sage Aristotle appeared in a dream to the Caliph of Baghdad al-Mamun (803–833), who subsequently had all the great philosopher's Greek works translated into Arabic and established a university, the "house of knowledge," in his capital city. The teachers at that university included the mathematician Mohammed al-Khwarizmi, whose treatise on calculus, which we refer to as Indo-Arabic (based on so-called Arabic numerals and on the introduction of the digit zero, which was of Indian origin) became the basis of modern mathematics.

This new system was introduced to the west by Leonardo Fibonacci. He was born in Pisa in 1180 to a writer in the service of the city government, who sent him to Bejaia, near Algiers, to attend to the economic interests of Pisa in that area. After Bejaia, Fibonacci travelled extensively in Egypt, Syria, and Greece. He returned to his homeland in the early part of the thirteenth century and wrote notes on what would become known as *The Practice of Calculation*, as well as an actual theory of mathematics. In fact, in 1202, he wrote the *Liber abaci* (Book of calculation), a kind of encyclopaedia of algebra, in which Arabic numerals, as well as arithmetic and geometric progressions and equations, were introduced. In 1220, he wrote *Practica Geometriae*, where he developed various problems in Euclidian geometry. Naturally, Fibonacci's interest in science was not "pure"; he adapted his treatises to the practical requirements of trade, using examples to demonstrate how mathematical ideas could be used to solve specific problems in trade or currency exchange. In this sense, his writings are of fundamental importance to correctly understanding the development of what are called "trade manuals" in the next century.

24. Pedanius Dioscorides, *On Pharmacy and Medicine*, detail of the *Herbarium of Medicinal Plants*, late eighth–early ninth century. Syria (?), Palestine (?), or southern Italy.

25. Miniature of Muthar ibn al-Hassan's *Symposium of Doctors*, thirteenth century. Biblioteca Ambrosiana, Milan.

16

THE CULTURAL IMAGINARY

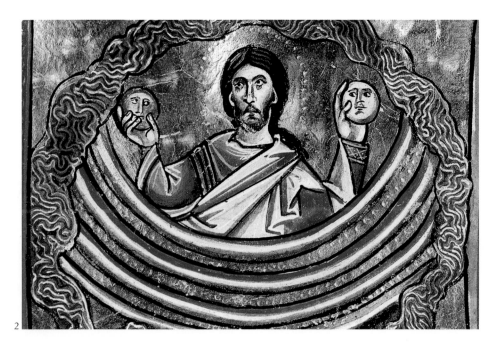

SPACE

History unfolds along two basic dimensions: space and time. It is impossible to define any historical event, institution, or structure without clearly identifying the geographical area to which we are referring. Perhaps looking at the concepts of space and time is the best way to characterize medieval men and women. When we reflect on their concepts of space and time, we come to appreciate the distance that separates us from them.

We are accustomed to the idea of an infinite space. Though it may disturb and even terrify us, it is also the reality in which we can situate ourselves, our physical bodies, within the universe. Medieval man, in contrast, occupied a specific place within a closed world. This fact made him similar to the humans of antiquity and the Bible, whose vision was like his. This conceptualization of space was described by Aristotle and later Ptolemy. It was a closed world within which there were spaces where one could not travel (the Asia populated by monstrous beings, for example, or the Africa of *hic sunt leones* [here there are lions]). It occupied what was essentially the Mediterranean area, over which was a perfect number of heavens where the planets moved as though fixed, while the earth remained motionless at the centre and everything was bound by the infinite Empyrean Heaven, the exclusive and privileged abode of God.

1. St Beatus of Liébana, *Imago mundi* (Mirror of the world). The map (1135–1219), commissioned by Ferdinand III of Castile, is centred on the Earthly Paradise and its streams, which flow and divide the world. National Library of France, Paris.

2. In the centre the Creator, with the features of Christ, holds the sun and moon as the world emerges from chaos. This is the way Honorius of Autun (1154–1180) depicts Creation in his *Imago mundi* (Mirror of the world).

3. Like the spheres, the circle is the basis for the construction of the calendar.

163

4. Thomas of Cantimpré, *De natura rerum* (On the nature of things); the astronomy teacher gazing at the firmament.

5. Giusto de' Menabuoi, *The Creation of the World*, 1374–78, in which the celestial spheres are emphasized, Baptistery, Padua.

The space of the cosmos was therefore hierarchically and rigorously structured. God was everywhere, but his special abode was the limpid, perfect, Empyrean Heaven, which was absolutely immobile and immutable, eternal and infinite. The Empyrean – the seat of God, the angels, and the souls of the blessed – encircled Creation, which had been willed into existence by the Creator and organized in concentric spheres consisting of a light substance called ether; it was governed by the twelve constellations and the seven principal planets (two of which were stars: the sun and the moon).

There was also a more immediate space. Between the eleventh and thirteenth centuries, people moved about but their spatial horizons alternated between the infinitely large of the entire cosmos and the infinitely small of the valleys and forests in

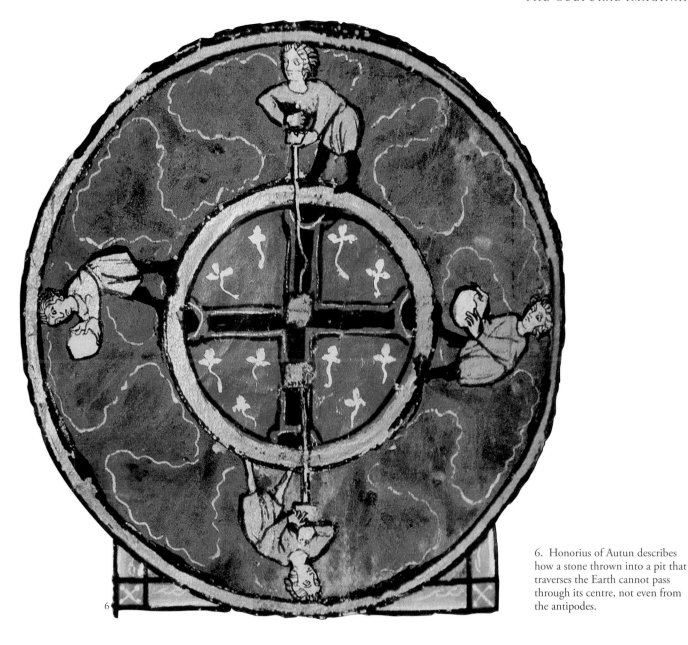

6. Honorius of Autun describes how a stone thrown into a pit that traverses the Earth cannot pass through its centre, not even from the antipodes.

which they normally travelled. An inhabitant of a nearby village was immediately a "foreigner"; conversely, no one who shared the Christian faith and was in some way connected with the Latin Church could be called a "stranger."

GEOGRAPHY

At the centre of this system of concentric spheres was the terrestrial globe – whose spherical form was known in antiquity; it was largely occupied by land masses. There were many debates on how these lands were configured. Opinions on the matter had already been formulated by Greek and Latin geographers of antiquity and were subsequently taken up by Arab cosmographers. Some imagined a single land mass

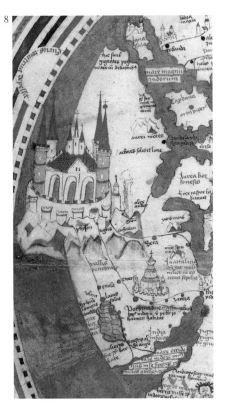

7. Reproduction of the T-O Map attributed to Honorius of Autun, twelfth century. Royal Geographical Society, London.

located in the northern hemisphere and, it was assumed, another corresponding mass on the opposite side of the globe (the antipodes). Although this theory was never completely abandoned, it was displaced by another, according to which the land masses formed a disc surrounded by the ocean and divided into three large continents: Asia to the east, as large as the other two continents combined, Europe to the north, and Africa to the south. The three continents were separated by a large horizontal body of water (consisting of the river Tania, which separated Europe from Asia, and the Nile, which separated Asia from Africa) and a vertical arm of the sea (the Mediterranean, which separated Europe from Africa). The two arms of the sea met to form a T, a sacred letter in the shape of a cross and symbolizing redemption.

At the centre of the world was the city of Jerusalem, where Jesus was crucified and resurrected. In the Far East (or, according to others, on an island in the western part of the ocean) an Earthly Paradise emerged, out of which the four great rivers of the world sprang: the Tigris, Euphrates, Nile, and Ganges. According to tradition, bizarre and disturbing creatures that were somewhere between human and savage, "monsters," lived at the unexplored edges of the world. Legend has it that the land of monsters and wonders par excellence was India, which was conquered in ancient times by Alexander the Great and subsequently Christianized by the apostle St Thomas. Only with the journeys of merchants and missionaries to Asia in the 1200s does the image of the world change and become more detailed.

There was also space for the souls of the dead at the edges of the world of the living. Hell (from the eleventh century on, approximately) and Purgatory were located in various places: islands in the ocean, mountains, volcanoes (Etna), and, finally, in a great pit in the earth's crust in Dante's vision.

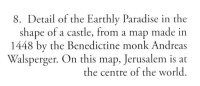

8. Detail of the Earthly Paradise in the shape of a castle, from a map made in 1448 by the Benedictine monk Andreas Walsperger. On this map, Jerusalem is at the centre of the world.

9. Twelfth-century miniature showing an inhabitant of India.

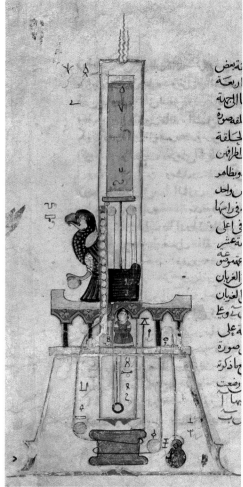

TIME

Our notion of time is basically linear; in contrast, the concept of time in the medieval world shares our linear idea, but it was also cyclical. On the one hand, time continually returned in the rhythm of work, months, seasons, and the liturgy, which each year repeated the life of Christ as a cosmic and temporal model through his role as *Kosmokator* and *Kronokrator*; on the other hand, time extended from God's creation to the Apocalypse, which is the end of the world that will signal the beginning of the eternal kingdom. This was cosmic time and was marked by the rotation of the spheres around the earth. For St Augustine, time was born with Creation. However,

10. Detail of the *Creation Mosaic*, the creation of the stars, Monreale Cathedral.

11. Drawing of a clock in an illumination from the *Book of Knowledge of Ingenious Mechanical Devices*, by al-Jaziri, who lived in the thirteenth century.

12

13

because humankind's fall redefined the relationship that God had established in and through Creation between Himself and humankind, and between humankind and Creation, original sin caused the birth of history, understood as a progression towards a final solution: the End of Time, which was mirrored in the physical end of human beings, the termination of their physical existence. Human time, that is the time of human beings and history, comes to an end with the "Last Four Things": death, judgment, heaven, and hell. The first two are personal and the second two are collective and final. Omnipresent God was the Lord of space, but He was also eternal and therefore the Lord of time. For this reason, He was represented at the centre of the twelve apostles as the sun surrounded by the twelve constellations and the twelve months of the year.

Human time, which is limited and linear, thus had a beginning and an end. It began with Creation and would end with the Last Judgment. Based on a calculation arrived at by adding the ages of the biblical patriarchs, the world was created in the year 5508, a date that remained in use in Greece and Russia. The West, however, measured time differently. Until the fourteenth and fifteenth centuries, the Iberian Peninsula began the count from the year 38 B.C., the year Augustus conquered that region. From the sixth to the tenth centuries, however, the calculation referred to

14

as "Christian" dominated in the West. It began in Rome in the sixth century and was based on the calculations of a Scythian monk, Dionysius Exiguus (Dennis the Small). He determined that Jesus had been born in the year 753 (in reality, it appears he erred by six or seven years and the year 746 or 747 is more probable). Since then, the western world has divided time into a period before Christ and one after Christ.

However, the year did not originally begin on 1 January: according to ancient Roman lore, the New Year was tied to traditions that the Church considered to be impious and pagan so, in order to combat these traditions, it was shifted. But every region of Europe had its own custom. In Rome and many areas of Italy and Germany, the New Year coincided with the western celebration of Christmas, 25 December (which, in its turn, was an ancient celebration of the solstice); elsewhere, it was 25 March (the Feast of the Annunciation), 1 September (according to Byzantine custom), or Easter (which is a flexible date, i.e., the first Sunday after the full moon of Spring).

The days were grouped into weeks and were given the old Roman names for the planets (but the *dies solis* or "day of the sun" became *dies dominica* or "day of the Lord") or, more often, the name of the saint whose liturgical feast was celebrated. Some days were particularly important for the expiry of civil contracts;

12. Detail of the reliefs on the façade of the Modena Cathedral: the creation of Adam and Eve and original sin.

13. The expulsion Adam and Eve from Eden, façade of the Cremona Cathedral.

14. Beato Angelico, *Last Judgment*. San Marco Museum, Florence.

15. Frieze depicting the cycle of the months
on the façade of the Cremona Cathedral.

16, 18. Roundels with the signs of the zodiac, which complete the
cosmological image of the hierarchies and the flow of time,
porch vault above the central portal of the Piacenza Cathedral.

15

16

for example, the feast of the Archangel Michael, 29 September, is the date when agricultural contracts expired.

The days and months were marked according to two systems: the liturgical feasts of the Church and labours on the farm. The months were usually represented on the portals of churches by the corresponding constellations and the typical work performed during that period: in June and July, reaping; in September and October, the harvest; in December, the killing of the pig; and so on. Even the hours of the day were segmented according to the Latin tradition and the Liturgy of the Day; there were Terce (third hour or 9:00 a.m.) Sext (midday), and None (ninth hour or 3:00 p.m.) or by counting the hours from sunset.

In the thirteenth century, for economic reasons, large mechanical clocks began to accompany the sound of the bells in the cities to mark the hours. Church time was by now beginning to correspond to the time of the merchant. It was becoming possible to conceive of time in a new way, no longer as something liturgical and cyclical but as something subject to both irreversible erosion and the laws of the market. This was a time that – contrary to what the scholastic philosophers were arguing – could be bought and sold, reduced to merchandise and a commodity.

"DESACRILIZATION" OF SPACE AND TIME

The advent of Christianity brought other changes in the relationship among humans, time, and space, particularly with regards to the sacredness of places. In the ancient world, especially in the countryside, many places were dedicated to specific deities. Ancient literature offers many examples, such as that of Pliny the Elder, who speaks of trees dedicated to divinities. Some species were protected because they were dedicated to particular gods and goddesses: the oak to Jove, the laurel to Apollo, the olive to Minerva, the myrtle to Venus, and the poplar to Hercules. Some

17. Depiction of the constellations and stars as the Serpent
and Ursa Major and Minor.

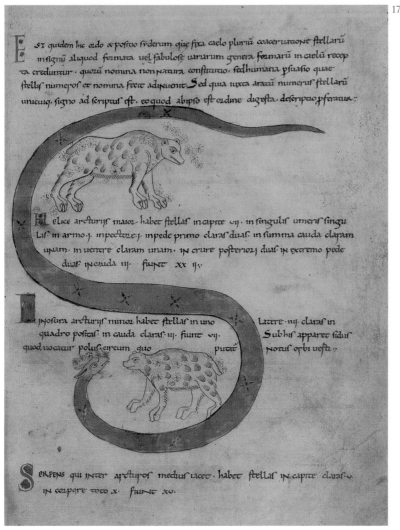

17

18

19. The image of the Virgin of Montserrat. Montserrat, an inhospitable place where a church was dedicated to her, had been a pilgrimage destination from the eleventh century.

19

20

of the places dedicated to deities are well known; they are usually woods, mountains, or streams, such as the sacred woods at Nemi, Monteluco Mountain near Spoleto, the *lacus Fucinus* (Lake Fucino), and the springs at Clitumno. But there must have been thousands of other such places, unknown to everyone except those who lived in communities near sites dedicated to some deity or which had tutelary gods. The abolition of paganism decreed the end or, at least the waning, of this relationship between the world of the divine and the natural world. This change occurred despite the fact that various Christian cults, especially those dedicated to Mary, the mother of God, replaced the old pagan cults associated with specific places, thereby reviving, at least at the level of "popular culture," mechanisms that were very similar to those in the pre-Christian era.

In addition to the "desacrilization" of the natural world, Christianity also brought about the desacrilization of time. In the Roman calendar, time was originally marked by the lunar cycle: the *dies fasti* (judicial days) were favourable for the conduct of one's daily affairs, whereas the *dies nefasti* were inauspicious. However the *dies nefasti* were not always sacred – only those days consecrated to the deity from whom they took their name were considered sacred. Studying the lunar cycle was the task of the *pontifex*, (member of the council of priests) who organized the calendar and summoned the assembly (*Kalendae*), which determined the days on which the Ides and the Nones fell. Beginning with the reform of the calendar under Caesar, however, the Calendes, Ides, and Nones were set down in writing once and for all on the basis of the solar month and thus no longer depended on the observations of the *pontifix*. The reform probably started, or at least supported, the process of concealing the sacred meaning of the archaic calendar, which, with its complement of feasts and celebrations of deities tied to "strong" periods of the year, remained part of the traditional religious mentality in more conservative areas. The seasonal rhythms of agricultural work undoubtedly contributed to the preservation of this tradition, which only the industrial revolution would make problematic.

NATURE AND CLIMATE

The peoples of the Middle Ages depended heavily on nature. This nature was wild and difficult to tame due to the technical capabilities of the period. The fact that, in contrast, the contemporary age is tied to the notion of a good, domesticated nature compliant with human intervention leads us to think that ancient and medieval peoples lived in greater harmony with the ecological system than we do. The opposite is probably true: nature was feared and not loved. Furthermore, the Bible taught that, after original sin, nature rebelled against humankind and, therefore, humans had to tame it. Francis of Assisi presents a version of this revolution in his *Canticle of the Creatures*.

That people in the medieval era were largely at the mercy of nature is shown by the effects that changes in climate had on human settlements and their operations.

21

22

23

24

During the Middle Ages, the climate was variable, even though the time span over which the changes took place was fairly long. The drop in temperature in the early part of the Middle Ages was probably one of the causes of the migration of people from the north to the south. The end of this mini-Ice Age, between the eighth and ninth centuries, corresponded to gradual economic growth in Europe, which, in turn, led to widespread improvement between the tenth and fourteenth centuries. At the end of the tenth century, the temperature of the earth's atmosphere increased dramatically and this improved the climate, at least in the northern hemisphere. This coincided with two important phenomena: reduced rainfall and the melting of the polar icecaps, with the resultant opening up of the North Sea, which allowed the Vikings to reach Iceland. In addition, the improved climate had positive effects on reducing infantile illnesses, which strike the respiratory tract primarily, and thus fostered population growth. At the same time, the reduction in rainfall and other forms of precipitation created conditions for improved agriculture. The result was that, between the tenth and thirteenth centuries, there was a dramatic expansion of agriculture. These were the times of the establishment of the great monastic orders, which drained marshes and cleared land, and the birth of the medieval city, which, we should remember, was made of wood for the most part. All these factors contributed to a population boom accompanied by an expansion of arable land.

20. View of Le-Puy-en-Velay, a Marian pilgrimage destination from the tenth century. According to tradition, the Madonna appeared to a Gallo-Roman matron who had gone to the mountain with a fever and healed her.

21. View of the chapel of the Virgin in Glastonbury, a pilgrimage destination from the sixth century and an important Celtic site dedicated to the cult of female deities.

22. *St Francis Preaching to the Birds*, miniature preserved in the Morgan Library and Museum, New York.

23. Two monks at work, detail of a miniature from Gregory the Great's *Commentary on Job*, Citeaux Abbey.

24. Water supply system to the west of Igny Abbey, Arcis le Ponsart.

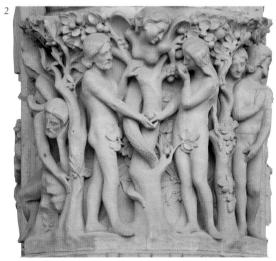

1. Fresco from the thirteenth-fourteenth century depicting the month of May with music and dance cortege, canon's cloister of the Cathedral of San Lorenzo, Genoa.

2. Sculpted figures of Adam and Eve on the base of the trumeau of the left portal of the Notre-Dame Cathedral, Paris.

3. *The Foolish Virgins*, apse of the chapel of Castel d'Appiano, Val d'Adige.

17

HOLIDAYS AND FEASTS

3

THE BODY

Called "the Age of Faith," the Middle Ages are usually associated with the spirit and thought of as an enemy of the flesh and all forms of corporeality. The age is also imagined as a time of negation and mortification of the body, as well as the devaluation of all things physical and, therefore, as affirming not only "spirituality" and "ideas" but the abstract itself. This distorted image of the Middle Ages as a completely "spiritual" epoch derives from two notions, both of which are erroneous, although they are based on a degree of truth. The first of these is the notion that the dominant philosophy of the age – at least up to the end of the thirteenth century when Aristotelian thought prevailed – was Platonism, which de-emphasized the importance of the body in relation to the soul and objects in relation to

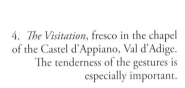

4. *The Visitation*, fresco in the chapel of the Castel d'Appiano, Val d'Adige. The tenderness of the gestures is especially important.

5. Personification of the virtues, detail: Humility, Mercy, and Fortitude. Hildegard of Bingen, *Scivias* (Know the ways of the Lord). Hessische Landesbibliothek, Wiesbaden.

6. Monks and the pleasures of life, miniature in a fifteenth-century Dutch edition of Boccaccio's *Decameron*. Bibliothèque de l'Arsenal, Paris.

7. The Maubuisson Abbey, north of Paris; latrines seen from below.

8. Plan of the Cistercian abbey at Tintern, near Bristol in Great Britain; dormitory and latrines.

ideas. But Platonism also triumphed in the fifteenth century, a period in which the classical cult of nudity emerged and there was such an explosion of sexual freedom that it would take two Reformations in the next century, one Protestant and the other Catholic, to stem the tide. The second notion is based on superficial knowledge of some mystical traditions, such as those associated with the techniques of mortification and purification of the body. From this emerges the image of a Middle Ages tormented by the uncleanliness of the body, which required the mortification of the flesh through fasting and physical punishment (self-flagellation, hair shirts, etc.). However, these practices already existed in the mystery religions of the pagan world and were known to Germanic peoples, especially the Celts, who used them for different purposes, from the initiation of warriors to shamanic techniques to foresee the future.

Furthermore, "sexophobia," which is often attributed to Christians even today, does not really pertain to either medieval man or woman. Christianity extolled virginity and continence, and it regulated sexual activity – as well as food consumption and entertainment – in a way that may have led to some "heroic" excesses in the form of extreme denial or outright self-inflicted torture. Discipline, sobriety, and self-control were central to Christian teaching and practice, but not, however, as techniques for self-inflicted punishment and mortification: rather, they were intended as means to achieve control of one's body in order to attain true freedom, which does not exist if the individual succumbs to uncontrollable impulses.

The Middle Ages were certainly not materialistic, but they were profoundly tied to physicality and even the carnal. Contrary to the tendency to "push back," into the past, the lack of personal hygiene, a state that emerged as historic reality between the late 1500s and the Baroque, the Middle Ages were very familiar with personal hygiene (hot baths were quite common) and with nudity, which was

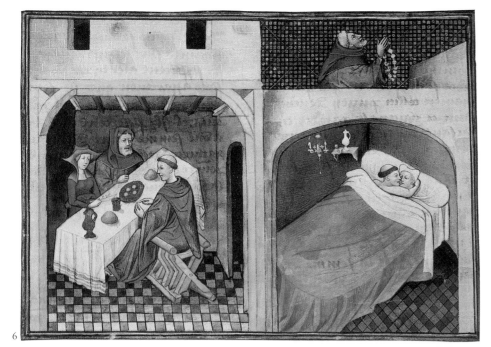

6

7

8

practised in many environments and on many occasions, though not promiscuously. Even in monasteries, the body was cared for: there were baths and latrines; provisions were made to wash, feed, and treat the infirm; ascetic practices were permitted, but always with the approval and under the supervision of a superior. These practices were sometimes very harsh but always commensurate with the physical and mental capabilities of those who undertook them. There were usually substantial comforts, which became the object of many satirical poems: monks who wore comfortable clothing, lived in well-heated accommodations, and ate well, sometimes abundantly. Even today many of the cheeses, preserves, and alcoholic beverages that we most appreciate originate in monasteries.

LOVE

Love was invented in the twelfth century, according to Denis de Rougemont, a scholar who devoted a great deal of research to the subject. The famous relationship between Abelard and Héloïse is important and informative. Peter Abelard was born in Pallet near the city of Nantes in 1079, studied in Tours and then Loche, and had Roscellinus as his teacher; he was the greatest philosopher of the Nominalist movement of the time. He soon moved to Paris, which was becoming one of the great cultural cities of the western world. His teacher there was William of Champeaux, but he soon clashed with him. In fact, Abelard was disappointed with William's teaching, as he felt his own thought was superior, a feeling that was naturally met with irritation. Abelard opened his own schools in Melun and Corbeil, but in 1114, at the age of thirty-five, he returned to Paris, where he began to teach in a school located on Mont-Sainte-Geneviève, a small hill to the south of the city, which would become the famous site of the Sorbonne.

9. The prophet Hosea forgives and embraces his wife. Gomer (Kings 17:8–24), detail of a miniature from the *Manerius* Bible (twelfth century). Sainte-Geneviève Library, Paris.

10. *The Kiss of Anna and Joachim*, the parents of the Virgin Mary, thirteenth-century fresco, north wall of the nave of the church of Notre-Dame. Pouzauges.

The novelty and boldness of his methods and ideas made Abelard a kind of symbol for the free and open-minded intellectual. He took advantage of his charm to seduce a young, intelligent girl named Héloïse, who had been entrusted to his care so that he could teach her philosophy. Héloïse was the niece of the canon Fulbert, with whom Abelard had taken up residence. Soon the passion between the two was as famous as Abelard's intellectual prowess. A child was born to the couple but was not given the name of a saint drawn from the Christian calendar, as was the custom; instead he was named after the instrument used for observing stars, Astrolabe. The choice of this name speaks to the climate of cultural and sexual freedom in which Abelard and Héloïse lived in these years. However, in 1119–20, the two were secretly married.

The situation could not be tolerated by Héloïse's uncle, who exacted vengeance by having Abelard castrated and forcing his niece to enter a monastery. Abelard reputedly embraced the monastic career, but without finding peace in his new condition; in fact, he found himself having to perform the duties of the abbot and was strenuously opposed by his monks. In the meantime, Héloïse, who had become abbess of the convent of Paraclete, maintained an intense correspondence with him, which has survived. Their love, now interrupted on the terrestrial plane, would continue in God. In these letters – some of which exhibit great artistry and sincere mysticism – the traces of their passion filter through. Abelard was persecuted, not for his relationship with Héloïse, which had, after all, been suspended, but for his ideas and his teachings, by the greatest mystic of the twelfth century, Bernard of Clairvaux, who accused him of spreading a poisonous philosophy that undermined the bases of faith.

Although Abelard repeatedly protested his Christian orthodoxy, he was condemned by the Council of Sens in 1141 and died in wretchedness and desperation the following year, surrounded, however, by the affection and admiration of the greatest cultural figures of his day. Abelard is undoubtedly one of the fundamental figures not only of the twelfth century but of western culture as a whole. His love for Héloïse was not merely a historical event; we can say that the two "invented" love as it would come to be understood in modern times – as passion and complete devotion on the part of two human beings for each other.

THE CARNIVAL

Today carnival is a festival especially for children, at best a playful masquerade, but in the past it had a different function. A wild celebration controlled by secular and ecclesiastical authorities and juxtaposed to the Lenten meditation, the carnival inspired great masterpieces of art across the centuries (we need only cite Brueghel and Goya), music (from Schubert to Berlioz and Paganini) and literature: Goethe studied the carnival as a natural manifestation and the great critic Mikhail Bakhtin, writing on his countryman Dostoyevsky, describes it in the following way: "The carnival is a festival of time that exterminates all and renews all; this is essentially the idea of the carnival."

So much passion and interest have also inspired research on the origins of this festival, which we certainly recognize as medieval, but which is considered by many to have ancient, indeed pagan, roots. Prior to the Renaissance, it was believed that the carnival descended directly from such Roman festivals as the Saturnalia and Lupercalia or Greek festivals like the Dionysian rituals. In all these celebrations, participants wore masks and acted as if in a state of delirium, playing tricks on passers-by. Many of these rituals disappeared, at least from the official calendar, when Christianity became established in the Roman world, but not without difficulty. The Lupercalia were abolished by Pope Gelasius I as late as 496 while similar festivals continued to be practised in the popular traditions in Italy as well as in Spain and France in subsequent centuries. Undoubtedly, some of their formal features – disguise, tricks, and wild ritual stone fights – found their way into the carnival.

11. Musicians and masks, detail of a miniature from the *Roman de Fauvel* (Romance of Fauvel). National Library of France, Paris.

11

12

12. Pieter Brueghel the Elder, *The Fight between Carnival and Lent*, 1559. Museum of Fine Arts, Vienna.

13. Goya, *The Funeral of the Sardinian Woman,* 1812–19, detail: demonic faces of the masked cortege.

13

14

14. Silenus holds a pitcher of wine and, in the background a satyr holds the mask of a drunken faun, detail of a large fresco in the Villa of Mysteries, Pompeii.

However, it is undeniable that the celebration as we see it in the Middle Ages was unknown prior to this time. What explanation can we provide? The unusual name has inspired many scholars to wonder about its origins and the word's etymology. For a certain period of time it was commonly believed that the word derived from the Roman phrase *carrus navalis* (boat float); this festival took place on 5 March, the Feast of Isis, and involved a pageant that included a boat (*Isidus navigium*) drawn by a cart. Apuleius provides a precise description in Book II of the *Metamorphoses*. Many scholars interpreted the custom of a carnival pageant with carts (such pageants have taken place from the Renaissance to modern days in Viareggio and Putignano) as a commemoration of the *carrus* (cart) and the sacred boat of Isis. During the 1900s, a new theory gained ground, which is widely accepted as the more probable explanation. The term "carnival" is to be interpreted not in the context of pagan practices but as a product of the Christian idea of Lent, with the word seen as a contraction of the expression *carnem levare* (to remove meat). The first recorded rituals bearing this name come to light at the end of the twelfth century and are described with the terms *carnelevamen, carnelevamine* or *carnisprivium*. In other words, it seems to have been a popular compensation for the sacrifices of the Lenten fast. This provides a good explanation of the "fight between Carnival and Lent," a rather famous motif in art and literature, where the carnal being celebrated is not only the one associated with the sin of gluttony. Brueghel's painting *The Old Man*, preserved in the Art Gallery of Vienna, is perhaps the most eloquent example.

It should not be forgotten, however, that not only the time of penance but the time of celebration was carefully regulated in traditional society. The "world turned upside down" motif of the carnival is not a completely destabilizing element. No matter how wildly people danced and participated in the orange, flour, and stone fights or in the masked parades, transgression was governed by rules and prohibitions: for example, people could not perform certain work, such as spinning yarn, during the carnival period. The unfolding of the celebration was set down with a certain precision: the carnival consisted of Fat Tuesdays and Thursdays, then it died and was buried, generally around Ash Wednesday. The conclusion of the carnival was often represented by a puppet who was carried in procession and then burned or by a flesh-and-blood person who escaped the flames amid applause. This was a sign that the abundance of the carnival would return the following year to brighten the spirits and, especially, the flesh.

The carnival was not the exclusive property of Christians, as Jewish communities had similar celebrations, modelled on those of the "Gentiles," especially on the occasion of the feast of Purim, which commemorates the rescue of the Jews from the Persian King Ahasuerus. During the feast, there is an abundance of food and drink. Purim fell at almost the same time as the Christian carnival, so it was easy for the two traditions to commingle. For this reason, Christians generally refer to this as the "Jewish Carnival." The sources describe similar street festivals and list foods that would make the inhabitants of the Earthly Paradise envious. Purim may have reached the heights of refinement in the homes of well-to-do Jews. Arial Toaff writes that in the Jewish part of Rome in the 1300s, the sumptuous suppers of the Jewish carnival consisted of twenty-four courses, including roast deer, cerci, mutton on a spit, roasted capon and chicken, grilled pigeon, skewers of fowl (partridges, Greek partridges, turtledoves), grilled marinated pheasant, stuffed duck and goose, fricassee of lemon dove, "goose sausages, tongue of veal, and sweets such as anise, biscuits, turnovers filled with marzipan, 'mostaccioli' (little moustaches) as well as other such delights."

THEATRE AND THE RITUAL OF ROLE REVERSAL

The carnivals were "naturally adapted" to plays, among which the most famous and most interesting is Adam de la Halle's *Jeu de la feuillée* (Play of the greensward). On the surface, this is a realistic play in as much as the actors portray the real people of Arras. The spectacle is part of an actual maypole festival or another feast that initiates a propitiatory cycle. The action takes place in a city-square; at the end of the play the characters leave the stage to go to actual places. However, at the same time the play contains elements of the carnival culture of laughter and pranks, as well as stereotypes (such as the physician and the prostitute) that expose the vices of the citizens (such as scatological vulgarity), "feral" elements, the courtship of Harlequin, fairies, and liturgical parodies. The ritual of subversion is also

15. Portrait of the poet Adam de la Halle within a capital letter from the *Chansonnier d'Arras* (Arras songbook), c.1278. Public Library, Arras.

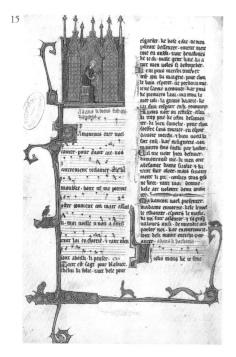

a well-known part of the carnival, as are the confession of sins and the expulsion of evil and sin from the community. The "fool," considered "pure," was generally entrusted with the task of exposing the defects of the city and its citizens, just as occurs in de la Halle's play.

There is no shortage of textual evidence of the correspondence between plays, such as Adam de la Halle's, and festivals organized in the city. For example, Giovanni Villani, in his *Nuova Cronaca* (New chronicle, book 8, ch. 70), describes the miracle play on the theme of Hell that took place in Florence in 1604: "for the day of the calends of May on the Carraia Bridge and along the Arno." This was on 1 May, which is the beginning of the spring cycle, and was organized by a local association, as in de la Halle's *Jeu de la feuillée*.

Another typical motif is the Nesnie Hellekan, or Hellequin, originally the king of the infernal hunt, probably of Germanic origin, which incorporates both the feral, subterranean, dark aspect (which the Christian tradition turns into the demonic or satanic) and the propitiatory aspect of fertility typified in the May festivals. The motif is also associated with the dark, infernal deity known as Hel, who had hellish features, as well as those of the god of abundance. The modern figure of Harlequin emerges from the normalization of the Hellequin figure.

But in the medieval world, as represented by *Jeu de la feuillée*, there were festivals in which the comical, festive, desecrating elements were not pure entertainment but folkloric rituals (although this was a folklore that, by this time, was mixed with Christian motifs and themes) of purification and celebration of particular times of the year.

16. Street jongleurs, detail of the frontispiece of a psalter from the early twelfth century, originating in Saint-Remy, Reims. St John's College, Cambridge.

16

18

BIRTH AND DEATH

1. Evangeliary cover in ivory called the *Diptych of the Five Parts*, containing a rich series of scenes from the life of Christ, from the end of the fifth century. Bottom scene: the *Massacre of the Innocents*. Museum of the Cathedral Works, Milan.

INFANCY

From the early 1960s, when French historian Philippe Ariès published a seminal study on infancy in the Middle Ages, the topic has been extensively debated. Ariès claimed that infancy is a cultural product and not a natural given. Prior to the modern age, infants were represented as miniature adults. The high rates of birth and infant mortality prevented people from considering infancy as a condition and an age in and of itself, rather than as a prelude to adult life, the only stage that was important.

2. *Adoration of the Magi*, detail of the Rachis Altar, seventh century. National Archeological Museum, Cividale del Friuli.

3. Eleventh-century icon with scenes of the infancy of Christ, St Catherine of Sinai Monastery.

4

5

4. *The Woman, the Son, and the Dragon*, detail of an Ottonian *Apocalypse*. National Library, Bamberg.

5. *The Birth of the Virgin*, 1313–14, detail of the fresco in King's Church, Studenica, Serbia.

6. Giotto, *Massacre of the Innocents*, 1304–06, detail of the fresco in the Scrovegni Chapel, Padua.

7. Gentile da Fabriano (1370–1427), *St Nicholas Saves the Three Men from Execution*, predella of the Quaratesi Polyptych, c.1425. Vatican Pinacoteca.

8. Benozzo Gozzoli (1420?–1497), *St Augustine as a Boy with His Mother Monica*, 1465, detail of the fresco in the Chapel of the Chorus, Church of St Augustine, San Gimignano.

Ariès' theories have been discussed and often refuted, but there is still no general agreement on what the status of the medieval child was. This is perhaps because the period is so long and complex that is does not permit easy generalizations. For example, it has been pointed out that Christ, the Madonna, and the Saints are often depicted as infants or with children who are miraculously saved, as in the case of St Nicholas, who brought back to life some children who had been chopped up and put in a barrel of saltwater. The convention of depicting children as small adults was ostensibly attributable to the lack of realism in medieval art (at least up until the late 1200s) rather than to a lack of interest in that age group.

The motif of *The Ages of Man*, on the contrary, offers images of infants in swaddling clothes and children are well represented. Similarly, we have toys for children that have survived and are not very different from those of the modern age. In his autobiography *De rebus a se gestis*, the chronicler Geraldis Cambrensis (Gerald of Wales), who lived between the twelfth and thirteenth centuries, describes how it was common for him as a child to build monasteries in the sand while his brother built castles and palaces; for this reason his father began to call him "little bishop," saying that he would provide him with an education suited to a career in the Church.

It is also true that the term used to designate children, *pueri*, is somewhat ambiguous. In Medieval Latin this word was used to signify "child" or "boy" but also "follower" or "hooligan." Even the age group that the term should designate is not very clear. In the case of the so-called "Children's Crusade" (also "Innocents" or "Little Shepherds"), the age of the child-soldiers is unclear. This is an age when adult life (military education for the aristocrats, work in the fields for the children of peasants, and marriage for almost all) began very early by our standards.

6

7

8

In the fifteenth century, devotion to child martyrs grew. Altars dedicated to "Innocents" and their holy relics, altarpieces, frescoes, and miniatures depicting the Massacre of the Innocents ordered by King Herod, one of the scenes that are typically part of the nativity narrative, were widespread during this time. This phenomenon occurred during a time when infant deaths were a daily occurrence. Alongside the more obvious causes of death, such as breech births, illnesses, and malnutrition, other causes and more specific reasons need to be identified: the recurrence of the plagues as well as the discovery that abortions and infanticides were not uncommon and were denounced with increasing vitriol by preachers.

DEATH

In traditional cultures, the most common response to the spectre of death is wonder, rather than fear; that is, a profound awareness that death is something unnatural and incomprehensible. There is therefore a desire to "tame it" and, in a sense, eliminate it, by preparing the body for resurrection of the soul for eternity. In one way or another, this element is an integral part of all funeral rituals in the world.

"Fear of dying," that is, the anguish one experiences as part of a difficult transition that one must face through some process of initiation, is something else. From this transition stem an infinite number of symbolic rituals to "accustom" the dead to the idea of being dead and, as such, to separate them from the community of the living. It is the source of a plethora of legends on the "revenants," or the dead who return from the grave, and the equally endless list of precautions to avoid, dominate, or control such a return. In addition, there are instructions on how to live life as if

9. Figure of blindfolded death on
horseback, detail of the splay of the central
portal lunette of the façade
of Notre-Dame Cathedral.

10. View of the chorus from the northeast
and the cemetery of the Church
of Saint-Nicolas, Caen.

it were a more or less long preparatory phase to the final passage. This is the core of Plato's teaching. But towards the end of the period we conventionally call medieval, the great revolution inaugurated by modernity occurred. The discovery of the fear of death is part of this process.

Between the fourth and the fourteenth centuries, we do not find terror in the face of death. In the Christian world, the dead are not isolated in a city designed and constructed specifically for them, the necropolis: instead, they are gathered in "dormitories." This is the meaning of the original Greek words "catacomb" and "cemetery." Death is only a temporary sleep that concludes with the resurrection of all humanity, according to the promise of Christ the Saviour. Therefore, cemeteries are inhabited places: the dead are buried in churches or near them. This is such a deeply rooted custom that hygienic practices originating in the Enlightenment that give rise to new pagan necropolises were initially opposed in Europe at the start of the 1800s.

In medieval thought and iconography, death is present but only as an image of the Apocalypse. Death was not feared, despite the fact that people knew it was a painful process, not only because they were convinced that life is a transitory state but especially because living conditions were so harsh (war, hunger, illnesses, etc.) that death appeared to be a relief, on the one hand, and because rituals of the "domestication of death" were so deeply rooted, on the other hand. People were accustomed to living in the shadow of death, waiting for it and not fearing it. It is as St Francis of Assisi wrote: "sora nostra Morte corporale / da la quale nullu homo vivente pò skappare" (Sister Death, / from whose embrace no mortal can escape).

But things changed during the fifteenth century, when life was radically better. Life became sweeter and more comfortable; abandoning this earth was therefore harder. Then the not entirely unexpected but still devastating plague of 1347–50, the Black Death, swept across Europe. It provided the terrifying spectre of a cruel death, which did not allow any time for people to prepare themselves, that mercilessly cut down the young and old, and that did not even permit acts of mercy because the dead were too many and the bodies were buried hastily or abandoned. In this climate, *Ars Moriendi* manuals, which provided advice on the "art of dying well," were produced and became devotional reading material in the secular world between the fourteenth and seventeenth centuries.

THE AFTERLIFE AND THE INVENTION OF PURGATORY

In the ancient world, the afterlife was visualized as a dark and terrible place. For this reason, the descent into Hades by heroes in search of revelation was the supreme test; there were also festivals and rituals to keep the ghosts of the dead away so that they could not return. The advent of mystery cults in the Greek world and then in Rome overturned this concept by proposing a less bleak image of the afterlife. This revolution was fully realized in Christianity, in which the afterlife is a place where divine justice is attained while the world in which we live is merely a smoky image of the real. As far as we know, during the first centuries of the spread of Christianity, believers awaited the Last Judgment and the resurrection of the body. They imagined that the souls of the dead experienced a state of prolonged sleep until that point. Several signs, however, seemed to contradict this notion. The first Christians adopted the pagan practice of the *refrigerum* (refreshment), which is recorded on epitaphs and in the catacombs. The term could refer to the funeral banquet, the happy memory of martyrs, and celebrations in honour of the dead, but it could also refer to the possibility of praying for souls for the purpose of obtaining peace for them.

12

11

11. War between angels and demons over the soul of a dead woman, detail of a miniature from the Rupertsberger Codex of Hildegard of Bingen's *Scivias* (Know the ways of the Lord). Landesbibliothek, Wiesbaden.

12. Procession of flagellants at the time of the Black Death in a miniature from 1360. Royal Library, Brussels.

13. Reliefs showing the parable of Lazarus and the rich man, from the left wall of the south portal of the Church of Saint-Pierre in Moissac. At the top, the feast, and to the side, Lazarus embraced by Abraham. In the centre, the death of the rich man and Hell, whose torments are depicted below.

14. The resurrection of the dead, detail of the lunette of the left portal of the left flank of the Reims Cathedral.

13

14

Among the Fathers of the Church, some, like St Augustine and Gregory the Great, admitted that, even though souls may not go to Hell or the Kingdom of Heaven, they receive either a reward or punishment at the moment of death. From this arises the need to pray for them. From the tenth century onwards, however, we find the first iconography depicting the judgment of the soul at the moment of death and not at the moment of resurrection. The motif became quite common beginning in the twelfth century, when theologians reflected on the concept and gave it the name *iudicium* (judgment). Because by this time the attention of the living was increasingly focused on the fate of the soul after death, the afterlife was no longer simply the final outcome, which was postponed until the End of Time. The world of the living and the world of the dead could communicate with each other through Masses of the living celebrated for the dead, as well as the intercession of the dead, especially saints, on behalf of the living or (a more disturbing fact which is present in the literature of the late Middle Ages) apparitions of the dead to communicate with the living.

It was especially in the famous Cluny Abbey that the "cult of prayer," especially Masses for the dead, became highly organized and spiritual. Cluny was designed as a sort of energy hub for prayer, with Masses for the dead performed on an ongoing basis, celebrated at the same time on many altars in the abbey church, and prayers recited by choruses of monks. Beginning in 1030, the reformed Benedictines of Cluny initiated the liturgical practice of the Feast of All Souls and the commemorative celebration of the dead on 1 and 2 November, which was connected with the Celtic-pagan belief in the holiness of the start of Fall, devoted to ancestors and respected as a tradition up to the eleventh century in rural society – a society that by then had become profoundly Christian – and the cult of saints and Masses for the souls of Purgatory. It is in the context of this daring and original cultural project that Cluny Abbey made an important contribution to the process of systematizing beliefs pertaining to Purgatory – a phenomenon studied a few decades ago by Jacques le Goff.

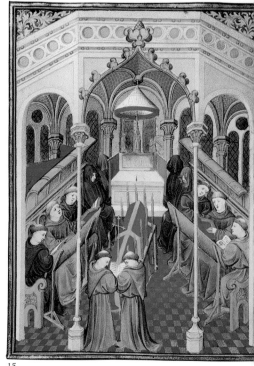

15

15. Monks during the offices of the dead, miniature from *King René's Hours*, Dijon, 1437. British Library, London.

16

16. Procession of the elect, detail of the lunette of the left portal, left flank of the Reims Cathedral.

17. Fresco by the Sienese school from 1346 showing the departure of souls from Purgatory, which is depicted as a hollow mountain and links up with the iconography of St Patrick and the well. St Francis Monastery, Todi.

From the twelfth to thirteenth century onward, the afterlife also began to have an increasingly well-defined geographic structure and to be seen as composed of three sites, as we find in the *Divine Comedy:* Hell for the damned, Paradise for the saved, and Purgatory, where those who are not stained with mortal sin but are nonetheless sinners spend a period of time. To these three places, two more must be added: Limbo for those who lived a just life prior to the advent of Christ but were not baptized and cannot live among the blessed, and, for the same reason, Limbo for infants who died without receiving baptism. These individuals are never permitted to experience the supreme joy of the Beatific Vision.

PENANCE AND CONFESSION

The early Church allowed pagans to enter the community of believers through baptism. At that point, no one could be excluded, except for the three especially serious sins of homicide, adultery, and apostasy (denying one's faith). In time the custom became less rigid and laity who were guilty of these sins could be re-admitted into the Church through a second (and in some cases a third) reconciliation. The sinner confessed to the bishop in private but he or she was required to ask for penance publicly. This kind of confession was called "public" or "canonical" penance. The condition of the penitent was made manifest by public acts of contrition and physical mortification, including fasts, simple dress, exclusion from Holy Communion, etc. In provinces far from Rome, such as the British Isles and especially Ireland, another form of penance called "tariff" penance spread. According to this practice, every sin constituted a kind of debt to God that had to be repaid in accordance with a penitential "price" or "tariff," generally established beforehand. These forms of penance were usually less onerous than those pertaining to canonical penance.

17

18

The Gregorian Reform of the eleventh century, however, suppressed the practice because it was considered to be a source of error relative to papal authority. At this point, the *Summae Confessorum* (Concise books on confession) or *Summae de Poenitentia*, (Concise books on penance), went into effect, in which regulations governing penance (for example, fasting), instructions on how to welcome and educate the penitent, and the legal consequences of the sin (which, at that time, also constituted a crime) converged. In addition, according to a Germanic tradition, which in turn was influenced by the Latin culture, the possibility of atoning for a sin by means of a sum of money called *composition* became common. As a result, many well-to-do individuals "composed" their sin by paying for prayers or Masses, while the poor and priests could perform their penance by making pilgrimages instead. As can easily be imagined, the practice led to many abuses and for this reason the so-called "indulgences" were invented. At the root of the indulgence is the concept that a sin breaks the law of God in two ways: the person performs an action that compromises the state of the soul and the person performs an action that is reprehensible in the face of society. In the first instance, it was necessary to repent and confess with true contrition; in the second, it was necessary to cleanse oneself thorough acts of mercy, prayer, Masses, pilgrimages, and so forth. There were abuses in this case as well, which disturbed many Christians from the fifteenth century onward, and in the 1500s such abuses comprised the principal argument in Martin Luther's protest to Rome.

Among meritorious acts, prayers for the dead and petitions for intercession were common. In this way, the concept of Purgatory was standardized and reinforced as a consequence of the growth in the practices of penance.

18. Cross-section of the Earth showing the horrors of Hell, detail of the miniature from Guillaume de Degulleville's allegorical *Pilgrimage of Human Life*, 1400–10. Royal Library, Brussels.

1. Hans Memling (1433–1494), *The Seven Joys of the Virgin* (1480). Donated to the chapel of the tanners guild of the city of Bruges by the patrons; the image contains a marine element in a panoramic view with port and ships. Alte Pinakothek, Munich.

2. View of Sognefjord, Norway.

3. Plan of the city of Elbing, in the State of the Teutonic Order. The new city emerges around an older nucleus at the foot of the castle.

4. Plan of the city of Lübeck, which grew around a market.

19

AN EXPANDING WORLD

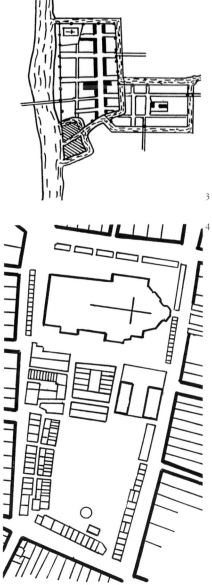

TO THE NORTH

In the middle centuries of the medieval epoch, Europe began to acquire the borders that we recognize today. In this gradual process, political, commercial, and missionary factors converged. With the reconfiguration of powers started by Charlemagne and continued by the Saxon emperors, peace and security were gradually restored and trade revived. In the meantime, the continental axis of economic activity shifted from the north to the east, while the Mediterranean had become a Muslim and Byzantine lake. The Christian-Germanic world was expanding towards the rivers Elbe and Oder, as dioceses and trade centres in Scandinavia were being systemically organized. Beginning in the tenth century, alongside the ancient cities of the Rhine and Danube, new centres developed in Germany supported by the imperial rulers and the aristocracy, who oversaw the expansion towards northern and eastern Europe.

Thus – from the Flemish coasts of the North Sea to the Russian rivers – new cities arose, usually around two foci: the "castle" or fortified fortress of the feudal lord, where the cathedral was also located, and the commercial quarter, where warehouses for the storage and marketing of merchandise mushroomed. In the meantime, renewed growth in the population and the cultivation of spaces that were once forests and swamps prompted the birth of new urban centres (called "*villes neuves*") whose revenue systems favoured the privileged classes in the sense that the feudal lords of those areas wanted to attract peasants who did not own land, recognizing that the resulting increased production – which would lead to greater food supplies, which were increasingly in demand in European markets as the population grew – would make them rich. On the borderlands, the Franks established several cities and sought to increase the importance of those that already existed. In the first group is the city of Hamburg and in the second Bremen. At the start of the ninth century, by order of Ludwig the Pious, the two centres created an archbishopric charged with organizing missions to Scandinavia and regions in the east. In the decades that followed, Bishop Anscario travelled to Denmark, where he was welcomed by the Christian King Harold. During the tenth century, three kingdoms had emerged in Scandinavia: Denmark, Norway, and Sweden, which were Christianized over a short period during the next century.

The movement of skilled warriors and seamen from Scandinavia had altered the destiny of the regions of Europe in many different ways. In its turn, the Scandinavian Peninsula had a rather complex history, especially in relation to the imperialist ambitions of the German crown and cities. Denmark had undertaken an ambitious expansionist policy westward – towards England – and eastward, conquering the lands of the Slavs and the Balts, and even subduing Norway for a short time. In the 1200s, however, the arrival of the Germans in the Baltic region had delivered a harsh blow to Danish power. Following several defeats, Erik V (1259–68) was forced to

5

5. Borgund Stave Church, built around the end of the twelfth century.

6. The western world in the year 1000.

Holy Roman Empire

Kingdom of Denmark in the year 1000

Missions of the archbishops of Bremen-Hamburg to Scandinavia

Scandinavian expeditions

Polish state in 992

Catholic missions

State of Kiev in 912

Expansion from 912 to 1054

Bulgarian Empire under tsar Samuel around 996

Muslim world at the end of the tenth century

Christian kingdoms on the Iberian Peninsula

Byzantine Empire

6

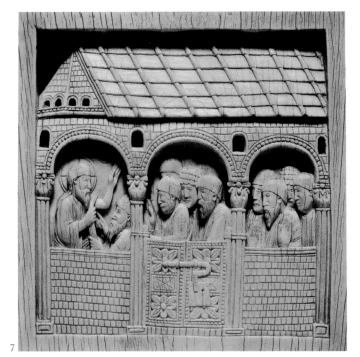

concede privileges to the Danehof, the legislative assembly formed of the high clergy and the aristocracy of the kingdom. In the decades that followed, up to the middle of the 1300s, the crown experienced a serious crisis. In the twelfth century, Norway was shaken by conflict over the election of a ruler in which the high clergy was opposed by the aristocratic "party." Despite Pope Innocent III's support for the clergy, the aristocracy succeeded in electing King Sverre (1184–1202) and establishing a hereditary monarchy. During the 1200s, Norwegian seamen explored and colonized new lands, such as Iceland, Greenland, and the Hebrides Islands (ceded to Scotland in 1266). The first stable dynasty in Sweden was the House of Sverker, who ruled, through ups and downs, from 1130 to 1250; it were succeeded by Count Birger, who established friendly relations with Norway and Denmark, granted privileges to the Hanseatic cities, and completed the annexation of Finland. In the second half of the century, there were several social upheavals that, with the Ordinance of Alsnö, laid the foundation for a hereditary noble cavalry exempt from taxes, which would keep the sovereign in check until the next century.

TO THE EAST

The Ottonians had created a network of cities along the Christian eastern frontier that performed the same function as Hamburg and Bremen on the northern border. The most important of these was Magdeburg, a lively commercial centre at the start of the ninth century. It was destroyed by the Slavs and rebuilt by Otto I; in 962, it became the seat of an archbishopric. Bishop Adalbert of Prague received his training in Magdeburg and decided to undertake a mission among the Slavs who lived near the river Oder; the Slavs, however, quickly rebelled against the bishop's sermons and

7. *Maiestas Domini* (Christ in Majesty), dedicatory ivory plaque of the Magdeburg antependium (altar frontal), 962–73. Emperor Otto I presents a model of the cathedral to the Lord. Metropolitan Museum of Art, New York.

8. *Christ before Pilate*, ivory carving of the Madgeburg antependium. Bayerschises Nationalmuseum, Munich.

martyred him along with his followers. Eliminating Adalbert did not save the Slavs of the Oder region from the arrival of new missionaries or from a military conquest that decimated them, as occurred under the assault of the Saxons. By the end of the tenth century, Magdeburg had six archdioceses, from which missionaries went out to Slav territories, in addition to the traditional seats in Hamburg and Bremen. The chronicles record that, around 1111, all the Slavs submitted formally to Henry X, called the Proud, Duke of Saxony. In reality, conversion and subjugation occurred over a lengthy period of time; only with continuous, aggressive campaigns did the Germans succeed in putting down Slav resistance. Other regions suffered invasions by the Danes in the second half of the century.

Bulgaria, the Balkans, Hungary, Bohemia, and Poland initiated moves toward political independence in the tenth century, in the face of pressures from powerful neighbours such as Byzantium and Germany, as well as the impact of invasions, such as that of the Mongols in 1241. After the tenth century, these regions gradually but consistently became an integral part of European politics, at least until the Turkish campaigns of the 1300s and 1400s, which resulted in the conquest of the most southern of these regions.

Bulgaria, a region populated by Slavs but occupied in the seventh century by the Mongols, had created an independent kingdom in the years following the

9. *Baptism of Boris*, khan of the Bulgars, miniature from a twelfth-fourteenth–century manuscript. Vatican Apostolic Library, Rome.

10. Slav settlements around the year 1000.

9

10

Russian Kiev at the end of the tenth century

Great Moravia under Svatopluk at the end of the ninth century

Bulgarian Empire during the time of Simeon (end of the ninth–start of the tenth century)

Croatia during the time of Tomisla (mid-tenth century)

11

12

amalgamation of the two ethnic groups, which by now were Christianized. In the early part of the tenth century, the Bulgaria of Simeon I (893–927) even threatened Constantinople but was subsequently subdued by the Byzantines, regaining its independence only in the twelfth century. The establishment of the Latin Empire of Constantinople in the thirteenth century gave the Bulgars the opportunity to expand their territory, even if only for a brief time. In 1217, the region of Serbia, which up to that time had been governed by the Bulgars and the Byzantines, acquired its independence and established a kingdom that grew to include Epirus, Macedonia, and Albania. Under Stephen Dušan (1331–55) the construction of so-called Great Serbia began at the expense of Byzantium. During the same century, however, both Bulgaria and Serbia were swallowed up by the Turkish invasion.

The Hungarian dynasty of the House of Árpád, established by Stephen I, called the Saint (997–1038), had created a kingdom whose boundaries were greater than those of modern Hungary. King Béla III (1173–96) annexed Croatia, Dalmatia, and Bosnia following a long war against Byzantium. In 1222, Andreas II (1205–35)

11. *Pious Women at the Sepulchre*, fresco in the church at Prilep, Macedonia.

12. A portrait of King Milutin, who holds up a model of the church, c.1320, detail of the nave fresco in the Church of the Annunciation in Gračanica, Serbia.

13. Nave of the Cracow Cathedral, 1346–64. The construction of the cathedral was sponsored by Casimir III the Great (1333–1370).

14. The Kingdom of Poland at the death of Casimir the Great (1370).

issued the Golden Bull, with which the high nobility and the clergy obtained – at almost the same time as the Magna Carta was being written in England – guarantees that their privileges would be protected by the institution of a Diet to control the actions of the ruler. Local assemblies were also created with the right to file grievances against the king; however, a few years later, in 1241, Hungary was overrun by the Mongols; the power of the king was re-established only many decades later under the House of Anjou (1307–82).

In the late Middle Ages, Bohemia was firmly bound to the German crown and the empire, of which it proclaimed itself a vassal in the tenth century. The Přemyslid Dynasty, which emerged during the ninth century out of the great landowning families, expanded its territory greatly during the 1200s under Ottokar II (1253–78). By opening up the frontiers of the kingdom to the Teutonic Knights, the king succeeded in annexing several neighbouring regions, including Austria, Styria, Carniola, and Carinthia, which was part of Slovakia. His kingdom was sufficiently powerful that in 1273 Ottokar aspired to the imperial crown. However, Rudolph of Habsburg was elected instead and intended to restore the territories usurped by the crown. The armies met on the Marchfeld and Ottokar died in the battle. The Přemyslid Dynasty remained in power for several more decades without being able to revive its past ambitions and in 1310 it was replaced by the Luxembourg dynasty.

In Poland in the tenth century, under the House of Piast, a kingdom in close proximity to Germany had been created. This powerful neighbour proved to be an obstacle to the creation of a great Slavic kingdom that was to have included Bohemia and Poland. However, the Poland of the Piast Dynasty undertook a policy of expansion to the northeast at the expense of the Slavic tribes that were still pagan. In the first half of the twelfth century, Pomerania and the territories between the Elbe and Oder were occupied. In 1138, the principal members of the House split the territories of the kingdom among themselves and the kingdom remained divided into many parts: Lesser Poland, around the city of Cracow went to the eldest son; Masovia, Kuivia, Greater Poland, Selesia, and Pomerelia, that is, the territories in the north, were given to the other member of the family as a duchy. The next century was

15

marked by wars among the political factions of Poland, which suffered a heavy blow with the Mongol invasion of 1241 and the German advance into the Baltic region. The unity of the kingdom was restored only during the time of Casimir III called the Great (1333–1370).

CONQUEST OF THE BALTIC

Around the year 1000, important merchant colonies were established on the Baltic. These were the product of the colonial rivalry between the Germans and the Scandinavians, who were aggressively establishing urban centres on the borderlands. It is not clear why many of these active and populous colonies declined from the eleventh century onward; it may have been due to the imperialism of the Germans, who completed the conquest of the Baltic in the centuries that followed.

The main protagonists of the conquest were the Order of Teutonic Knights and the Sword-bearers, who had come into existence, with the support of Pope Innocent III, to conduct crusades against the pagans in the Baltic region; these two orders merged in 1237. The military campaigns were especially cruel. The pagans had only two choices: if they refused to convert, they were forced to do so, not by missionaries but by the armies; if they accepted the conditions imposed on them, they became prey to the merchants and the savage Saxon colonization and risked being rapidly as-similated. Resistance continued for much of the twelfth century, and the campaigns finally concluded with different results for the principal ethnic-tribal groups. The Latvians, who were the first to accept conversion but continued to put up resistance throughout the thirteenth century, were defeated and had to acquiesce to German colonization. The opposition put up by the Prussians was more tenacious and they

15. The majestic monastic castle of the Teutonic Knights of Marienburg, whose construction began in 1280. The Palace of the Grand Master of the Order was built in its interior between 1382 and 1389.

16. The spread of the Order of Teutonic Knights.

16

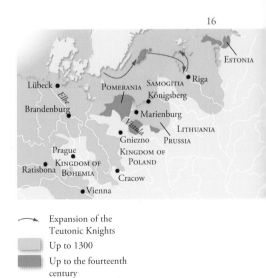

→ Expansion of the Teutonic Knights

Up to 1300

Up to the fourteenth century

17

withstood the violent offensive of the Teutonic Knights until around 1230. In 1226, Prussia was entrusted to the government of the Teutonic Knights and from 1234 the territory and its new conquerors were placed under the direct protection of the pope. In 1249, the Balts were forced to sign a treaty whereby they agreed to abandon their traditional customs; however, the conflict was protracted into the second half of the century and in 1250 those Baltic tribes that had remained free joined forces and resisted until they were almost annihilated. Finally, the Lithuanians managed to retain their independence a little longer by taking advantage of the conflict between the Germans and Poles over the control of the region. They became allies of the Poles in the 1300s and accepted political and military subjugation. They also converted, and from 1370 onwards, the region, with the newly established German emporia,

18

Extent of the principality of Kiev at the start of the tenth century

Extent of the principality of Kiev at the end of the tenth century

Boundaries of Great Moravia at the start of the ninth century

Kingdoms and principalities of Eastern Europe

Boundaries toward the end of the tenth century

19

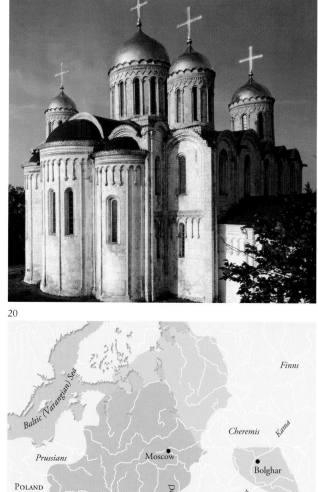

20

Area of the Russian principalities

Area of Slav expansion eastward

Bulgars of the Volga

21

became part of the Hanseatic League. In 1386, with the Teutonic Knights in decline, part of Lithuania became a Grand Duchy under Polish rule.

Between the ninth and eleventh centuries, the Slavs of what would later be Russia united with the eastern Vikings to create a great state with the city of Kiev as its centre, a state that extended to the north as far as Finland. Around the middle of the twelfth century, the decline of the kingdom coincided with the rise of the city of Moscow. During the 1200s, the Mongol invasion produced the empire of the Golden Horde, while Kiev passed into Polish control. Under Ivan I (1325–41) the Principality of Moscow achieved independence from the Tatars, though they paid tribute to them. Thus the reunification of Russian lands was initiated, a process that continued for about a century and a half.

EXPANSION IN THE MEDITERRANEAN

Some historians have used the term "commercial revolution" to indicate a complex set of economic, social, and technological realities that are believed to account for the reduction in agriculture as the driving force of the European economy and the establishment of various other activities: trade, artisanal production on a manufacturing scale, and the instruments of trade and credit. The city is the natural place in which this change occurs, a change of which it is partly both the cause and the effect. But the city alone does not explain the change, just as improvements in the climate and the population explosion after the tenth century cannot be considered the only causes of the change in agriculture. In all these elements, we can identify factors and components of the new type of economy, social dynamic, and distribution of property and labour that were already established in the eleventh and twelfth centuries and reached maturity in the 1200s. However, it was definitely "chance" that brought all these factors together to produce the "commercial revolution," which was clearly visible in the thirteenth century.

In some Italian maritime cities, economic activities and political independence dated from the early Middle Ages. In these centres – to which could be added Provençal cities like Marseilles or Catalan cities like Barcelona – social classes dedicated specifically to trade and shipbuilding developed a complex relationship with the old urban aristocracy or the new feudal nobility of the late Middle Ages. These new classes were responsible for the establishment of a new and bolder way of doing

17. Saint Sophia Cathedral in Novgorod, 1045–50.

18. Map of Kievan Rus.

19. The Cathedral of the Dormition of the Mother of God, 1158–60, built by order of prince Andrei Bogolyubsky, who wanted to make his capital city, Vladimir, the first city of Russia.

20. Russian principalities of the twelfth century, where Moscow would emerge.

21. Wood inlay depicting a boat, c.1300. Museu Nacional d'Art de Catalunya, Barcelona.

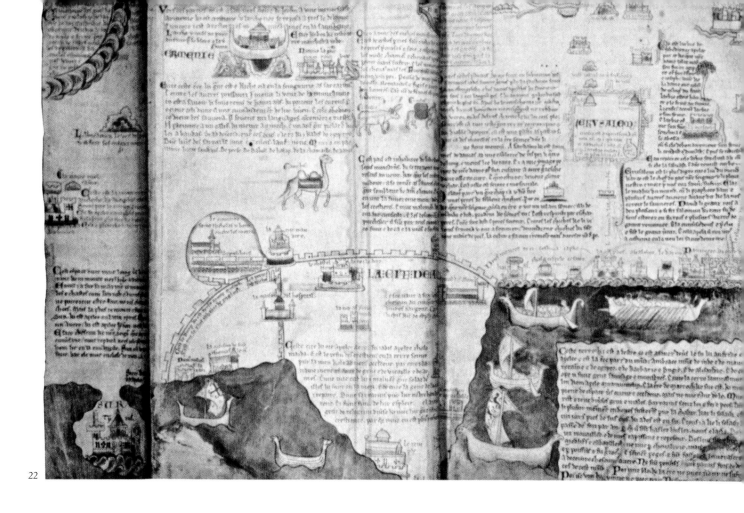

22. Detail of Matthew Paris's thirteenth-century *Iter de Londino in Terram Sanctam* (Journey from London to the Holy Land) with the port of St John of Acre, where pilgrims landed from 1291 onward. Corpus Christi College, Cambridge.

business: that of forming "companies," "commendums," partnerships, and *societates*, which involved pooling their capital and accepting certain risks in order to realize specific gains. Because trade was largely conducted along the waterways, there was a need for ships and sailors. For this reason maritime cities were dotted with shipyards, skilled workers, and sailors.

During the twelfth century, a profound change took place, as evidenced by the fact that, during the First Crusade, everyone had travelled overland, with the exception of the ships of Pisa and Genoa, which arrived later to consolidate the conquests. During the Second Crusade, ships were used, but only by the Byzantines and the Normans of Sicily; even the great Third Crusade was planned as an overland journey by the Germans of Frederick Barbarossa, although the English and the French preferred to travel by sea. From the 1200s onwards, however, it was no longer considered possible to reach Constantinople by land, not because the journey was risky or too long (it had been so even before) but because, in the meantime, the ship had become a normal means of transportation. Even the proud representatives of the feudal aristocracy and the knights had put aside their aversion to the sea and navigation.

This revolution was economic and, in part, social; it was not yet technological in that – except perhaps for its scope – the increased maritime mobility did not lead to substantial changes in navigation, which continued to be traditional in the Mediterranean. In general, Mediterranean ships continued to be of two basic types until the fourteenth century. The first consisted of a light and long oared galley,

which accommodated few sailors and passengers but needed 150–200 rowers; it was a fast ship, although the rowers had to touch port and rest practically every day. The second type was the round ship with high sides and large hold as well as a single large sail, and it was well suited for trade. It was useful for the transportation of heavy merchandise and did not require a large crew or need to stop frequently at ports. On the negative side, it was slow and difficult to control and defend. To these two basic types were added the cargo ships, which were primarily transport ships with hatches on their sides that could be lowered to load or unload animals and were sealed with tar during the journey.

The construction of a ship required many elements: wood for the ship's skeleton, tar, hemp for the rigging, and linen for the sails. A busy shipyard therefore stimulated imports and the clearing of forests, which was necessary in order to procure the lumber required. There was a circle of interdependence among shipyard activity, urbanization, and the development of trade, which also included the mainland, where forested areas were populated once they were cleared and the land could be tilled.

MARITIME CITIES, SHIPYARDS, WAREHOUSES

By around the year 1000, some Italian-Byzantine cities facing the sea had already achieved a high standard of living and robust commercial activity. From the beginning of the ninth century, Amalfi, Naples, and Salerno struck their own coin, the

23. The port of the island of Majorca, an important hub for Mediterranean trade. Altarpiece of Sant Jordi, by Pedro Nisart, dated from end of the fifteenth century. Diocesan Museum, Palma, Majorca.

24

24. The port of Venice in a drawing from the end of the fifteenth century by the German canon Bernhard von Breydenback. National Library of St Mark's, Venice.

25. Plan of the city of Genoa and its port in the fifteenth century:
.... districts
_____ city walls in 1155
_._._ city walls in 1320
_ _ _ city walls in 1346

25

"tarì," which was a reproduction of the Arabic coin: a sign that the Islamic world, and not only Byzantium, was the ideal area for trade. Among all the Italian-Byzantine cities, however, Venice embarked on the most important future, succeeding in the following centuries at combining land and trade interests with agricultural and financial activity in a vast maritime empire. The cities of southern Italy, as part of the Norman kingdom, never ceased their commercial activity, but were unable to develop it in parallel with the political structure, as occurred in Venice. Between the ninth and tenth centuries, navigation in the Adriatic was made secure through force and treaties and at the start of the eleventh century the Venetian network of commercial interests extended from Constantinople to the Syrian-Lebanese-Palestinian coast and from North Africa to Sicily. In spite of repeated imperial prohibitions coming from both the east and the west, Venice sold such items as wood, iron, and slaves from Istria, Slovenia, and Croatia. At the same time, other Italian maritime cities set off on the road to political autonomy; these included Genoa and Pisa.

Coinciding with the First Crusade, these three cities established the east-west routes that connected their ports to Constantinople and to the colonies that the cities had established both in the Byzantine Empire and along the Syrian-Lebanese-Palestinian coastline. With the support of the crusader princes, the frequent conflicts that developed in the twelfth and thirteenth centuries among the cities often originated in tensions "overseas." For example, the hostility between Genoa and Pisa began over the question of which city would exert hegemony over the islands of Corsica and Sardinia; this hostility continued in Constantinople as well as in Acre and Tyre (the two main ports of the crusader kingdom), where the Venetian, Pisan, and Genoese "quarters" were contiguous.

These trading colonies of the Italian cities developed in urban areas that were distinct in that they had fortifications and faced the sea. They even had port infrastructures, warehouses, and arsenals, and they were populated by citizens from the homeland who spent part of the year on one shore of the Mediterranean and the rest of the year on the other shore. These were commercial emporia of great importance, where merchandise arrived from the great trade cities of the hinterland, such as Damascus or Aleppo, and even from points beyond, along the Silk Road that connected south-west Asia with China. From there, precious cargoes of spices, which were necessary for medicine, food, the preservation of foods, and especially manufacturing, as well as art (for example colouring agents used to dye fabrics in the west, as well as in painting and glass production) travelled to Europe. Also included were wool cloth, hemp fabric, foodstuffs, lumber, unrefined metal, and arms, which were produced in the west and were increasingly in demand in the east. The sale of weapons was lucrative, although the popes tried everything, including excommunication, to stop the sale of arms to the Saracens by Christian merchants. In this way, during the 1200s, the balance of trade (which up to that point had favoured the Orient) was reversed and, due to the flow of gold into the coffers of the Latin merchants, Europe was able to strike gold coins from the fourth to thirteenth centuries, a privilege that previously had been almost exclusive to the Byzantines and some Muslim rulers.

27

If Venice had restored its control over Constantinople with the Fourth Crusade, the Pisans and Genoese turned their attention to the Egyptian ports of Alexandria and Damietta, where they established trading colonies in defiance of the pope, who had prohibited trade with the Muslim world. Genoa then tried to expand its commercial activities beyond the Bosphorus Sea into the ports of the Black Sea, from which they traded alum with the Tatar Golden Horde and the Russian principalities, taking advantage of the trade routes along the rivers Volga and Don that originated in the Baltic, as well as the caravan routes from central Asia that reached ports in the Crimean Peninsula and allowed them to acquire grain from the Ukraine to supply the west.

26

26. The Arsenal of Venice showing a ship under construction, detail of a drawing dating from the fifteenth century by German Canon Bernhard von Breydenback. National Library of St Mark's, Venice.

27. Hartmann Schedel, view of Constantinople, colour engraving, Nuremburg, 1493.

1

INTERNAL AND EXTERNAL ENEMIES

HERETICS

The Gregorian Reform and the troubles that plagued the political and ecclesiastical institutions of the eleventh century brought changes to the practice of preaching and, more generally, to the relationship between the clergy and the laity. The decisions taken by the councils, however, did not resolve the problem of the "care of the souls"; in fact, the problem seemed to be on the verge of becoming involved with new needs.

What was missing was a real reform in preaching that, in addition to specifying requirements, would alter its content by updating it to reflect the times. In the face of these deficiencies, the laity increasingly demanded a role in the religious life, thereby coming into conflict with the clergy's professed need to retain control of the content in order to ensure that sermons conformed to Christian doctrine.

1. Benozzo Gozzoli (1420?–1497)
Meeting of St Dominic and St Francis, fresco, 1450–52, Church of San Francesco, Montefalco (Perugia).

2, 3. Religious authorities (2) and lay authorities (3); detail of the Exultet hymn dated from the mid-thirteenth century preserved in the Museo Diocesano in Salerno. The Gregorian Reform is the foundation of the secular nature of the state.

The first signs of demands for greater participation in the life of the Church on the part of the laity were already manifest in the second half of the eleventh century with the formation of the so-called "patarini" movement, but it was particularly from the mid-twelfth century on that the problem began to appear urgent, with the development of non-conformist or heretical movements.

In 1173, Peter Waldo, a merchant from Lyons, established the community of *Pauperes de Lugduno*, or "the Poor Men of Lyons," vowing to spread his ideal of prayer and poverty through preaching. His petition was rejected first by the bishop of Lyons and then by the Church of Rome, which condemned the movement as heretical on the grounds that only clerics were allowed to preach. If he wished to live a life of prayer and poverty, he could enter a monastic order. Waldo's example found followers, especially in Lombardy and Tuscany where the memory of the "patarini" movement was still fresh: this movement had included penitential brotherhoods, such as the "Poor Men of Lombardy" (who lived in common and shared the fruits of their labour) and the "Umiliati," a movement born among the underclass of wool workers in the great city, which would later be reintegrated into orthodoxy, at least in part.

During the eleventh century in Germany and in the south of France, as well as in central and southern Italy, Catharism (from the Greek "katharos," meaning pure) developed and spread. The sermons of the Cathars appeared similar to those of the "patarini" from the time of the reform. Because of the similarity of the two terms, the movements became confused in public opinion and the words "heretic," "Cathar," and "patarino" acquired the same meaning. In reality, the Cathars stressed the need for the Church to be poor, especially since wealth was something material and, on the basis of those passages in the Bible where Jesus underscores the irreconcilable difference between His kingdom and this world, they preached an equally irreconcilable difference between spirit and matter, Light and Darkness, Good and Evil. Creation became a sort of enormous illusion whereby Satan (whose powers increased to the point where he became a sort of anti-God) had hardened the human spirit that yearned to return to the Light. The sexual act, therefore, became a grave sin, not in itself (as it might be in terms of Christian morality) but because it caused procreation, that is the creation of a prison for another spirit.

4

4. Pope Innocent III receives the Rule of the "Umiliati" in 1199, which he approved in 1201 revoking the excommunication issued by Lucius III, miniature. Ambrosian Library, Milan.

5. The spread of the Cathar Heresy from the East to the West.

6. Meeting of St Francis and St Clare, detail of the *St Clare Panel*, Convent of St Clare, Assisi.

7. St Dominic with his followers in Rome, as he receives the staff and the pilgrim's Bible from Sts Peter and Paul, detail of a fifteenth-century manuscript. Conde Museum, Chantilly.

5

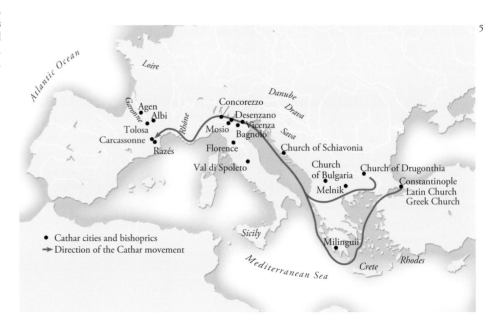

• Cathar cities and bishoprics
→ Direction of the Cathar movement

It is probable that some form of Manicheism reached Europe in the early twelfth century through the Byzantine Empire and the Balkans or perhaps via pilgrims returning from the Holy Land; in fact, some of its preachers were referred to as "Bulgars."

Naturally, Cathar propaganda would not have been effective had it not been framed in terms of popular Christianity, whose most common tactic, in times of disappointment with the reform that had brought about the enormous power of the clergy within the Church, was denunciation of the worldliness of the religious hierarchy. There is no doubt that many adhered to the cult with the intention of becoming better Christians. In the 1200s, a crusade was launched against the Cathars, which extended into Provence and Languedoc and lasted for decades, supported by the French monarch and his allies, as well as the feudal lords from the north of France, who saw an opportunity to subdue the rich and autonomous lands of the Midi.

A REVOLUTION: THE MENDICANT ORDERS

Pope Innocent III was somewhat sceptical in the face of these "spontaneous" groups. Their autonomy with respect to the Church hierarchy made them susceptible to the charge of heresy. But in 1210 he surprisingly approved the initiative of a thirty-year-old citizen of Assisi, Francis, the son of Pietro Bernardone, who, together with some companions, had written a "rule for living" that prescribed total poverty, manual labour, and a form of preaching that consisted primarily of setting an example rather than sermonizing. For Innocent III, Francis was the ideal devout individual: he lived a life of absolute poverty and purity, but at the same time constantly referred to the Church for instruction and teaching.

6

Francis certainly did not want to establish an order and Innocent was diffident in the face of new institutions. He therefore gave verbal approval (but without committing himself in writing) for the "rule for living" proposed by the group from Assisi. He also granted Francis the right to be tonsured, that is, to have his hair cut in a style that identified a person as a member of the clergy, and authorized him to preach. In this way, the Franciscan experience was inserted into the disciplinary body of the Church.

Francis of Assisi also inspired the establishment of a group of women penitents, led by a young lady from the nobility of Assisi, Chiara Scifi. In addition, he founded a lay confraternity that, modelled on his experience, intended to live according to the Franciscan spirit without abandoning their professions and families. These were, respectively, the "second Franciscan order" or the Order of Poor Ladies, and the third order, called the Franciscan Tertiary. By now, the *fraternitas* founded by Francis had become an order because of its enormous popularity; it was confirmed by Pope Honorius III and between 1221 and 1223 Francis wrote two additional Rules for the order. Those were his last important public acts. Ill and perhaps embittered, he withdrew from the public scene, leaving the direction of the order to some of his followers, but not without insisting on rigorous rules for always living off one's work and in accordance with the Rule interpreted literally, without compromise.

7

To some extent, the experience of a Spanish cleric, Dominic de Guzmán, canon of Huesca Cathedral, paralleled that of Francis of Assisi. The Franciscans had taken the name "minor friars" to underscore their vow of humility. Dominic's followers took the name "preaching friars" since Dominic, who was aware of the challenge heretics posed to the Church but also of the effectiveness of their propaganda based on

8

9

8. Scenes from the life of St Dominic, detail of Andrea di Bonaiuto's (1343–1377) fresco *Allegory of the Church*, 1365–67. Cappellone degli Spagnoli, Santa Maria Novella, Florence.

9. Lorenzo Lotto (1480–1556), *The Trial by Fire of Orthodox and Heretical Books*. The predella contains scenes depicting the miracle of St Dominic before the Albigensian theologians, in which only the heretical works burn. Kunsthistorisches Museum, Vienna.

preaching, had chosen to contest their work not only by leading a life of poverty but also through works. Dominicans thus needed to prepare themselves well since their primary function was to hear confessions and preach. Dominic saw his confraternity become an order in 1215. When he died in 1221, five years before Francis, the Dominicans were already a powerful force that had spread throughout Europe.

THE INQUISITION

During the thirteenth century, both the Church and the emperor firmly opposed the spread of Catharism. The Council of Verona of 1184 issued several harsh *constutiones* (decrees): the powerful, on any level, were obliged to punish Cathars, under penalty of excommunication, by removing them from public office and confiscating their possessions, while commoners were obliged to report anyone suspected of heresy to the bishops. The bishops themselves were obligated to visit all the population centres of their respective dioceses at least twice a year for the purpose of identifying heretics, isolating them, and reporting them to the lay authorities so they could be punished.

In 1231, when armed repression of the Cathars in the Midi of France had already been underway for some time, Pope Gregory IX increased these sanctions. It is from this moment on that the term *inquisitor* – which up until that point simply designated the person charged with an inquiry – assumed the meaning of "inquisitor" that we have become accustomed to give it. This is the start of the so-called "Bishops' Inquisitions," which proved to be ineffective as many people protected and concealed the heretics. The bishops themselves were unhappy with the growing centralization of power in the Roman See, which reduced their own privileges, and they worried that the persecution of heretics might give rise to an endless series of excuses to carry out political and personal vendettas. Gregory IX reacted by conferring authority on the order of Preaching Friars, to whom in 1221 he entrusted the repression of the heretics as well as the reform of the Church.

10

11

The papal bull *Ille humani generis* (That human race) of 8 February 1232 entrusted the *negotium fidei* (business of faith) to the Dominicans, and ordered bishops to support them without reservation. On 21 August 1235, the pope named Dominican monk Robert "the Bulgar" general inquisitor for the whole Kingdom of France because he himself had been a Cathar before converting. Soon after, the Franciscans were also given the task of inquisition, which until that time had been reserved for the Dominicans. The search for heretics was to proceed in parallel with systematic preaching that could respond to heterodox teachings and demonstrate the influence of "good Christians" on the general population.

In addition, the Holy See skirted the obstacle represented by the resistance of the bishops by relying increasingly on secular authorities, who liked nothing better. They, in fact, considered heretics to be a civic danger as well and were certainly not displeased by the possibility of enriching themselves with goods confiscated from the condemned. In theory, lay officials had no special authority to identify and condemn heretics, which was the responsibility of the Church. They could only carry out the sentences. However, in terms of practical politics, the path was open for a number of pressures to be exerted, both direct and indirect, that would lead in time to many cases in which ecclesiastical tribunals were subordinated to lay authorities, as we can see clearly in cases like those against the Templars and Joan of Arc. The decretals (papal letters), acts of councils, and manuals make it possible to generate a picture of the inquisitorial procedure, with the caution that, in practice, there were undoubtedly many dispensations and abuses and many provisions that were ignored or abused, as the sources indicate. The inquisitors visited the places where they were to conduct investigations on the recommendation of commissions charged with controlling the expansion of a given heresy or on reports that were kept anonymous in order to protect the informant from vendettas on the part of relatives or friends of the individual identified. A *tempus gratiae* (grace period) was instituted and a "general sermon" invited all those who had somehow come into contact with heretical groups to appear, atone, and receive

10. The Fourth Lateran Council of 1215, which condemned Catharism, in a drawing by William of Tudela and an anonymous assistant, c.1210–30.

11. The monumental apse of the Albi Cathedral, whose fortress-like structure appears to be a warning to the defeated Cathars.

213

a penance. A certain period of time, usually a month, was given for heretics and witnesses to present themselves.

Once the period came to a close, the inquest was set in motion against suspects who had not voluntarily turned themselves into the inquisitors. Accused suspects who were considered to be especially dangerous or flight risks were arrested. Although it was possible to condemn an accused on the basis of evidence, the Church preferred that the accused confess and for this reason judges could, at their discretion, adopt restraining measures, such as preventive incarceration, which could be made harsher by the application of chains, fasting, and sleep deprivation. If the evidence was insufficient to either condemn or prove the innocence of the accused and confinement did not induce the prisoner to confess, the use of torture was permitted. If the accused confessed under torture, he was forced to confirm the substance of his confession later, after the torture was terminated. The confirmation was recorded in the transcripts of the trial as "spontaneous," which explains why torture is mentioned only infrequently in such transcripts, although it was used quite often. The harshest punishments, in ascending order, were confiscation of goods, prison, and death. The latter was reserved for "unrepentant heretics," that is, those who believed in the heresy and refused to abjure and ask for forgiveness – as well as repeat offenders, those who formally retracted their confession and gave indications that they would return to committing the same error.

THE POOR, BEGGARS, AND THE SICK

With Francis of Assisi, the very symbolism of the Christian faith was changed forever in many respects, including the treatment of the poor and the downcast in society. Behind every pauper and unfortunate soul, Francis saw Jesus. One of his first actions was to wander through the countryside of Assisi restoring abandoned or crumbling churches and, as Christ was poor and naked, Francis also chose to live in poverty and nakedness.

The 1200s were a time of misery, but also of sudden and extraordinary fortunes. Taking as his model the King of Kings, who chose to be born poor in a stable in Bethlehem, Francis chose poverty voluntarily, thereby sending a message that was also a challenge to his society. If his was a world where money triumphed, he demonstrated that he did not seek it (like the poor, who find themselves in that condition through no choice of their own); instead, he considered money to be "less valuable than stones." If his was a world in which people increasingly appreciated science and culture, a world of universities, he would live like a perfectly ignorant person, a "madman" or "troubadour," demonstrating that there is perfect happiness in abject poverty freely chosen and that to live in poverty can mean to live happily.

This was poverty as a joyous choice; this was living by doing penance without exhibiting the labour and pain associated with the penance. Francis's was not only an ascetic of renunciation; he subverted the values of his century, upset judgments, and appeared to live Christianity as a perpetual paradox and, at the same time, with simplicity and absolute adherence to the letter of the Gospel. From such a man, who could have had everything in life and rejected everything in order to follow the example of Christ, we might have expected a harsh judgment against the Church of his day and the weakness of priests. Many perfectly orthodox ascetics had expressed similar views, which were also typical of heretical preaching. Francis, instead, stressed the need to love and respect priests without expecting from them demonstrations of Christianity superior to those they were capable of giving.

12. St Elizabeth clothes the naked and tends to the ill. Walraff-Richartz Museum, Cologne.

13. The naked St Francis in the streets of Assisi, illumination from the *Legenda Major* (Major account of the life of St Francis). The Capuchin Historical Institute, Rome.

14. Assisting the lepers, from a miniature called the *Franceschina della Porziuncola* (Franciscan Church of Porziuncola), Assisi.

13

14

15

Francis knew that, because of his simple and poor lifestyle, he could be taken to be a "perfect" Cathar. But he was able to remedy this situation quite easily by distinguishing himself on the basis of his charitable deeds. Cathars could not eat anything that was the "product of procreation"; therefore, they could not eat meat, eggs, or milk products. Francis always ate whatever was brought to him. In addition, Cathar teachers preached that the world is an illusion created by the God of shadows and matter, and that Creation was the product of an evil God. Francis responded by writing the *Canticle of the Creatures*, which is not only a great poem but a perfect anti-Cathar theological treatise.

In choosing poverty, humility, and unquestioning obedience, Francis did not intend to impose a universal model on others, recognizing that such an austere lifestyle was only for him and for those who freely chose to adopt it. But for those who did adopt it, the lifestyle was uncompromising and did not allow for any concessions. He did not reject money, culture, and comforts in themselves but because he felt his life was based on the renunciation of these things. And he saw with increasing dismay that the Franciscans were becoming cultured and accepting gifts and riches (even though technically these things were not held by the order but by the Holy See). With the excuse of being better able to serve their neighbours, some of them asked him to soften the Rule he had written in 1221. Francis agreed to write a second Rule in 1223, but he expected the Franciscans to be absolutely faithful and to accept it "without comment," which is to say, without interpreting its provisions. In 1224, on Mount Verna, he received the Stigmata. His participation in the suffering of Christ gave Christianity a new face in that it was no longer a religion of triumph, symbolized by Christ in majesty, but a religion of participation in the suffering of the poorest in the world and a religion of the resurrection, both of which are represented by Christ suffering on the cross.

15. Sano di Pietro (1406–1481), *St Bernard Preaching in the Campo*. St Bernard's sermons on the topic of property, trade, commerce, and against usury are famous. Siena Cathedral.

1

1. Mohammad Siyah Qalam, *Nomad Camp*, early fifteenth century, a product of central Asia with strong Chinese influence, Topkapi Soraya, Istanbul.

2. The caravanserai or rest places for travellers of Ribat-i-Sharaf, 1114–1154. It is located on the well-known caravan route that leads to Bukhara and Samarkand in the Iranian region of the Khorasan.

2

21

THE DISCOVERY OF ASIA

3. Camel caravans in a detail from a sixteenth-century map. Ducal Palace, Venice.

TRADE ROUTES BETWEEN EUROPE AND ASIA

The Romans were aware of the "incense trade route" that brought precious Indian or Chinese spices by sea from the far side of the Arabian Peninsula to the Mediterranean. They also had trade relations with the Far East, although these took place through intermediaries; direct contact with the heart of Asia remained uncommon. Europeans knew little about Asia but the Arabs, who were accustomed to travelling on that continent and engaging in trade with its peoples, knew much more. Up to the ninth century, merchants in the Persian Gulf travelled to China while ships from Java, aided by favourable monsoon winds, reached the Arabian Peninsula.

Trade also flourished by overland routes: the ancient Silk Road connected the fertile Chinese Plains of the rivers Yang-Tse and Huang-Ho, shielded by the Great Wall, to Arabian and Iranian cities (Shiraz, Isfahan, and Baghdad itself), crossing the Gobi Desert and the oases of Turkistan, reaching even as far as the Himalayas. Small kingdoms had been created between China and Persia; they were vassals of one of the two great empires and their merchandise was transported by caravan. The trade was organized in convoys that made short trips from oasis to oasis; the cargo was then transferred to other similar convoys. In general, people travelled relatively short distances but merchandise, ideas, and religious cults made long journeys in a relatively short period of time.

4

5

4. Fourteenth-century Chinese painting showing a Mongol caravan. Private collection.

5. The Kingdom of Prester John in a sixteenth-century map by cartographer Visconte Maggiolo. National Library of France, Paris.

The goods most in demand included gold and silver from Sumatra, Malaysia, and Korea, sandalwood, bamboo, camphor (whose valuable essence was extracted), aromatic compounds like incense and musk, and precious stones like rubies and sapphires from Ceylon and India. Perhaps the richest trade was that in spices: pepper, nutmeg, clove, and cinnamon. Some of these products were used in cooking, as were less precious and therefore cheaper foods, which were exported in larger quantities (cane sugar, rice, cereals). Heavy and cheap merchandise was usually transported by sea; it was not convenient to transport such bulky material overland on pack animals such as donkeys and camels. Westerners in the emerging communes (for whom knowledge of Asia was limited to the Anatolian Peninsula or Asia Minor and the regions closest to the Lebanon-Palestine coastline) knew nothing of these great civilizations. The information about Asia provided by the ancients had, for the most part, been based on imagination. Westerners were, of course, very interested in the provenance of the spices that had become such an important part of their lives, as had gems and expensive fabrics, which princes and the Christian liturgy used extensively, but they were willing to accept fairy tales about the origins of this merchandise.

Towards the middle of the twelfth century, a letter relating to Prester John reached the west – including the courts of Pope Alexander III and Emperor Frederick I – delivered by a Byzantine intermediary. The letter spoke of the many wonders of Asia and of a great and powerful Christian kingdom that existed there, led by a mysterious king-priest called Prester John. Written almost certainly as propaganda, the letter contained allusions to historical facts; for example, the organization of some Turkish-Mongol kingdoms in central Asia and the existence of various Christian-Nestorian communities scattered along the Silk Road between Iran and China.

THE MONGOL ASSAULT

During the twelfth century, there was a true re-awakening of the Mongols, who were nomadic shepherds living in what is modern-day Mongolia, southwest of Manchuria. Arabs called them Tatars, a term from which the Latins derived the term "Tartars," which to them resembled the pagan Hades, i.e., Tartarus; it was an elegant pun. In the middle of the Asian desert, south of Lake Balkhash, a new nomadic "empire" was created called Qara Khitai. To defend itself, the ruling Song Dynasty asked for help from another Turkish-Mongol people, the Girgut, who had settled between Mongolia and Manchuria. But these same peoples soon invaded northern China. The Chinese empire showed signs that it, like the Western Roman Empire during the fifth century, might collapse under pressure from the "barbarians." However, the vast territory between the great Siberian rivers and the Great Wall was populated by nomadic tribes who were continually at war with one another. Given this, they were not particularly dangerous until they found a khan (leader) capable of unifying them.

Little is known about the early days of Temudjin; even the date of his birth fluctuates between 1155 and 1167. He was the son of a tribal leader living on the upper Onon River, east of Lake Baikal, and, according to legend, spent his infancy and early adolescence enmeshed in the battles and vendettas that took place among various tribes. His ascent began when he entered the service of the khan of the Kerait, a Turkish-Mongolian tribe converted to the Christian religion, specifically the Nestorian confession. Temudjin married the daughter of the leader of the Kerait, whose name was Borte, and from that marriage acquired the base from which to expand his dominion, defeating and assimilating neighbouring tribes. In 1206, the entire Gobi region was under his control. In the great Kurultai (tribal assembly) convoked at the source

6

of the Onon River, he was proclaimed Great Khan, that is, supreme leader of all the Mongols, who now discovered a kind of "national" unity. It was at this time that he was given the name of Genghis Khan, "Lord of dominion."

After unifying the Mongol peoples in 1211, Genghis Khan set off on his campaign to conquer China. Between 1219 and 1220, the Mongols subdued the Iranian-Persian kingdom of Kwarezm (between Lake Baikal and eastern Iran). Bukhara and Samarkand were captured, after which the conqueror headed north towards the Russian steppe, conquering the kingdom called "Great Bulgaria" and dispersing its people.

Genghis Khan was both a conqueror and organizer of peoples; however, he was not an institutional reformer. His "legislation" was based on the traditions and needs of the Mongol people, who were herders of horses, camels, and goats. As the various tribes moved constantly in search of pastureland, sometimes expanding and at other times shrinking their area of activity, Genghis Khan similarly gave his "empire" a mobile political organization, although without neglecting the need for a hierarchy. The tribes remained independent of each other; however, at the head of each tribe, there was an "imperial" family, the so-called "house of golden lineage," which was considered sacred because it was believed to descend directly from the highest deity of the Mongol people, Tengri (the sky god). The nucleus of the tribe was always the "ulus" (nation or people), which was the entire tribe and its patrimony. In the empire, this concept was changed to refer to the totality of conquered lands, which then became the "ulus" of the imperial family. Each khan continued to enjoy autonomy, but all khans were obligated to show great loyalty and respect for the Great Khan, who ruled his lands through a well-organized and efficient system of attendants and couriers.

6. Portrait of Genghis Khan (1162–1227), the creator of the great Mongol Empire. National Museum of the Palace, Taipei.

7. Map showing the growth of the Mongol Empire up to the death of Genghis Khan.

8. Mongol siege of Baghdad in 1258, miniature from the second half of the thirteenth century from Rashid al-Din's *Universal History*. National Library of France, Paris.

9. Prisoners of Genghis Khan. National Library of France, Paris.

10. Fourteenth-century miniature depicting a battle fought by Genghis Khan at the start of the thirteenth century. British Library, London.

7

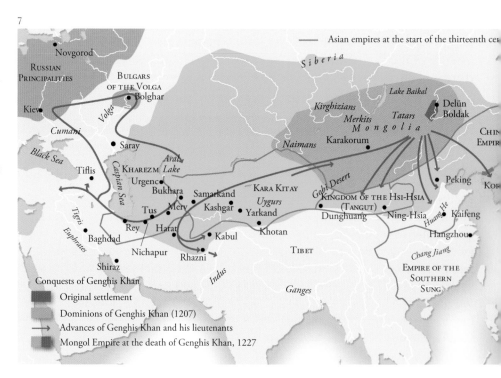

8

9

10

The beliefs of the Mongols were predominantly animistic and shamanistic. However, they coalesced in a cosmic monotheism that made them particularly disposed to accept the Buddhist, Christian, and Muslim religions. The religious dimension is one of the most interesting aspects of the personality of Genghis Khan as a model for all the Mongol leaders. He was extremely tolerant in religious matters, but this was not true or genuine "tolerance." Like his people, Genghis Khan possessed a magical, rather than a genuinely religious, vision of the world. And he tried to identify in the various cults those forces that could assist him; this explains why there were priests in his court and why liturgies from most of the religious cults were recited there.

THE *PAX MONGOLICA*

When Genghis Khan died in 1227, his empire extended from Siberia to the Kashmir and Tibet, and from the Caspian Sea to the Sea of Japan. He was responsible for enormous genocides and mass deportations, and had both founded and razed cities, but he had built a solid, peaceful empire where an inflexible but equitable *pax mongolica* (Mongol peace) allowed people with different languages, heritages, and religions to live together. He was succeeded by his son, Ögedei, and the Mongols quickly resumed their policy of conquest. The nephew of Genghis Khan, Batu, descended upon Europe. Kiev fell under his assault in 1240. A quiet terror overcame Christianity. *The Annals of Novgorod* describe these terrible men, whose language and origins were unknown and who appeared to be more savage than human: a punishment from God for the sins of humanity. The myth of Gog and Magog resurfaced. In the spring of 1241, the warriors of Batu Khan, having conquered the territory between the

11. Anonymous portrait of Kublai Khan from the thirteenth century.

12. The Mongol Empire at the end of the thirteenth century.

13. The Mongol court hands letters to the ambassadors of Pope Innocent IV, miniature from a fifteenth-century edition of Vincent de Beauvais' thirteenth-century *Speculum Historiale* (Mirror of history). Conde Museum, Chantilly.

11

Volga River and the Black Sea, which would be the nucleus of the kingdom of the Golden Horde, swept down on Poland, Bohemia, and Hungary. The best Christian cavalry was unable to withstand the assault of the horde, whose notorious cruelty was combined with discipline and exceptional strategic ability.

The danger appeared to be extreme, but Batu was forced to withdraw from the portion of Europe he had conquered, partly because the victories had cost too many lives and his campaign was in danger of becoming an insane advance without supplies or logistical support, and partly because Ögedei's "Sippe" recalled the Mongol leaders to the city of Karakorum for the assembly. Guyuk (1241–48) was elected khan but he was unable to resume the campaign against Europe. After his rule, the Mongols changed course along with a change in policy and they no longer aspired to conquer Europe and the Mediterranean but cast their eyes on China, where in 1279 the Song Dynasty collapsed and a non-Chinese ruler ascended the throne for the first time since the year 1000. This was the great Kublai Khan. Thus began what is recorded in Chinese history as the Yuan Dynasty of foreigners.

The order brought about by the *pax mongolica* and the well-organized caravan routes of the Tatar Empire permitted people to travel in relative security and fairly quickly, bringing Europeans into direct contact with the riches of China and the Far East. Many western merchants set off along these caravan routes in an attempt to avoid using the Arab intermediaries who, in the past, had been necessary to acquire the precious merchandise of the Orient. The Venetians in particular, who were always interested in all things pertaining to Asia and its products, had discussed the possibility of establishing a relationship with the Mongols for some

12

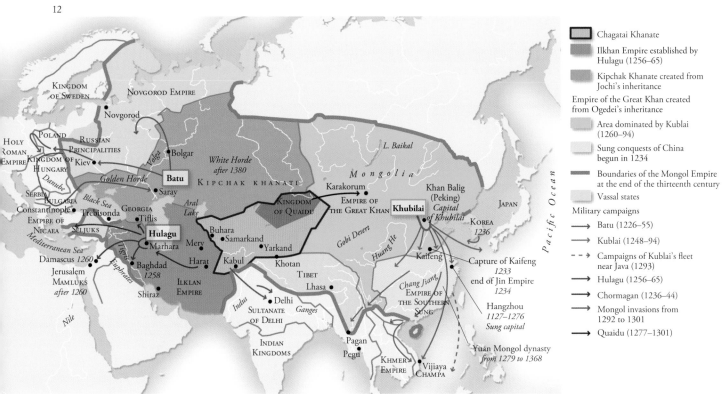

time. In 1260, two merchants from Venice, Maffeo and Niccolò Polo, left from Constantinople and headed to the Mongol khanate of northern Russia. From there they proceeded to Bukhara in Uzbekistan, and then to the summer residence of Kublai Khan, north of the Great Wall. They stayed with Kublai Khan for about a

14. Zhu Derum, *Primordial Chaos-Hanlun*, horizontal manuscript, ink on paper. Yuan Dynasty, 1349. Shanghai Museum.

223

15

15. Marco Polo crossing the bridge over a river in China, detail of a miniature from the *Livres des merveilles* (Book of wonders), end of the fourteenth–start of the fifteenth century. National Library of France, Paris.

year and visited the splendid city of Peking; after the long return journey, they arrived in Venice in 1269. It appears that they had promised the Great Khan that they would return with news and gifts from Europe. In 1271 they set out once again for the Far East, encouraged by the new Pope Gregory X, who had high hopes of converting the Mongols. This time they travelled for a longer period and Niccolò's son, Marco, who had accompanied them, remained at the court in China and in the service of the Great Khan until 1272. Marco narrated his experience in the book called *The Travels of Marco Polo*, which is undoubtedly one of the masterpieces of medieval European travel literature.

EUROPE AND CHRISTIANITY IN ASIA

In addition to arousing tremendous terror, the appearance of the Mongols had revived eschatological fantasies regarding the mysterious Christian peoples of the Orient, such as those that had polarized Europe following dissemination of the myth of Prester John. Batu Khan's campaign, which at one point seemed directed towards the valleys of the Rhine and the Danube, had been interpreted by some as revenge for the theft from Cologne of the remains of Magi kings, whom the Mongols supposedly considered to be their royal ancestors. These legends created a widespread feeling of hope that the men from the steppe could be understood by building on their common Christian faith, whether this was real or imagined. The new pope Innocent IV, while repeatedly suggesting that he was in favour of a crusade against the Tatars, was more inclined to establish peaceful and diplomatic relationships with them. The news that members of the Nestorian Church were respected by the Mongols, although exaggerated to some extent by the Nestorians themselves and by the excessive optimism of westerners, had some basis in truth. In order to establish contact, westerners considered approaching

16. *Bahram Gur Slays the Dragon*, Mongol miniature from a Persian poem, c.1335. The Cleveland Museum of Art.

Mongolian Asia in two ways: to the south across the khanate of Persia and to the north along the road through Russia and the Asian steppes.

Responsibility for these expeditions, which were both diplomatic and missionary (but they also partly served to assess the real strength of the Mongols) was entrusted to Dominican and Franciscan monks, who wrote interesting diaries about their experiences, which to some extent – like Giovanni del Pian del Carpine's *Historia Mongolium* (History of the Mongols) – are still considered important for understanding the history and geography of Asia.

Not only the pope but the king of France, Louis IX, was interested in the Mongols of Persia, especially because he hoped to secure their help against the Muslims during a crusade that he organized in 1248. To this end, he sent messengers to the Great Khan. These were two Franciscans, William of Rubruck and Bartolomeo da Cremona, who spent about three years (1253–56) completing their round-trip journey from Acre in Palestine. However, in the thirteenth century, both the Mongols of the Golden Horde and those of the khanate of Persia converted to Islam. This left the Great Khan, who as "Chinese emperor" wanted to promote a kind of conciliation between Buddhism and Taoism. In 1294, Giovanni da Montecorvino, a Franciscan monk, established the first Latin bishopric in Peking in the Sino-Mongol Empire, and early in the 1300s, other Franciscans followed suit. The missionary activities of these religious figures was extensive and unselfish, but the fall of the Sino-Mongol emperors in 1368 encouraged China to close itself off, particularly to westerners, who were seen not only as undesirables or barbarians but also as foreigners who had been protected by the despised Yuan Dynasty. Thus, the West found itself blocked from the Far East via overland routes, but continued to attempt to reach it by attempting to circumnavigate Africa and Asia to again reach the Indies. At the end of the fifteenth century, Christopher Columbus hoped to again establish contact with the Great Khan.

17. Late nineteenth-century portrait of Flemish monk William of Rubruck, ambassador of the French King Louis IX, at the Mongol court in the thirteenth century.

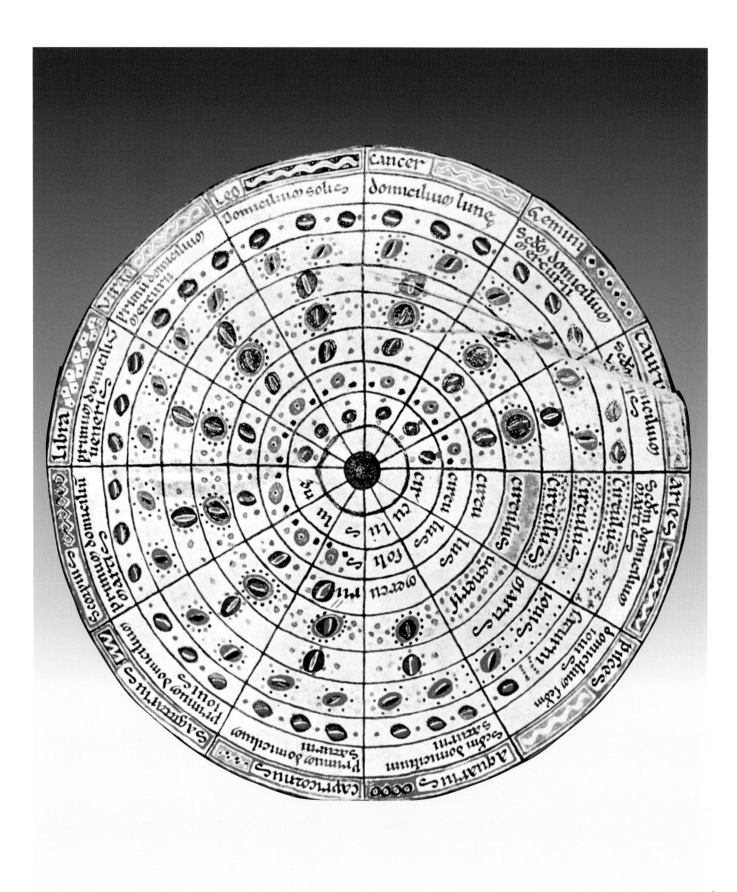

22

SCIENCE AND MAGIC

THE REBIRTH OF MAGIC AND FOLKLORE

Beginning in the eleventh and twelfth centuries, a renewal of social life coincided with the reintroduction into the west of branches of the scientific and philosophical culture of the classical age and Late Antiquity through rediscovered Greek and Latin manuscripts, sometimes mediated through Arabic and Hebrew commentaries and translations. Italy played an important role in transmitting the knowledge contained in these texts, and between the eleventh and twelfth centuries, centres were established where manuscripts were translated from the original Greek and Arabic. In Monte Cassino and Salerno, many treatises on medicine were translated into Latin; in Sicily, at the court of the Norman king William the Bad, translations were made of the works of Plato, Aristotle, Ptolemy, and Diogenes Laertius. At around the same time, that is to say, the middle of the twelfth century, Jacobus Venetus produced the most complete Latin translation of the works of Aristotle, while a few years later Gerardo da Cremona translated approximately seventy works from the Arabic, many of which dealt with astrology. In certain places, for instance the Chartres School, interest in philosophy, particularly Neoplatonism, was accompanied by investigations into the "magical" disciplines, which were understood as more profound methods of deciphering the occult causes of natural phenomena.

The legacy of the Chartres School in the study of natural magic found many enthusiasts. In the twelfth century, we have John of Salisbury in particular. In the next century, there were Vincent de Beauvais, Albertus Magnus, and Roger Bacon. In their writings, in addition to an appreciation for natural magic, a clear distinction was made for the first time between this kind of magic and ceremonial magic, which was considered to be permeated by Satanism and therefore illegal. For example, in the pages of his *Polycraticus* (a treatise on politics), John of Salisbury condemned divination because it involved the summoning of demons.

The distinction between natural magic, which was legal, and ceremonial magic, which was not because it was Satanic, was not always easy to make. Roger Bacon wrote a treatise titled "The Secret Workings of Art and Nature and the Vanity of Magic" to illustrate the differences between the two practices and to condemn ceremonial magic, which was essentially considered a fraud. He looked favourably, however, on traditional healers, who were experts in natural magic, which was based on ancient, empirical knowledge. The encyclopaedists of the thirteenth century, figures such as Vincent de Beauvais and Albertus Magnus, participated in discovering the correspondences that link humankind and nature. In doing this, they accepted and justified, for example, traditional beliefs regarding the secret power of minerals (such as coral, malachite, diamond, and amber – the latter was considered a mineral). They were supported in their conviction by ancient texts, especially Pliny's *Historia Naturalis* (Natural history) and by the encyclopaedists of the early Middle Ages, who

2

1. The universe, shown on a disk used to generate horoscopes, including the prediction of illness, from William of Conches's *Dramaticon Philosophae Magistris Choncis* (Dialogue on natural philosophy), thirteenth century. Library of the Faculty of Medicine, Montpellier.

2. Vincent de Beauvais, *Speculum Naturale* (The mirror of nature).

3

3. Precious stone dealers, illustration from Juan de Cuba's *Hortus sanitatis* (Garden of Health), printed in Mainz in 1491 and preserved in the University Library, Pavia.

4. A couple asks an astrologer to predict the future for their two sons, fifteenth-century miniature. Universiteitsbibliotheek, Ghent.

epitomized that knowledge. In the twelfth century, Marbod of Rennes wrote a famous treatise on the properties of stones, which was full of information on the magical and therapeutic powers of gems. These ideas were subsequently taken up by Albertus Magnus in his work *On Minerals* and by de Beauvais in *The Mirror of Nature*. Among other things, both authors (although with a degree of scepticism on the part of Marbod), as well as Bacon, were inspired by a strictly magical text called the *Tabula Smaragdina* (The emerald tablet). They took seriously the beliefs of the alchemists regarding the transmutation of metals and the art of turning base metals into the noble metals gold and silver

NECROMANCERS, ASTROLOGERS, ALCHEMISTS: "HIGH" MAGIC

There was, however, a type of ceremonial magic that was widely condemned: the art of necromancy, that is, divination through communication with the spirits of the dead, which in the Middle Ages became "negromancy" (black magic). This was a series of magical practices and rituals used to attain occult or elicit objectives.

But what instruments did the "negromancers" use? It is possible to identify some of the basic features of these instruments by examining a few of the books used by "sorcerers." The most famous books are those believed to contain information regarding the legendary magical powers of the biblical King Solomon. The mythic ruler is said to have written a number of texts on magic; perhaps the most well known of these was the *Clavicula Salomonis* (Key of Solomon). In this text, in addition to prayers to God, there is an emphasis on the need for the officiant to meet certain ritualistic requirements, including purity, fasting, and cleanliness. However, the purpose of the ritual appears to have been anything but religious, as it was often designed to acquire magical instruments for the purpose of sowing death, discord, and destruction. Invoking demons so that they might grant someone power was combined blasphemously with prayers and incantations, as well as with appeals to the prophets of the Old Testament and to God himself to curse the demons so they would be compelled to obey the will of the invoker.

Astrology apparently did not possess the same threatening unknowns as the magic of the necromancer. However, especially in the 1200s, it became an increasingly worrying phenomenon. Thomas Aquinas was fervently against astrology and against the interest it was generating, as he emphasized the incompatibility of astrology and free will. What is especially interesting is the popularity of these techniques among the powerful elite – the use of magic and astrology was popular in many of the communes and seigneuries of the Middle Ages. The correspondence between Galeazzo Maria Sforza and his ambassadors in 1474 is important in this regard as in these letters the Duke of Milan angrily comments on and expresses concern over the unfavourable prognostications that his astrologers, Girolamo Manfredi, Marsilio of Bologna, and Pietro Bono Avogaro, had produced for him. In the courts of Europe, some forms of divination connected with astrology also played an important public and official role. The stars were constantly consulted prior to constructing city walls or putting up buildings, going on a trip, or engaging in battle. In the 1300s, Charles V of France established a college of astrologers in Paris who were charged with producing horoscopes and translating the best texts available on the subject into the vernacular. In the next century Matthias Corvinus of Hungary did the same thing in his court at Buda.

4

5

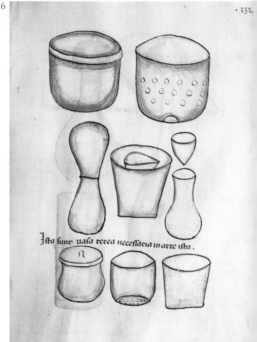

6

HERMETICISM

But it was above all the rebirth of Platonism and Neoplatonism (more properly, the philosophy of Plotinus), along with the arrival of hermetic texts that explains the renewed popularity of magic, which spread from Florence to the entire continent over the course of the next two centuries. What were the hermetic texts? The Greek manuscript *The Hieroglyphics of Horapollo* arrived in Florence in 1419 and ignited interest in Hellenic mystical literature, establishing the basis for the "Egyptian myth" that would become especially popular in eighteenth-century esotericism.

The rediscovery of hermetic texts culminated in Ficino's translation of the *Corpus Hermeticum* (Writings attributed to Hermes Trismegistus) in Florence in 1463. This work represented the full realization of a concept that had developed slowly during the two or three preceding centuries, which bound tightly together the sky and the earth, the cosmos and individual elements, and made humankind the centre of the universe. In summary, it was the actualization of the ancient notion of the human being as microcosm, mirror and synthesis of the macrocosm. According to Marsilio Ficino (1433–1499), the sorcerer or magician captures, coordinates, and organizes

5, 6. Distiller with coil (5) and heat-resistant jars for fusing metals (6), Aldini MS, fifteenth century. University Library, Pavia.

7

7. Hippocrates, Galen, and Avicenna discuss zoology, illustration from Juan de Cuba's *Hortus sanitatis* (Garden of health), printed in Mainz in 1491 and preserved in the University Library, Pavia.

the celestial forces, directing them to favour the interests of humans and their health – both physical and spiritual. This was particularly important to a scholar and physician who was also the son of a physician. Defending the dignity of magic as a beneficial art and divine science, Ficino cited the biblical Magi, pointing out that the word "magus" did not mean "creator of curses or maledictions" but rather "wise man" and "priest." Inspired by the teachings of Plato and the Neoplatonists, he believed that using appropriate techniques and materials to create an image similar to its superior model exerted a force and an attraction on the model itself. This was the principle of "universal sympathy," of the great chain of being connected by similarity. For Ficino, the cosmos was no longer a mass of neutral elements but an animated whole. There is therefore a harmony of the cosmos, from the stars to the pebbles, a continuous interweaving of occult properties that commingle and complement each other; the universe is alive and composed of secret correspondences that human beings, especially a particular type of human being, are tasked with investigating.

Aware of the illicit implications that magical art could invoke, Ficino emphasized that while satanic creatures could be attracted, invited, or induced to establish contact with humans, these demons could not be constrained to follow human bidding. The theoretical and speculative aspects of Ficino's writings did retain the traditional figure of someone who performs magic. Magic did not take place where there was no concrete "doing": drawing effigies, making signs, burning aromatic compounds, and making talismans. Ficino's magus was thus not only a physician and priest; he was also someone who understood physical substances and metals, a shaper of objects; in short, he was an artificer and an artist. The connection is quite clear between this line of thinking, which was pursued in Florence during the second half of the fourteenth century, and the environment in which the concept of the artist as a quasi-superhuman being developed. It is no coincidence that in the next century magic would find some of its most loyal and fervent enthusiasts among artists.

THE ATTACK ON MAGIC

There was, however, a good portion of society, especially among the lay citizens of the middle class, which was developing a slightly different attitude towards magic. The Dante of the works written in the Florentine vernacular represents this tendency to some extent. In his work magic was strictly tied to fraud and deception perpetrated by the devil, the only creature who has the power (though more apparent than real) to alter nature and its laws. This "fraudulent magic" was performed primarily through divination, which was punished in the fourth pit of the eighth circle of Hell. Here "fraud" is subdivided into its various manifestations: in the first instance, theft, falsehood, simony – "with such vile scum as these" (*Inferno* XI: 58–60). Among the "falsifiers" are the fortune tellers, from those who were famous in antiquity to contemporaries, including Michael Scot, in addition to "the wretched, who the needle left, / The shuttle and the spindle, and became / Diviners" (*Inferno* XX: 121–3).

Dante was not the only artist to depict city dwellers between the 1200s and 1400s, from the high culture of the professionals, such as physicians, notaries, and legists, to the class of merchants and businessmen. In Tuscany, for example, even faced with a certain interest arising from philosophy, theology, astronomy, and physics, as well as from bestiaries, herbaria, and treatises on the properties of stones, and found in the work of such authors as Brunetto Latini, Bono Giambino, Dino Compangni,

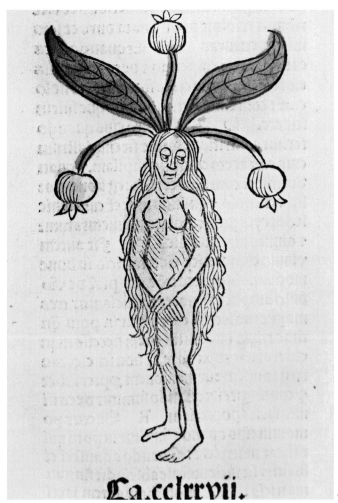

8

ℭa.cclᵣᵣvii.

9

Francesco da Barberino, and Cecco d'Ascoli, many people remained completely un-interested in magic, if not hostile to it, because it lacked philosophical or empirical content and was therefore sometimes seen as a prank or fraud.

The novellas of the 1300s are important in this regard. Such figures as Tuscans Giovanni Sercambi and Franco Sacchetti (authors of collections called *Il novelliere* [Novellas] and *Trecentonovelle* [Three hundred novellas], respectively) provide evidence (though with different nuances) of the rejection of all forms of thought or action that deviated from the certainties of the bourgeoisie as well as of a Christianity that lacked intellectual curiosity. Whether it included important philosophers or fraudulent preachers, the world of magic was looked upon with suspicion and, wherever possible, ridiculed, in the same way as those (generally the "rustic" folk – thereby illustrating the divide between the city dweller and the peasant) who, victims of superstition and stupidity, were easy prey for deceptive practices. More importantly, "learned" or high magic, which had already been established in the courts of Europe for a century, as noted above, was never even taken into consideration. It was ignored, along with that current of thought in which the border between the new science and magic appeared to be less than clear.

8, 9. Male mandrake root (8) and female mandrake root (9), illustration from Juan de Cuba's *Hortus sanitatis* (Garden of health).

The growing interest in magic and the aversion to it by a part of society were two tendencies that could only lead to friction with the ecclesiastical and secular authorities over magic and those who practised it (or were accused of practising it). The emergence of a heretical non-conformism during those same years, and the danger it represented for Christian discipline, made the Church of Rome more circumspect and prompted it to establish the instruments of an inquisition capable not only of uncovering heresy but also of identifying its social and cultural underpinnings. The same instruments, supported by new reflections on theology and demonology as well as by the inquisition, were used to monitor the performance of magic rituals.

WITCHCRAFT

The treatment of magic and heresy as interchangeable practices emerged incrementally before the Inquisition, beginning around 1233 with the papal bull *Vox in Rama* (Voice in Rama) issued by Pope Gregory IX and concluding in 1326 when Pope John XXII's decretal *Super illius specula* (Upon his watch-tower) permitted the application of the usual procedures of the Inquisition in trials involving magic. The phenomenon that paid the highest price in this process was the cluster of practices that, in time, would come to be defined as "witchcraft." It should be emphasized that this term covers many different elements; elements that can be seen as a single phenomenon only when interpreted very narrowly (by "hunters" of witches).

In Italy, for example, a vigorous revival of classical culture led to the resurgence of the figure of the witch from antiquity, initially only through comparisons of these figures to individuals who practised a basic form of magic or women who performed abortions or perhaps augmented rudimentary knowledge of midwifery with some sort of magical ritual. The first to strongly suggest this parallel, in the first half of the 1400s, was Bernardino of Siena, a Franciscan preacher of the reformed movement called the Observance. In France, the convergence of anti-heretical and anti-magic sentiment prompted episodes of persecution on a large scale, such as the witch-hunts of Arras and Lyons (1459–60).

Something similar, at least in part, happened in areas of modern-day Switzerland. For example, in Pays de Vaud, in Franconian Switzerland, a number of fifteenth-century trials have been studied. These show a clear link between accusations of heresy, familiar to residents of the area who remembered the Waldensian Heresy, and accusations of witchcraft. Here we see that the first "hunts" persecuted males primarily, not women, as would occur subsequently.

In French- and German-speaking regions, elements of Celtic and Germanic tradition played a role similar to that played by the classical witches in Italy; that is, they served to frame contemporary magic ritual within familiar cultural parameters. Here we find the figures of "women of the night" and "women of abundance," who were associated with the Hades-Hell tradition as well as with fertility myths and rebirth myths in Celtic-Germanic lore. Many aspects of these complex traditions (magical flight, the ability to enter buildings through closed doors and windows, and conversance with the netherworld) are part of the imaginary of the late Middle Ages, as well as the modern period, in terms of the main features of the witch. Contrary to what has long been claimed with respect to the presumed cruel persecution of witches in Spain, that country actually avoided the uncontrolled explosions of violence that sowed terror elsewhere. Other regions of Europe (modern Great Britain, northern Germany, Scandinavia, and the whole of Eastern Europe) experienced the phenomenon much later – a timeframe that goes well beyond the usual chronological boundaries of the Middle Ages.

10

10. Heretics being burned at the stake, miniature from cosmographer Gauthier de Metz's *Imago mundi* (Mirror of the world), c.1464. Royal Library, Brussels.

11. An allegorical medieval vision after a period of famine, wars, and general insecurity. This image from a fourteenth-century manuscript depicts the practice of using spells and incantations in witchcraft.

11

23

LANGUAGES AND LITERATURE

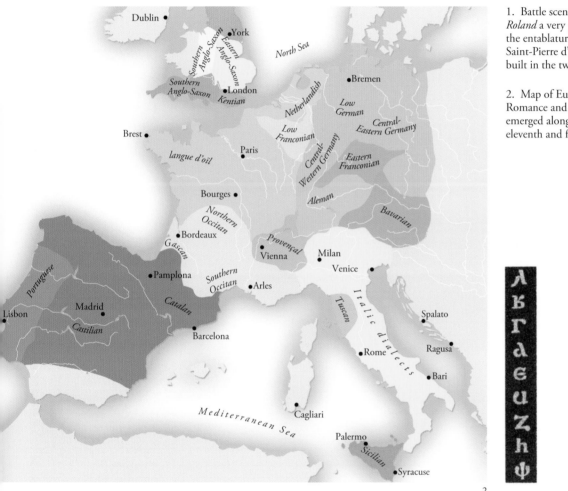

1. Battle scene from the *Song of Roland* a very popular tale, frieze on the entablature of the central portal of Saint-Pierre d'Angouleme Cathedral, built in the twelfth century.

2. Map of Europe showing the various Romance and Germanic languages that emerged alongside Latin between the eleventh and fifteenth centuries.

2

3

LATIN AND THE "VULGAR" LANGUAGES

Although Latin remained the principal language of culture and official communication on the continent of Europe well beyond the Middle Ages, the "vulgar" tongues soon acquired an important function. In the early Middle Ages, three cases are noteworthy:

1 In the second half of the fourth century, the Arian bishop Ulfilas translated the Bible into Gothic. Ulfilas was of Greek origin, but his grandparents had been

3. Fragments of the Gothic script from Ulfilas's translation of the Bible, Codex Argenteus, sixth century. Uppsala University Library, Uppsala.

235

captured by the Goths. It appears that the young Ulfilas, who knew several languages very well, performed diplomatic services for the Goths at the Byzantine court. After several years of such service, he was appointed Bishop of the Goths in 348. During the years of his bishopric, among his many tasks he completed a translation of the Bible into Gothic, using two scripts: the letters of the Greek alphabet and Gothic runes. From his original synthesis of these two fonts, he produced the first literary Germanic characters.

2 In 843, after a lengthy dispute between the heirs of Ludwig the Pious (son and heir to Charlemagne), the two rivals signed a peace agreement and divided the empire between them. Charles the Bald acquired "western France," which corresponded roughly to modern France, and Ludwig the German acquired "eastern France," the area between the Rhine and the Elbe, the historical nucleus of the future Germany. In addition to the text of the treaty written in Latin, the brothers also produced versions written in their respective vernaculars, which were substantially different despite a common Frankish substratum.

3 In 813, during the Council of Tours, people became aware that the sermons addressed to worshippers in the churches were not very effective because they were delivered in Latin, which was not understood by the majority. It was decided that from that moment on sermons would have to be delivered in the vernacular. However, we must wait until the twelfth century for the vernaculars to be used as literary languages as well. In France, the "chanson de geste" and profane poetry quickly adopted either the "langue d'*oc*" or the "langue d'*öil*," which permitted production of a greater number of works. In Italy, the first literary work in the vernacular is Francis of Assisi's *Canticle of the Creatures*, which may have been composed at different times but whose final edition is generally dated to 1226.

COURTLY LOVE

Across the Alps, writers of both prose and poetry developed a keen interest in storytelling and the study of love. In chivalrous literature, love was the central, or at the very least an important, element. Courtly love is often not only described but also analyzed and discussed. This trend is evident in some of the works of one of the most famous

4. *Lancelot*, from a fifteenth-century manuscript. British Library, London.

5. Lancelot's dream, miniature from a manuscript of *Lancelot du Lac* (Lancelot of the Lake), Arras, c.1260. National Library of France, Paris.

4

5

6

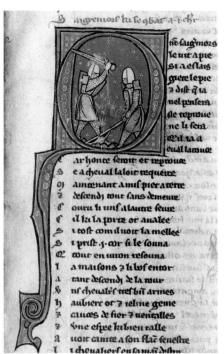

7

8

storytellers of the Middle Ages, Chrétien de Troyes; for example, *Erec et Enide* (Eric and Enid) deals with the issue of the conflict between chivalrous duty and love, and concludes with a hymn of praise for the virtues of matrimony and conjugal fidelity – if freely chosen – as opposed to adultery. Other romances went well beyond this. *Lancelot*, part of a cycle of tales that narrate the deeds of the Knights of the Round Table and the quest for the Holy Grail, proposes the thesis that the knight must discharge his duties to his lady even at the cost of transgressing the laws of chivalry. Thus when Queen Guinevere is stricken by remorse because passion and jealousy prevent her lover from undertaking what was considered to be a knight's supreme adventure, i.e., the quest for the Holy Grail, Lancelot reassures her by affirming that his first duty is to offer the queen that which he represents at that moment, which is to say, the best of the knights. The amorous adventure in *Lancelot* is similar to that in *Tristan et Iseut* (Tristan and Isolde) and was retold and readapted so frequently during the Middle Ages that it became almost mythical. It is the story of a mad love that leads the lovers to their death. The legend of Tristan and Isolde, which is rooted in myth and folklore, represents the notion of courtly love taken to its extreme. Love was generally seen as a force that inspired noble and beautiful actions, and as a moral sentiment that elevated the minds of men, inspiring them to undertake bold adventures. It was the product of an aristocratic society, for which the chivalrous poem in a romance language represented the highest cultural expression. It offers us a picture of moral life that differs from the spiritual model in that power, courage, profane love, and masculine desire play a major role. The barrier that made the women of the courts – at least those that were married – unobtainable became the obstacle the knights had to overcome, often through role-playing, a game that became more complicated when the object of desire was a woman of superior social status, such as the wife of one's feudal lord.

6. Miniature of *Estoire del Saint Graal* (History of the Holy Grail), northern France, c.1290. National Library of France, Paris.

7, 8. Stylized capital letter (7) and miniature (8) from a manuscript of Chrétien de Troyes' *Perceval*, Arras, c.1260. National Library of France, Paris.

9

10

During the Middle Ages, marriage was essentially a matter of relationships between families and lineages. The interests of the family prevailed over the desires of the individual, which meant that passion was generally absent from marriages. Furthermore, families often sought to arrange a good marriage for the first-born son – to be sure that the patrimony was not dispersed – but were unconcerned about the marriages of the other children. Young bachelors anxious for adventure and hoping perhaps to eventually find an advantageous marital arrangement flocked to the courts of the lords in order to work for them. This was the chivalrous milieu in which the "fin'amour" (fine love) celebrated by the Provençal troubadours became established in an adapted form. In the court environment, the love between a young knight and the wife of his lord – even if the relationship was not consummated – created a serious dilemma regarding fidelity in terms of the code of chivalry: should one be faithful to the rules of the game of love or to one's lord? As we have seen, the literature of the period provided a variety of answers to this question.

ANNALS, CHRONICLES, NOVELLAS, SAGAS, LIVES

Beginning in the eleventh to twelfth century, there was a proliferation of folkloric themes in the medieval world (which is visible in the art of the cathedrals as well as in literature). Alongside the "learned" or high culture of the schools and universities, a substratum of ideas emerged that may have circulated orally in the preceding centuries but was brought dramatically to light by the cultural revival. This unwritten culture, frequently called by the ambiguous term "popular," was rooted in the different pagan cultures of the peoples who populated Europe. By this time, however, the traces of those cultures were being re-read from a Christian perspective. Indeed, we can say that the melding of motifs and themes with different origins represents the major innovation of the middle centuries of the medieval epoch. The "myth" of the Holy Grail is perhaps the most well-known cultural artefact of those centuries. Born in the twelfth century in the pages of *Percival*, an unfinished work by Chrétien de Troyes, the myth underwent an infinite number of iterations and re-writings in the era that followed. The Grail was originally a mysterious cup containing the consecrated host, which the Fisher King consumed. He was the wounded king and his illness coincided with the misfortune that struck his kingdom. In succeeding versions, the "myth" transformed the Grail into the cup containing the blood of Jesus Christ, thereby fusing different fables – perhaps of Celtic origin – with the Christian story. Through a large number of romances, the protagonists of the quest for the Grail became the Knights of the Round Table in the service of King Arthur.

Although the Middle Ages are usually associated with chivalrous literature in the cultural imaginary, we should not forget that many other literary genres were established during those centuries. The Roman annals inspired the monastic and royal annals of the early Middle Ages. Alongside these, there were stories, part fact and part myth, that narrated the deeds and migrations of the Germanic peoples up to the time they settled to the west of the Rhine and proceeded to establish the Roman-barbarian kingdoms. Among these, the stories of Gregory of Tours, Bede, and Paul the Deacon are noteworthy. In the late Middle Ages, there was also a proliferation of chronicles pertaining to the crusades or celebrating the life of the communes, in both Latin and the vernacular. Although many of these chronicles concerned themselves with concrete and contemporary events, they were presented as "universal" chronicles and the narration generally began with a biblical episode.

9. Codex Foroiulensis, early ninth century, containing the *Historia Langobardorum* (History of the Lombards) by Paul the Deacon. National Archeological Museum, Cividale del Friuli.

10. Page from the Venerable Bede's *Historia ecclesiastica gentis Anglorum* (Ecclesiastical history of the English people), seventh century. Universitäts-und Landesbibliothek, Münster.

peccatorum · pdnm inunt ·

It is also possible to connect the Norse prose sagas and poems with the Roman-Germanic tales. The content of these sagas originates in the ancient history of the Nordic peoples, but the legends were transmitted orally up to the time of the Christianization of the Scandinavian people. The two main authors are Icelander Snorri Sturluson, who composed the *Eddas,* and the Dane Saxo Grammaticus, the author of *Gesta Danorum* (Deeds of the Danes).

Despite the Christian influence, these texts are important for understanding the mythology and religion of the Scandinavian people (largely similar to that of the Germanic people), which would otherwise have left traces only in folklore. There were also two forms that originated in Late Antiquity and acquired great importance in succeeding centuries – the *Passiones* (Passion plays) and the *Vitae* (Lives) of the saints. Hagiography represents an important literary genre by which to understand the Middle Ages, once we move beyond the simplistic distinction between imaginative elements and real events in the biographies of saints, a distinction already made by the Bollandists in the seventeenth century. The exemplary *Lives* of the saints, which were numerous in the preceding centuries, are brought together from the 1200s onwards in large collections that were then used for preaching and as inspiration for the figurative arts. The most famous of these is Dominican friar Jacobus de Voragine's *Golden Legend*.

A typical product of the culture of the Italian communes (especially Tuscan) is the novella, a genre related to the *exempla*, which were short stories that the popular preachers of the late Middle Ages inserted into their sermons to make the homilies more interesting. From the anonymous *Novellino* (One hundred ancient tales) of the late 1200s to the masterpiece *The Decameron* (or outside Italy, Chaucer's *Canterbury Tales*, which was indebted to Boccaccio's work), collections of novellas represent one of the many original forms of storytelling produced by the culture of the Middle Ages.

11. Fulda sacramentary, c.980 with scenes from the life of St Boniface. Biblioteca Capitolare, Udine.

12. Saint-Lazare, soldier and bishop, detail from a miniature in an edition of Jacobus de Varagine's *Legenda Aurea* (Golden legend), dated 1400–10. University Library, Glasgow.

13. Mirror case with courtly scenes, the work of a French wood carver, c.1350. Civic Museum of Ancient Art, Turin.

14. Couple on horseback in a rural scene from a Franco-Flemish devotional book dated to the end of the fifteenth century and created for personal use by the Benedictine monks of San Martino alle Scale in Monreale. Public Library, Palermo.

15. Miniature showing a falconer and a court scene from a fifteenth-century edition of Boccaccio's *Decameron* preserved in the Vatican Apostolic Library, Rome.

15

13

14

THE SPREAD OF CHIVALROUS LITERATURE IN ITALY

In France, the passion for chivalrous love seems to dwindle during the 1200s. Even though the century produced some of the most interesting chivalrous epics, the courtly ideal increasingly became a ritual in which conventional deeds prevail over the unrestrained and perilous passions we find in the original works. The tragic story of Tristan and Isolde loses its power and sweetness in romances such as *Floire et Blancheflor* (Floris and Blancheflour) and *Aucassin et Nicolette* (Aucassin and Nicolette), in which the pure love of the young lovers triumphs over the wishes of society.

In the meantime, between the twelfth and thirteenth centuries, the "langue d'*öil*" was extraordinarily successful in penetrating Italian territory, as seen by the spread of manuscripts written in French but produced in Italy, in addition to the many French terms found in the vernacular translations of French texts as well as in original prose compositions. The pre-eminence of the "langue d'*öil*" was widely acknowledged and was attributed primarily to the rich literary production in which it had been adopted for use in popular poems and romances. The commercial relationships between Italy and France were conducive to the transmission of literary themes as well as the language itself. The region most affected by these exchanges, for obvious geographic and historical reasons, was Piedmont, but the region that today is Treviso, which included the cities of Padua, Verona, Ferrara, and Bologna, soon assumed a leading role in this regard with the establishment of a form of literature known as "Franco-Venetian." With respect to the many literary genres that flourished across the Alps, the chivalrous epic was the most popular genre in the Lombardy-Veneto region, so much so that it played a vital role there. Initially, this form of literature was known through French manuscripts or passed on by French troubadours. These epics, such as the well-known *Chanson de Roland* (Song of Roland), were subsequently reproduced in the vernacular, and eventually original works in Franco-Venetian, which also derived their subject matter from the very rich tradition of the French area, began to be composed. Other regions of Italy, in particular Tuscany, soon developed the same passion for this material.

The romantic story of Tristan spread rapidly in Italy during the 1200s and 1300s. The so-called *Tristano Riccardiano* (an Italian adaptation of the prose *Tristan*) emerged in the Tuscan mercantile commune context, as the palaeographic and linguistic features of the numerous manuscripts that have come down to us show. Some elements of the text itself confirm this indirectly. The gift of arms and horses to Tristan when he knights his squire recalls the Florentine Guelph practice of offering this type of gift to knights; the colours of Arthur's shield, gold and blue, and Tristan's coat of arms, vermilion, are those adopted in the coats of arms of Florentine families during the first half of the fourteenth century. But the most sensitive adaptation of the original story in order to fit with the taste of the public addressed in the vernacular version is found precisely in the different concept of love that emerges from these pages.

16. Three scenes from a version of *Tristan and Isolde* from the start of the fifteenth century which has a conclusion that differs from the traditional one, allowing for the possibility of reconciliation: King Marco returns to Tristan's bedside. Austrian National Library, Vienna.

16

Since the conflict between loyalty to the lord and fidelity to one's lady was possible only in the context of feudal chivalry, the public in the Italian cities was given a very different image of the love between the two young people. There is no trace of the pessimism of the lovers, who, in the original story, are secretly aware of the fate that awaits them. The *Tristano Riccardiano*, on the other hand, evokes different sentiments, with joy as the dominant note. Even if the passion between the two people is the result of having drunk a magic potion, as in the original in the vernacular version it seems clear that there was already a strong mutual attraction between them and, at the moment of his daughter's departure, Isolde's father expresses his wish that she marry Tristan and no one else. In the later French versions of the legend, we find the expedient of the potion losing its importance: a sign that the taste and sensibility of the public had changed, as had occurred in Italy. An even more important aspect of the new version is the negative way in which the figure of Marco is presented. The conflict between him and Tristan becomes a contest between an unjust and treacherous king – because peaceful coexistence between the king and his knights, and thus the wellbeing of his kingdom, would require Marco to forgive the two lovers and acknowledge their passion – and the most valorous and courteous of his knights. The *Tristano Riccardiano* tempers the harshness of the legend and makes it conform to the taste of the urban classes, who want to read beautiful stories of chivalry but are by now removed from the feudal world that produced those stories.

The poetry of the French troubadours and the German *Minnisänger* (troubadours), who also sang of courtly love, saw its best and most original representatives in the Italian adaptations created at the *Magna Curia* (Great Court) of Frederick II of Swabia. In that court, an authentic, poetic "school" (in the sense of a circle of intellectuals engaged in a productive relationship) emerged in which the French poetic tradition was fused with influences from various cultures, particularly Greek and Arabic, and gave birth to a new kind of poetry that expressed its themes in an elevated and pure language, a truly elevated form of Sicilian. Among the poets of the Sicilian School, Frederick II himself and his sons Enzio and Manfred are particularly important. The poetry of the Sicilian School, together with Francis of Assisi's *Canticle of the Creatures*, represent the foundations of Italian literature.

17. Detail of a miniature on the education of Tristan, from Ulrich von Türheim's *Tristan* (1240–50). Bavarian State Library, Munich.

18. Detail of a miniature from an early fifteenth-century edition of *Parzival* by Wolfram von Eschenbach (1170–1220). University Library, Heidelberg.

... AND IN GERMANY

In Germany, the highest achievement in chivalrous literature is found at the start of the 1200s in Wolfram von Eschenbach's *Parzival* (Percival). Although closely related to Chrétien de Troyes' *Perceval*, Wolfram's version includes two introductory books in which he narrates the story of Gahmuret, the hero's father, and Percival's childhood, spent with his mother in the woods of Soltane. In addition, in the last four books he concludes the story that Chrétien left unfinished, using what is probably a literary device, namely, a book by the Provençal poet Kyot, who was supposedly his source and guide, although there is no other source of information about either the poet or the book. Wolfram interweaves the adventures of Parzival and those of Klingsor and Lohengrin. On the one hand, this introduces an element of deep and sincere spirituality into the romance, which is quite different from the light-heartedness of Chrétien's work; on the other hand, he profoundly alters the Grail component, which, in the romance of the poet from the Champagne, had an essentially courtly and "Celtic" flavour (although the debate on the presumed Celtic nature of the images and symbols in Chrétien continues, as I will explain), while in the German version we find a strong Oriental element, though this is an Islamic-Oriental element – more specifically, Arabic and Persian – which is largely imaginative.

19

20

Although *Parzival* is still inspired by themes treated by Chrétien in *Eric and Enid*, Wolfram expresses high praise for conjugal love, whereas Chrétien's dialectic is interpreted as a more radical opposition between the spiritual mission and the worldly nature of chivalry, between the quest whose object is the meaning of life and adventure for its own sake. The hero often finds himself in error, having lost his way. Not only does he avoid asking Amfortas the question that will free him from his suffering; he also distances himself from God and actually makes an enemy of Him before being redeemed. The hero finally asks the Wounded King Amfortas, "Uncle, what ails you," and the king is magically healed while the Grail Knights, on bended knee, recognize Parzival as their new young king. The sacred relic here is not the cup that contained the host and later the blood of Christ, as in Chrétien's romance; nor is it the chalice of the Last Supper and Joseph of Arimathea; it is a precious stone called the *lapsit exillis*,

Wolfram's definition of the grail has set off a plethora of hypotheses. Seeing the *lapsit exellis* as the *lapis elixir*, which can be interpreted as the "philosopher's stone," would allow us to establish a closer connection with the Arab-Muslim hermetic culture, which permeates Wolfram's work, as noted. This is an indication that the circulation of culture between the Orient and the West during this period is indisputable.

19. Composition of the philosopher's stone, from a fourteenth-century Arab manuscript. Riccardian Library, Florence.

20. The knight Wolfram von Eschenbach with his squire in a miniature from the Manesse Codex, early fourteenth century. University Library, Heidelberg.

1

24

THE NEW FIGURATIVE ART

GIOTTO'S REVOLUTION

The great shift in the figurative arts in the second half of the 1200s began with sculpture, especially the work of Nicola Pisano (he was from Puglia, where he absorbed the classicism of Frederick II's court), who was active in the 1260s in central Italy. The first artist to translate his aesthetic ideas into striking images was Cimabue. Compared to the work of the painters of the preceding generation, such as the Florentine Coppo di Marcovaldo and Guido da Siena, Cimbaue's work appears to be

1. Cupola mosaics from the Baptistery of Florence, attributed to Coppo di Marcovaldo.

2. Cimabue, *Crucifix*. Santa Croce Museum, Florence.

3. Pulpit in the Baptistery of Pisa, the work of Nicola Pisano, 1260.

4. Giotto, *Death and Ascension of St Francis,* Bardi Chapel, Santa Croce, Florence.

5. Giotto, *Crucifix,* Malatesta Temple, Rimini.

free from the Byzantine forms that continued to dominate in the last decades of the thirteenth century. The first decades of the fourteenth century were marked by revisitations of Cimabue's work by Giotto and Duccio di Buoninsegna.

Giotto had several commissions in Florence, Assisi, and Padua, but we need to look at his later work in the Bardi and Peruzzi Chapels in Santa Croce (1320–25) in order to understand the "narrative" innovation in his painting style. The commissions came from two of the wealthiest and most influential Florentine families during a time when the city was expanding rapidly and the crisis was still far off. The subject matter selected is important: for the Bardi Chapel, it was stories of St Francis drawn from his official biography, written by Bonaventure. The episodes chosen focus on important moments in the life and death of the saint, including his embrace of poverty, the casting off his clothing in the presence of the Bishop of Assisi and his father, Bernardone, the approval of the Franciscan Rule, the test by fire before the Sultan, and Francis on his deathbed with the incredulous Gerolamo looking for the Stigmata. There are also scenes of the miracles – the apparition of St Anthony to Francis in a church in Arles – and visions, such as those of the monk and Bishop of Assisi, Guido. The central episode in the life of Francis, the receiving of the Stigmata, is on the exterior in the top register of the chapel. Alongside the scenes from his life, there are four paintings of saints belonging to the Franciscan order. We thus have an interpretation of the meaning of the Franciscan experience, both that of the founder and the order, in a fourteenth-century context where the charismatic and innovative aspects of the movement are set aside in favour of a formal redefinition of the movement.

6

6. Giotto *Ascension of St John*, Peruzzi
Chapel, Santa Croce, Florence.

7. Duccio di Buoninsegna,
The Temptation on the Mount.
The Frick Collection, New York.

7

In the Peruzzi Chapel, the theme is linked less directly to actual events in favour of frescoes depicting episodes from the lives of John the Evangelist and John the Baptist, in which both naturalism and classicism emerge with full force. This was a lesson that Giotto's followers would apply in the Church of Santa Croce in the following decades. We can say that, with Giotto, medieval representation was eclipsed in the transition from flat figures to the transparent rendering of planes, through which it was possible to see open spaces. In addition to Giotto's classical naturalism, Duccio di Buoninsegna developed a style that combined Italian-Byzantine and Neo-Hellenic culture with the French taste for illuminated manuscripts, demonstrating his attachment to the Gothic, which was dominant across the Alps, but always adding personal touches. This trend in painting was much more pronounced than other developments at the time. Even if we set aside past value judgments that saw a dramatic move towards "modernity" in the arts of Florence, as opposed to the presumed ideological backwardness of Siena, there is no doubt that the production of works that are so novel and characterized by such precise and stylistic choices corrresponded to the political and cultural experiences of the city.

SACRED AND PROFANE ART

An outstanding disciple of Duccio was his fellow citizen Simone Martini, who came to prominence with the commission of a *Maestà* (Majesty) executed in 1315 for the Palazzo Pubblico in Siena. His work aligns perfectly with the realities of this aristocratic city, which was quite different from the bourgeois Florence of Giotto's works. Martini was influenced by French miniature art and the ideals of chivalry as expressed in the style that came to be known as International Gothic. Not coincidentally, his work as a painter brought Simone into the two places that were best positioned to express the courtly culture: the Naples of the Anjou and the papal court at Avignon.

The final decades of the 1300s were marked by social unrest and religious tensions. On the one hand, there was the attempt by the subaltern classes to acquire a political voice; on the other hand, there were various spiritual impulses, wherein mysticism coexisted with the first attempts to renew the religious orders, which would become the grounds on which the Friars Minor of the Observance would develop. These often diverging tendencies were occasionally translated into artistic works at the end of the century, giving the resulting work a popular and didactic quality that also suggested the dawn of a new, extraordinary artistic period.

Beginning in the 1300s, we witness the spread of the use of both allegorical and profane subjects to illustrate or celebrate specific moments in the life of the commune. At the beginning of the century, Giotto painted a fresco on the theme of "the commune robbed by many" (subsequently destroyed, according to Giorgio Vasari) in Florence's Palazzo del Podestà (Bargello). We have a general idea of the content: the commune was depicted as a ruler sitting on a throne protected by the four cardinal virtues but assailed by figures who threaten his authority. This has been interpreted as an image of the ruling bourgeoisie concerned with defending itself against the other social classes, but, given its location in the Palazzo del Podestà, the work could also be read as a condemnation of the political parties. The fresco in the Hall of Justice of the Palazzo dell'Arte della Lana (Guildhall of the Wool Guild), c.1340, also in Florence, is easier to interpret. Here, a battle between the four cardinal virtues and the vices is depicted, at the centre of which we see the Roman consul Brutus, the

8

8. Simone Martini, *The Dream of St Ambrose*. San Martino Chapel, Lower Basilica of St Francis, Assisi.

9

9. Simone Martini, *Guidoriccio da Fogliano*, 1335. Palazzo Pubblico, Siena.

10. Simone Martini, *Our Lady of Humility*, before 1343, Notre-Dame-des-Doms Cathedral, Avignon.

10

symbol of justice. Also Florentine is the famous manuscript called the "Biadaiolo," datable to the end of the third decade of the century, in which the illustrations, which chronicle the famine that struck much of Tuscany in the preceding years, depict daily life with great realism and a flair for description – unimaginable in the monumental Tuscan art of the time.

But the most important examples of this type of painting come from Siena. In 1314 the walls of the Palazzo Pubblico (the Hall of Peace) were frescoed with episodes from the Surrender of Giuncarico Castle. In 1335, we have Simone Martini's

11. Ambrogio Lorenzetti, the *Effects of Good Government*, detail, 1338–40. Palazzo Pubblico, Sala della Pace, Siena.

masterpiece dedicated to Guidoriccio da Fogliano, captain of the Sienese army that assaulted Montemassi. He is shown on horseback, riding alone against a mainly empty landscape interrupted only by fortified towns in the distance. A few years later, between 1338 and 1340, also in the Palazzo Pubblico, Ambrogio Lorenzetti produced the largest secular pictorial fresco cycle of the century. The compositions – Good Government and its effects on the city and in the countryside, as well as Bad Government and its effects, juxtapose allegorical depictions of the Virtues (in Good Government) and the Vices (in Bad Government) with extremely realistic scenes in which urban and rural landscapes are enlivened by scenes from daily life. In addition to these frescoes, there was an outstanding depiction of the territory dominated by Siena in the Sala dei Nove (Mappamondo), unfortunately destroyed.

There is another type of secular fresco, also public in nature but completely different from what had been seen up to that point. These were the so-called "defaming" paintings intended to serve as punishment or to bring notoriety to specific criminal acts. Those who could be the subject of such a painting were corrupt officials, counterfeiters, assassins, and traitors. This kind of punishment was often applied to those who were guilty of treason against the commune and, as such, it acquired a public dimension.

In addition to serving a celebratory or polemical function, in the 1300s secular subjects were also painted purely for aesthetic pleasure. These images, inspired by French Gothic illuminated manuscripts dealing with courtly life, were frequently commissioned by patrician families for their residences. In the decades that followed,

12. Francesco del Cossa, *The Month of April*, detail of the lovers in the Triumph of Venus. Schifanoia Palace, Ferrara.

with the growth of interest in history and classical art, people began to prefer subject matter drawn from the works of the ancients or from vernacular adaptations of these works, as opposed to characters from French romances or the *Decameron*. Boccaccio, with his *Genealogiae* (Genealogies of myth) continued to be one of the major figures in the artistic culture of his day.

THE FIFTEENTH CENTURY

However in some cities – not necessarily the major population centres – in which public institutions and the organization of collective labour and not been definitively established or were more easily replaced by other models, new types of patronage and a new kind of artist emerged, characterized by greater freedom from traditions and conventions. The concentration of power in the hands of the elite meant that enjoyment of works of art could become a completely private matter, separate from the public sphere. At the same time, the humanistic culture, and later that of the Renaissance, saw the birth of a new concept of the artist, who, though not yet completely divorced from the tradition of the workshop (which was the training ground for many important figures of the 1400s), began to assume an increasingly individualistic character and a more precise awareness of his role as an intellectual. This artist created and shaped aesthetic taste and, at the same time, reflected on his relationship with the ancients and the models of classical antiquity in order to go beyond the purely artistic framework to generate an ethics and a concept of the world that are new, at least in part.

13

13. Piero della Francesca, *The Annunciation*, detail of the St Anthony polyptych. Galleria Nazionale dell'Umbria, Perugia.

The figurative arts in the fifteenth century are therefore situated midway between innovation and the continuation of traditional models. Also contributing to the evolution of this sector of the arts were advancements in panel painting involving the transition from tempera to oil painting, which became consolidated in Italy after the middle of the fifteenth century. The need to depict both limpid backgrounds and plastic forms in the foreground in the same painting led to the use of more aqueous mixtures called "thin tempera," along with others that were denser and more compact, called "thick tempera," where the emulsion was usually oil or resin. Thus, we slowly arrive at the technique of oil painting (using walnut or linseed oil), which, combined with turpentine, gave greater lustre to the paintings. To the innovations in technique, however, we must add more important changes in terms of the conceptualization of figurative space. So-called "perspective" profoundly revolutionized painting as well as sculpture, architecture, and urban planning.

The invention of "perspective" is attributed to Brunelleschi who, using Euclidian geometry, applied the principles of optics to pictorial representations. The painting

14. Paolo Uccello, *The Presentation of Mary in the Temple*, Prato Cathedral.

was to be the point of intersection of the pyramid of vision produced by light rays that connect the eye of the spectator to the object viewed. Fifteenth-century "perspective" in painting was best interpreted by Piero della Francesca. In the last part of his life, Piero wrote three treatises on geometry and perspective: *Libellus de quinque corporibus regolaribus* (A short book on the five regular solids), *De prospectiva pingendi* (On perspective for painting), and *De abaco* (The abacus treatise). In these works, he clarifies his own point of view with respect to painting, which can also be deduced from a study of his works: it involves monumental images constructed with geometric and mathematical precision and enlivened by the application of colour that take into account variations produced by the distance between the subject and the object in space. Even though the relationship between Piero and classical art, understood as a deliberate search for a clean and rigorous style and a revival of particular aspects of ancient art, is often pointed out by critics, there are also strong connections between his work and the subject matter of religious art.

THE RENEWAL OF ARCHITECTURE

15

15. Filippo Brunelleschi, *Hospital of the Innocents*, detail of the façade, Florence.

16. Filippo Brunelleschi, interior view of the basilica of San Lorenzo, 1420–70, Florence.

17. Leon Battista Alberti, Malatesta Temple façade, from 1450, Rimini.

18. Frontispiece of the 1535 edition of Vitruvius, *De achitectura* (On architecture).

From a theoretical point of view, the humanists' claim that there is a precise correspondence between humankind and the cosmos also informs the arts and science of the fifteenth century. Even in philosophy and science, the ancient certainties of Aristotle and Aquinas were gradually abandoned and people began to observe nature with greater detachment and to further develop ideas that already existed in the culture of the 1200s and 1300s (for example, the scientific investigations of the Franciscan monk Francis Bacon and the Oxford Calculators). Indeed, artistic and scientific investigation were closely connected, as we see in the Paolo Uccello's studies on perspective based on mathematical principles, the architectural projects of Leon Battista Alberti and Filippo Brunelleschi, where aesthetic innovation and mathematics coincide, or the impassioned questions posed to nature by Leonardo da Vinci in his desire to extract its secrets (on human and animal anatomy, flight, the behaviour of liquids, and so forth), which would be useful in his work as a painter and engineer.

Among the various arts, architecture unquestionably epitomized the fifteenth-century renewal with increasing clarity. It reflected the careful studies that several artist-builder-architect-engineers had conducted in order to obtain new solutions to the problem of representing space, taking into account classical models through which perfect forms could be attained. Although it consisted of many forms, hence its stylistic eclecticism, medieval architecture was based on the solid tradition of workers guilds and it often produced impressive results by using mathematical calculations and technical devices derived from actual practice. At the same time, the use of symbols and allegories drawn from the eleventh to the fourteenth centuries appears to be inspired by a free interpretation of this legacy.

On the contrary, the key to Renaissance architecture appears to be theories aimed at producing well-designed forms suited to human beings and their proportions – forms that contain, for example, their own raison d'être in a system of theological symbols. Renaissance architecture takes into greater consideration the relationship between the monument and its environment than did its medieval antecedent and, in so doing, proved to be useful to the oligarchical or seigneurial system of government, which tended to be absolutist in nature and within which architecture performed a particular function. The scale and proportions of the architecture no longer accounted for the specificity of the monument, which became readable only within a scenario or context designed for it. As a result, there are no Renaissance buildings that are not tied to the evolution of the city in that period. As well, architecture and urban planning tended increasingly to dovetail. The new method of planning city-squares, churches, and palaces was based on mathematical and geometric rules that permitted the architect to design a work without necessarily having to build it. Indeed, the architect distinguished himself from his medieval counterpart precisely on the basis of his ability to design and the fact that he was not obligated to work as a master mason at the same time. With respect to the other defining aspect of the Renaissance (namely, the "rediscovery" of antiquity), we must keep in mind that the classical tradition – which was never really lost during the Middle Ages – was revitalized during the fifteenth century as a consequence of the rigorous study of the ruins of ancient monuments, especially Roman ruins, as well as their reinterpretation in the light of literary sources, which included the important works of Vitruvius, whose treatise *De architectura* (On architecture) was discovered in the Abbey of Monte Cassino between 1414 and 1416, and subsequently circulated and cited. It was published in print form in 1486.

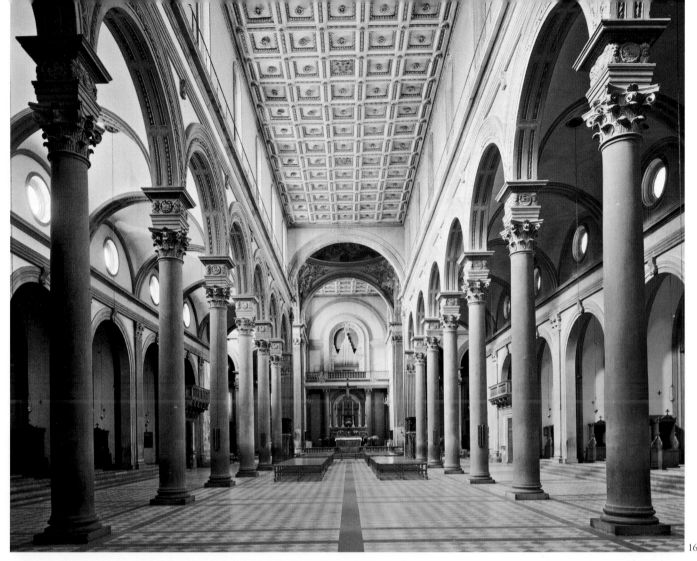

16

17

18

1

25

THE FOURTEENTH-CENTURY CRISIS

HUNGER

The fact that the demographic crisis of the 1300s manifested itself in widespread hunger well before the appearance of the plague has led historians to think that its cause was primarily an unfavourable relationship between the growth in population and the growth in production. In the absence of an authentic revolution in farming methods and technologies, the great increase in population during the preceding centuries had been made possible largely by the expansion of arable land; but toward the end of the 1200s, all the available land was being ploughed and, consequently, production did not increase.

On the other hand, the population continued to grow. It was, therefore, inevitable that nutrition should suffer, at least for the more disadvantaged social classes. In the first two decades of the 1300s, the European continent underwent a period of cooling and a general deterioration in climate. The cold and humidity brought illness and hunger, and both of these things caused socio-economic destabilization, which affected particularly the less well-to-do classes, who were already weakened. The first symptom of the great difficulties threatening Europe was the great famine of 1315–17. The fact that successive years of poor harvests invariably led to an increase in prices and exposed the most vulnerable social groups to hunger is a reality of all pre-industrial economies. Even the prosperous Europe of the thirteenth century was not immune from famine.

When it did appear, however, famine was usually local in nature and the development of the network of roads allowed the authorities, especially those in the city, to contain its effects by importing grain from regions that had not been hit by bad harvests. In this way, they were able to keep the increase in prices and the subsequent death toll within acceptable limits. The famine caused by the disastrous harvests of the 1315–17 years, however, was distinctive for its magnitude, since most of Europe found itself in great difficulty, with the exception of a few regions that had been spared by the whims of the weather. A series of negative climactic conditions damaged the harvests to such an extent that they produced a long-lasting and devastating crisis never seen before. There were manifold increases in the prices of cereal crops, which caused the death of many people and animals due to malnutrition and illnesses resulting from malnutrition. In the city of d'Ypres, roughly 2,794 people out of population of 20,000–25,000 died between 1 May and 1 November 1316: more than one in ten of the inhabitants.

THE PLAGUE

However, it was an unexpected and imponderable event that caused the collapse of the European population. A disastrous epidemic swept through Asia in 1346 and in

2

1. Pieter Brueghel the Elder, *The Triumph of Death*, c.1562. The plague struck Europe in waves during the fifteenth and sixteenth centuries, before the pandemic of 1630. Prado Museum, Madrid.

2. *Hunger*, detail of an illustration from the *Comment on Revelation*, by St Beatus of Liébana in 786. The *Apocalypse* from which this miniature is taken was executed in 1047, commissioned by Ferdinand I of Castile and his wife Sancha of León. National Library of Spain, Madrid.

3

4

3. The effects of the plague, miniature from the second book of *Croniche* (Chronicles) by Giovanni Sercambi (1348–1424). State Archives, Lucca.

4. Victims of the plague, detail of the Toggenburg Bible, c.1411. National Museum, Berlin.

1347. It was carried to Europe, perhaps by Genoese ships travelling between the Black Sea and the Mediterranean with shiploads of grain from the Crimean Peninsula. The disease spread to the port of Messina, then to other locations in the Tyrrhenian Sea, and eventually everywhere. It is important to underscore that the first manifestations of the plague were unclear and perhaps not alarming. It arrived in Italy and the western Mediterranean in the fall of 1347. It then went into a kind of "hibernation" during the winter because the conditions from December to March were not favourable to the propagation of the agents of the contagion, especially fleas. It reappeared with a vengeance in the spring. Between March and May, the disease spread from the coastline to the interior with incredible speed. The cities not yet affected witnessed the progress of the epidemic with terror, anxiously awaiting news concerning its spread, and searching nervously within their own city walls for signs of the disease. The plague raged on the continent for three long years, between the end of the 1347 and the summer of 1350.

Not since the sixth century had Europe experienced such a terrible pandemic: there had been localized epidemics among the people of Europe from the eleventh to the thirteenth centuries, but always with only limited harm to the population. Now, the violence of the epidemic and the situation of the population, weakened by many years of famine and massed together in urban centres where hygiene was precarious, triggered a truly continental calamity. The sources describe the rapid course of the illness, citing the appearance of the primary symptoms: the buboes, on the thighs and groin and the transition from the bubonic plague to the secondary pulmonary plague that caused the victim to cough up blood.

Europe emerged from the pandemic seriously debilitated. In some areas, such as England, it appears that twenty-five percent of the population died during the plague; elsewhere, in certain areas of France, Germany, and Italy, the death toll reached thirty to thirty-five percent and sometimes higher. The plague disappeared during 1350–51; however, it continued to incubate and spread surreptitiously throughout the continent, reappearing from time to time between the fifteenth and sixteenth centuries until the next pandemic in 1630.

Population growth remained stagnant until, toward the end of the fifteenth century, the population of Europe began to grow once again. During this time, it is estimated that the population of the European continent was sixty percent of what it had been two centuries earlier, at the end of the thirteenth century. We have to wait until the end of the 1700s for the voids caused by the thirteenth-century collapse to be filled. Just to provide a few figures, in an area where the sources do not allow precise calculations, it appears that the population of England in 1348 was 3,700,000 (according to some sources, it was closer to 5 million), while in 1430, the population barely reached 2,100,000–2,300,000 (a decrease of about forty-four percent according to the more optimistic estimates, which is lower than that recorded in certain areas of Italy, where it surpassed fifty percent). In Florence, the population in 1348 was perhaps 100,000; a century and a half later, there were perhaps 60,000 inhabitants.

WAR

This grave situation, which as we have seen quickly became chronic, cannot be attributed solely to the plague. The fourteenth and fifteenth centuries were a time of war on the European continent. Though not excessively bloody for the combatants, they were ruinous for the inhabitants of cities. More than clashes on the battlefield, these wars consisted of raiding, pillaging, setting crops on fire, and blocking the trade arteries. These actions resulted in the slow hemorrhage of wealth and a chronic state of famine and epidemics due to the conditions these phenomena created.

The so-called Hundred Years' War devastated large areas of France between the fourteenth and fifteenth centuries with guerrilla tactics, raids, and sieges, which reduced France to desperation and misery. Many citizens without food sought refuge in the cities, where at least some charitable organizations provided the minimum required for daily survival. But this influx of unfortunate souls through the city gates threatened the lower classes because they reduced the cost of labour by introducing a surplus workforce. During the 1300s, in both the cities and the countryside, the poorest – when they did not resort to begging – were the targets of discontent, which the epidemics and frequent wars intensified. The result was rioting that often originated in the countryside and spread into the cities, usually involving the disenfranchised and the marginalized but sometimes also small artisans and producers who were slightly better off.

Between the second and the sixth decades of the 1300s the countryside in France was repeatedly pillaged by mobs of "pastoureaux" (little shepherds), who combined their protests against the wealthy and the feudal landlords with a generalized sense of apocalypse and the idea of a crusade that would purify Christianity of its internal enemies. Among these mobs, a confused version of the Christian idea – perhaps fuelled by the Franciscan experience and by heretical elements – of the poor as inheriting the earth acquired momentum: the wretched and the disenfranchised were in reality the "Chosen People." These issues underlay the revolts of the French peasants called "jacqueries" (perhaps derived from the name Jacques, applied to farmers),

5

5. *War*, detail of an illustration from Beatus of Liébana's *Comment on Revelation* of 1047 (see fig. 2). National Library of Spain, Madrid.

6. Late fifteenth-century drawing of an English archer holding the type of longbow used in the Hundred Years' War. Christ Church Picture Gallery, Oxford.

7. Drawing of the siege of Calais by the English in 1426, Warwick Manuscripts, 1484–90. British Library, London.

which led to the burning down of many castles between 1356 and 1358. But these elements were also present in the Paris revolt of 1356 headed by the provost of the merchants of Paris, Étienne Marcel. In addition, the depopulation of Europe after the epidemics and wars made the old citizen armies and the feudal cavalries obsolete. What was needed were professional armies that were always mobilized and well trained and made fighting wars a permanent occupation without diminishing the workforce and production. As well, neither the oligarchies nor the seigneuries were happy with the fact that the subaltern classes on their lands were armed and expert in military matters. Thus a new, and in a sense economic, military institution was born: the "compagnie di ventura" (free military companies). This was a kind of commercial organization whose members were armed and expert in matters of war. Governments wishing to hire an army drew up a contract with these companies, which was known as "condotta" (from which the term "condottiere" derives, to

6

7

8. The chart shows the decline in population between 1345 and 1410.

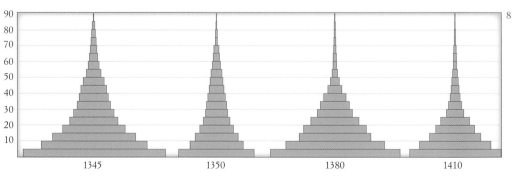

8

9

10

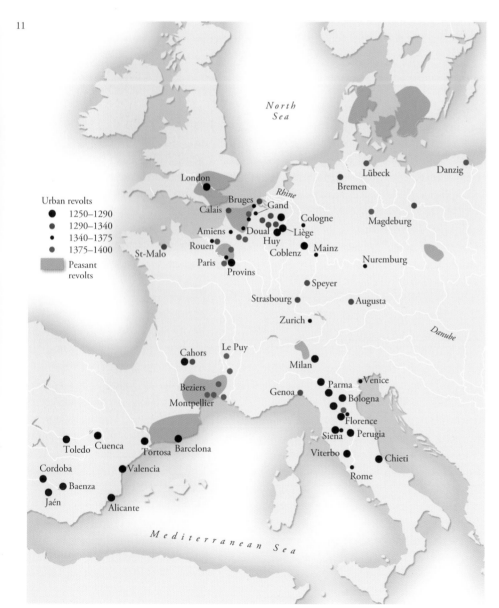

11

North Sea

London
Bruges
Calais
Gand
Rhine
Cologne
Amiens
Doual
Liège
Huy
Rouen
Coblenz
Mainz
St-Malo
Paris
Provins
Speyer
Strasbourg
Augusta
Zurich
Lübeck
Bremen
Danzig
Magdeburg
Nuremburg
Danube

Cahors
Le Puy
Milan
Beziers
Parma
Venice
Montpellier
Genoa
Bologna
Florence
Siena
Perugia
Toledo
Cuenca
Tortosa
Barcelona
Viterbo
Chieti
Cordoba
Valencia
Rome
Baenza
Jaén
Alicante

Mediterranean Sea

Urban revolts

● 1250–1290
● 1290–1340
• 1340–1375
● 1375–1400

Peasant revolts

9. Mercenaries receiving their pay, detail of Giotto's fresco in the San Martino Chapel, Lower Basilica of St Francis, Assisi.

10. John Ball, an English priest, rides to meet Wat Tyler, leader of the peasants' revolt of 1381. British Library, London.

11. Revolts of the peasants and city-dwellers from the mid-thirteenth century to the end of the fourteenth century.

12

designate the leader of such a company). Such groups played an important role in the conflict among the Italian "signorie."

However, these unique groups of armed and well-organized military men in a world such as that of Italian society, which was very rich despite the socio-economic crisis, essentially prevented the establishment of any sort of lasting peace because peace would have left the mercenaries unemployed. In the Italy of the fourteenth century and the early part of the fifteenth, it was almost impossible to establish a lasting peace. Unemployed mercenary companies resorted to sacking and became much more dangerous in peacetime than they were in times of war. Hiring a company, however, meant that the government paid a kind of tax to these professional soldiers (thus the Italian term "soldato" [soldier] was born, derived from the term "assoldato" or mercenary since the Roman *solidus* was solid gold coin) to prevent them from running riot.

THE ECONOMIC CONSEQUENCES

The decrease in population was reflected especially in the countryside and coincided with the profound reconfiguration of agricultural lands, marketing of products, and salaries. The most conspicuous phenomenon was undoubtedly the "lost villages" ("wüstungen" in Germany, "villages désertés" in France). These were settlements, usually located in inaccessible areas (mountains, the edges of swampland, and other terrain that was not very fertile), where farming was difficult but had been made necessary by the demographic pressures of the eleventh to thirteenth centuries. Now, conversely, the demographic crisis opened up vast empty spaces in the most fertile lands, in lowlands or on gentle hills, and villages located in inhospitable areas were therefore abandoned. In the meantime the crisis caused the collapse of the prices for cereal crops, while the cost of labour rose due to the fact that fewer men worked the land. This prompted a reutilization of lands once designated for the cultivation of cereal crops: it was now more remunerative to grow crops with "industrial" applications (hemp, linen, hops or dye plants, for instance, madder and woad, etc.) or to transform the lands into pastures for animal breeding.

Even feudal lords experienced hard times. The fall in the price of cereal crops and the increased labour costs reduced their income, which was also undercut by the devaluation of the currency, which affected income in the form of cash payments. In the meantime, there was a tendency throughout Europe for small property owners to sell their land, which caused estates and wealth derived from property to become concentrated in the hands of a few, while large property owners increasingly turned to indirect management of their estates. They rented their land or, as occurred in Tuscany, drew up a special contract called the "mezzadria" (sharecropping) whereby the harvest was shared by the landlord and the peasant who worked the land. Behind this process, widespread among the well-to-do classes of the 1300s and 1400s, it is possible to see a slow process of estrangement from the land on the part of a class of owners who preferred to live in the large cities or in the vicinity of the courts of rulers in order to enjoy the fruits of the income from their properties rather than tend to their possessions personally.

The distancing of the ruling classes from the administration of their lands does not, however, affect the whole of Europe during this time. Indeed, in certain areas like southern Italy, Spain, and eastern Europe, local lords established themselves even more firmly at the centre of their estates and the population decrease encouraged

them to expect even more from the peasants working their lands, who were forced to bear the brunt of the crisis. We generally find this situation in areas that did not develop a genuine urban culture or a proto-middle class.

The first signs of the crisis appeared quite soon even in the cities, particularly in the levelling off of production, the marketing of certain products (especially textiles), and the resulting stagnation in the relationship between the gold currency (used in international trade) and the silver or base metals used to pay salaries. Up to about 1320, this relationship was characterized by the constant increase in the value of gold, a sign of the health of international trade. This tendency began to reverse between 1320 and 1340, causing several problems. In the meantime, a series of large loans made by the Florentine banks (the Acciaioli, Bardi, and Peruzzi families, etc.) to European monarchs, loans that were never repaid, set off a series of bankruptcies, which in turn caused grave problems for mid-sized and small businesses that had entrusted their capital to those large banks. The results of an economic and financial stagnation closely connected to a much wider crisis were chain bankruptcies, the sale of personal possessions, new concentrations of wealth, and general impoverishment.

THE IMPACT ON CULTURE

A widespread religious feeling and the sense that divine justice was no longer confined to the heavens but would appear imminently on earth as well as the appearance of problems related to the moral issue of equality were the confused but powerful elements of a collective religiosity that signalled the development of what in the modern world we are accustomed to calling a "social issue."

Undoubtedly, this was a disorganized and passionate religiosity; the socio-economic circumstances had created terror and people were unable to find an explanation for the succession of poor harvests, epidemics, wars, and the terrible news

12. Hieronymus Bosch (1453–1516), *The Adoration of the Magi*, 1485–c.1500, detail, in the foreground, an abandoned house, in the background the flourishing city. Prado Museum, Madrid.

13. Accountants at work with their ledgers, from an illuminated codex. Royal Library, Brussels.

14. Andrea del Castagno (1421–1457), *Niccolò Acciaioli*, c.1449–50. Uffizi Art Gallery, Florence.

15

16

17

15,16. The Three Living (15) and
The Three Dead (16), from Jean Le Noir's
(active 1335–75) *Psaltery of Bonne of
Luxembourg*, paint on parchment, before
1349. The Metropolitan Museum, Cloisters
Collection, New York.

17. *Imago mortis* (Image of death), drawing
in an illustrated manuscript from 1493.

that arrived from time to time (such as that pertaining to the strange celestial phenomena often reported by the chronicles or the advance of the Turks on the Anatolian Peninsula or the Tatars in the southern portion of Russia). The most immediate response was to attribute all these events to the work of the Devil and to see the forces of evil that were inflicting pain and suffering on the faithful as coinciding with the imminent end of the world, which, according to the apocalyptic tradition, would be announced by the appearance of the Anti-Christ.

This religious sensibility was permeated by fear and in part fomented by popular preachers, who exploited this fear to increase donations to the Church and the purchase of indulgences. It was recorded in the literature and the art of the period in the form of "Triumphs of Death," "Danses Macabres" (Dances of death), and "Encounters between the Living and the Dead." These terrifying subjects demonstrate the depth of the crisis and the speed with which it was growing. The people of the 1300s had a fear of death, or at least exhibited such a fear, which was unknown in previous centuries. This was undoubtedly because death was a more vivid presence in society during the years of the crisis; in the years preceding, people had learned to live better and to become more attached to existence.

The religiosity of the times often expressed itself as participation in various groups, such as the "fraticelli" (little friars), who professed a more spiritual Church, free from terrestrial concerns. But religious fervour also expressed itself in the spread of lay devotional confraternities in which people prayed, made pilgrimages, and flagellated themselves as a sign of penance (one famous example is the so-called "devotion of the Bianchi" of 1399), but numerous works of charity were also performed, such as almsgiving and the establishment of hostels for the poor, the sick,

18

19

and abandoned children. In short, the religious sentiment offered an initial but incomplete response to the "social issue."

The new devotional climate also witnessed the birth, especially in Italy and Flanders, the most populous areas of Europe, of a different way of understanding the mystical experience: the *modern devotion* represented by such figures as Bridget of Sweden, Catherine of Siena, Enrico Suso, and Thomas à Kempis. This form of devotion was characterized by a less liturgical and formal but more intimate and immediate adherence to religion experienced as human value. In this climate what is today perhaps the most famous treatise of Christian meditation of all time, *The Imitation of Christ*, (generally attributed to Kempis) was produced. Such cults as the one devoted to St Sebastian, considered as the protector from the plague, were either born in this time or strengthened.

18. Andrea di Bartolo (1460–1524), detail of a portable altarpiece with St Catherine of Siena. Accademia Gallery, Venice.

19. Vincenzo Foppa (1427–c.1515), *The Martyrdom of St Sebastian*, detail c.1485, detached fresco from Santa Maria di Brera. Brera Art Gallery, Milan.

26

TOWARD THE RENAISSANCE

A NEW ERA?

The long-lasting social, economic, and spiritual fever that turned fourteenth-century European society upside down did not fail to provoke a response on the part of the ruling classes. This response took the form of a genuine economic and productive realignment, with the concentration of property in a small number of hands and the reduction of estates to a number of small parcels of property representing only one aspect of this process.

Following the chain reaction bankruptcies of the 1340s, banking houses learned to adopt a more flexible structure so that the failure of one branch did not mean the collapse of the entire system. Furthermore, the monopoly in textile production, which was in the hands of Flemish merchants up to the 1300s (in Tuscany the merchants were content with finishing or dying imported Flemish fabrics) tended to free up space for imports from England, Holland, and Italy. Decentralized "industrial" activities expanded in the sense that such activities were no longer concentrated in the city but in the countryside, where the workforce was more docile and cheaper. Merchants also took advantage of the waterways, which were essential to the manufacture of textiles, metallurgy, and paper production. In terms of agriculture, with the reduction in land designated for cereal crops and the increase in the cultivation of "industrial" plants, textile manufacturing poured into the markets not only wool cloths but also canvas, linen, and hemp – production stimulated by the new fashion trends that included shirts and undergarments. The demand for silk also grew while glass manufacturing developed substantially.

In summary, after the middle of the 1300s it appears that the European population, though diminished and impoverished, generally consumed more goods. The volume of merchandise in circulation increased, as did the volume of so-called "poor" products (wines, foodstuffs in general, and fabrics). This phenomenon was conducive to the employment of new types of ships with larger frames able to withstand the rigours of ocean travel; the ports on the Baltic Sea and the North Sea also grew in importance. Thus, the ocean-going cargo ship par excellence was born, the tall and wide-bodied "cocca" (or Hanseatic cog), a vessel capable of transporting large quantities of merchandise. In the face of such progress in the fields of commerce and manufacturing, financial instruments either improved or new forms were created, for example, "double entry accounting," "letters of exchange," etc. The surplus earnings from these activities were in part reinvested in property. In this way, a new entrepreneurial ruling class developed, especially in Italy, a class with characteristics that today we would call "capitalist"; at the same time, they lived the life of the nobility, in some cases intermarrying with the old feudal aristocracy, thereby rediscovering and reviving aristocratic traditions.

Was this the dawn of a new age? The term Renaissance entered the Italian cultural lexicon as a calque of the French "Renaissance," which was coined in the 1800s

1. Hans Memling (1433–1494), *Tommaso Portinari* (1470–72). Metropolitan Museum of Art, New York.

2. Beato Angelico (1395–1455), *Perugia Triptych*, 1437. In this scene from the life of St Nicholas, Angelico gives us the image of a fifteenth-century port. Vatican Art Gallery.

3. Pietro de' Crescenzi (1230–1320), *Livre des profits ruraux* (The book of rural benefits), Bruges, 1470. Miniature showing work on the manor being done under the watchful eye of the landlord. Morgan Library and Museum, New York.

2

3

4

5

4. Piero di Cosimo (1462–1521),
Venus, Mars, and Cupid, detail, c.1490.
Gemäldegalerie, Berlin.

5. Page from a 1460 edition of Vergil's
Aeneid. National Library of France, Paris.

by French historian Jules Michelet to describe the period before the modern age. This period corresponded roughly to the sixteenth century (although it had already started in part in the preceding century) and was seen as a time during which, following the stagnation and barbarism of the Middle Ages, civilization, culture, and ancient art were revived and enlivened by innovation. Although this model is widely rejected today, there is no doubt that many aspects of life and culture in Europe changed profoundly during the first decades of the 1300s through the 1400s.

HUMANIST CULTURE

We are accustomed to describing Italian culture of the 1400s as humanistic, that is to say, as characterized by a desire to distance itself from medieval traditions and establish a special relationship with the Greco-Roman civilization, which is taken as a model to be admired but not slavishly imitated. We are also accustomed to seeing Humanism as the preparatory phase of the Renaissance. Such terms as Humanism, humanist, and humanistic are modern, but they are rooted in the cult of the *humanae litterae* (humanistic letters), the philosophical and literary culture that developed particularly in the Rome of the so-called "Golden Age" between the first century B.C. and the first century A.D. The search for a specific stylistic model – which would also provide an ethical model – meant choosing some things and discarding others. In addition to restoring the most beautiful and correct form of the literary Latin language – the language of Cicero and Vergil – people also looked to the moral and political values of the authors of the golden period of Latin civilization. They were inspired by its ideals of moderation and serenity, as well as by the political ideal of aristocratic freedom, which was especially appreciated by the elite of the Italian cities of the fourteenth and fifteenth centuries, who – not unlike Romans in the first century B.C. – were uncertain as to which form of government to prefer: republican or seigneurial/princely.

In addition to the idealism and the intellectual achievements of Humanism, the new culture was not without compromises, particularly with regard to the hierarchical and dogmatic structures of the Church. The humanists were often clerics who placed their knowledge at the service of their faith. Their scientific investigations never attacked religious doctrine, at least not explicitly. Even the relationship between *virtus* (strength or manliness) and *fortuna* (fate or luck) was lived in a completely non-fatalistic way (since fatalism and predestination contradict Christian dogma regarding God's omnipotence and the human being's free will). Stated differently, they praised the best features of humankind: intelligence, boldness, and wisdom. Their frequent references to ancient mythology, inevitable in a literature and art that explained existence through the classical referent, are compatible with presenting Christianity through an allegorical reading of symbols and myths that point to Christian values. Certainly, there was no lack of ardent opponents of "paganism" in the humanistic style. Humanistic figures would enjoy success in the next century and would be an important influence on the Lutheran Reform but not until in the mid-1400s can we say that the popes and many pious citizens accepted without reservations the style and values that this movement proposed.

Furthermore, the work of the humanists was neither free nor neutral: on the contrary, because they were often people of humble origin, humanist artists and scholars needed resources and tranquility, both professional and personal, and therefore sought out patrons and protectors, which they usually found in the great princes of their time. The protection offered by such figures was often generous but not free, in the sense that the prince expected to gain fame and glory through the artist and the works that he protected and financed. The majority of the artworks of the 1400s, including the best, were in fact commissioned celebratory artworks.

THE AGE OF INNOVATIONS

Humanist thought is rich in practical achievements. The scholar was rarely an ivory-tower intellectual: more often than not he was an artisan, and art and technology went hand in hand in his workshop. The fifteenth-century painter knew mathematics because he had to execute his works according to the laws of perspective as well as those of the marketplace. He had some knowledge of chemistry because he worked with raw material to produce his colours and also had to study their properties when they came in contact with wood panels or, in the case of frescoes, plaster walls. The sculptor knew the laws of geometry but also the rules of the sculptor's art and the secrets of stone and marble. The metal worker cast statues in bronze, but he also cast church bells and cannons. The world of the fifteenth century was not abstract or bookish: it was a world of artisans who lived and worked in contact with the world and people with their practical problems. This link between humanist culture and the exercise of power explains a series of inventions and discoveries during the 1400s that changed the face of the known world. Gunpowder had been known for many centuries in China, where it did not have military applications. In Europe, up to the 1300s it was used to make rudimentary cannons that fired stone cannonballs. The princes of the fifteenth century and their engineers, however, perfected the firearm and made it a siege instrument so effective that it forced military architects to invent new protective structures.

The printing press was also used prior to the 1400s for the rudimentary reproduction of short texts or designs etched on wood and then stamped onto paper. However,

6

7

6. Antonio del Pollaiolo (1431–1498), *Hercules and Antaeus*, c.1475. Uffizi Art Gallery, Florence.

7. Gutenberg's printing press in Mainz.

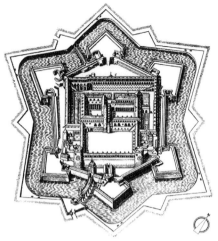

8

9

8. Detail of a drawing that shows the conquest of the city of Rouen by Henry V after a six-month siege in 1418–19. British Library, London.

9. Sixteenth-century plan of the Sforza castle in Milan.

it was during the 1400s – and especially when Johann Gensfleisch, called Gutenberg, invented moveable type around 1455 – that it became a new, formidable instrument for the spread of culture and propaganda. Similarly, cosmography – which was renewed through the ancient knowledge rediscovered by the humanists – became important in the fifteenth century not as a speculative science but instead as an instrument with which to expand knowledge of the earth and enrich rulers who had the daring and resources to sponsor oceanic voyages of discovery.

SHIPS AND CARTOGRAPHERS

The great protagonist of medieval Mediterranean navigation was the galley, but between the 1200s and the 1300s important innovations were made in the field of transportation as a result of the increased volume of merchandise circulating in the Mediterranean. In particular, the importance of the Baltic region and the coast of Flanders to the exportation of various products, particularly fish and manufactured goods (wool products), necessitated a different type of transport ship: the galley was not very efficient for trade and was not suitable for travel on the Atlantic since it could not withstand stormy seas. The new types of ships were the "cocca" (Hanseatic cog) and "caracca" (carrack). These were ships with large holds and several sails, though they were still not very agile, and they were capable of travelling on the Atlantic Ocean, though not far from the coast, between the Baltic Sea and the Straits of Gibraltar.

More or less in the same decades, sailors began to use the magnetic compass – perhaps imported from the Chinese by way of India and Arabia – and the sextant, instruments that made it possible to determine the position of the ship as it made its way along the coastline or on the high seas. There was also substantial progress in cartography as medieval maps were replaced by nautical charts and very precise drawings of coastlines and ocean floors called "portolani" (descriptive atlases).

In the fifteenth century, interest in geography and cosmography was part of the cultural renewal of the period. In 1410, Ptolemy's *Cosmographia* (Cosmography) was once again in circulation in the west in Jacopo d'Angelo da Scarperia's Latin

translation. While cartographers had increasingly better navigational instruments at their disposal, the writings of cosmographers concentrated on some basic questions, such as: How wide was the ocean that separated Europe form Asia? Was it possible, sailing constantly westward, to reach the Far East without circumnavigating the African continent and passing through the southern portion of the ocean?

The idea that the limits of the ocean were insuperable prevailed for a long time. This was due to the difficulties of the undertaking and not because people believed the earth was flat, a notion found in the Bible but invalidated when Aristotle's writings resurfaced in Europe. Things changed in the 1400s. The fact that Ptolemy's *Cosmographia* was again in circulation prompted the theory of the more or less balanced distribution of land and water and thus an increased distance between the coastline of the Iberian Peninsula and China. Florentine geographer and astrologer Paolo del Pozzo Toscanelli did not entirely accept Ptolemy's theory. He developed his own calculations of the distance and provided a more optimistic estimate than Ptolemy's. Toscanelli laid out his theories in a letter from 1474 to the canon of Lisbon, Fernam Martins. The two men had met during the Council of Florence and had evidently discussed the possibility of reaching China by sailing westward from the Iberian Peninsula.

BEYOND THE MEDITERRANEAN

In practical terms, the voyages of discovery were initially directed towards Africa in search of a route to sail around the continent. It was probably with this in mind that two brothers from Genoa named Vivaldi set sail from Genoa in 1291 to explore the ocean beyond the Strait of Gibraltar; they never returned. The Genoese sailor Lancelotto Malocello reached the Canary Islands in the early part of the fourteenth century; the island of Madera was discovered between 1340 and 1350; and the Azores archipelago between 1327 and 1332. In the meantime, news began to circulate concerning the gold to be found in Sudan and Mali, and expeditions to reach the mouth of the Niger River were launched. In 1487 Portuguese navigator Bartholomew

10. Albino Canepa's fifteenth-century nautical map. Società Geografica Italiana, Rome.

11. Facsimile copy of *Ptolemy's Atlas* produced in 1472 by a Florentine workshop. Vatican Apostolic Library, Rome.

12

14

13

Diaz sailed around the Cape of Good Hope, opening up a route towards the Indian Ocean, and in 1497 Vasco de Gama sailed from Lisbon to the coastline of India. The great organizer of these first extraordinary maritime undertakings was a Portuguese prince, Henry "the Navigator" (1394–1460). He established a centre for studies in the Algarve region in southern Portugal, which attracted sailors, astronomers, and cartographers.

However, the most important and revolutionary undertaking of the century was not the circumnavigation of Africa but rather the problem of the distance to China posed by Toscanelli and Martins. Information about Christopher Columbus's biography is not always completely reliable but between 1478 and 1479 he settled in Portugal, where he married the daughter of Bartolomeo Perestrello, from the city of Piacenza, who had become the governor of Porto Santo on Madera Island. Interest in cartography and the belief that the coastline of Asia was not too far from that of Europe stem from his time spent in Portugal. Columbus studied the ancient mapmakers, but he also interviewed sailors and collected legendary accounts pertaining to the western islands. Toscanelli's 1488 letter to Martins reinforced his own ideas.

Columbus soon began to develop the idea of a journey across the ocean travelling westward toward the Orient rather than reaching it through a long and dangerous circumnavigation of the African continent. Gathering information from Pliny, Arabian geographers, Pierre d'Ailly and Aeneas Sylvius Piccolomini, he produced a coherent cosmographic system, although it contained colossal errors: for example, he believed that the earth was much smaller than it actually is and he calculated the distance of the equator to be 30,000 km (one-fourth its actual distance). He also believed that to reach the Cipango Islands (Japan), a trip of

5,000 km from the Iberian coast would suffice, whereas the actual distance between the two coasts is 20,000 km.

A commission of scholars meeting in Salamanca examined his arguments carefully and refuted them one by one. Today, we are able to see how much more correct the scholars of Salamanca were than Columbus with respect to the actual alignment of the continents on the earth's surface. The fact remains that both the scholars and Columbus were unaware that there was a continent between Europe and Asia and that this continent was not far from the point where Columbus believed the coastline of Asia to be located. This misapprehension lasted for some time because Columbus never admitted that he had erred in his calculations and that the land he discovered was not part of the Asian continent. Following the Salamanca meeting, Columbus's hopes of obtaining financing from the Catholic kings faded. However, he gathered all his resources and knowledge in order to persuade the rulers to help him and in the end he was succeeful. On 17 April 1492, the Santa Fe Convention was signed, by which Columbus was granted the titles of admiral, viceroy, and governor of any lands he discovered. On 3 August of the same year, three ships of modest size (two caravels and one carrack, which was slightly larger) set sail from the port of Palos, financed with Spanish and Florentine capital. On 12 October, Columbus came within sight of an island he identified as one of the coasts of Cipango and which the indigenous population called Guanahani. He gave it the name of San Salvador (the identification of this island is uncertain, although there is a tendency to claim that it is the island of Watling in the Bahamas). On subsequent expeditions, Columbus reached Cuba (which he identified as Cipango) and Haiti (today the island of Hispaniola), which he believed to be Cathay. From 1492 to 1504, Columbus made four other journeys between Spain and what was by now being referred to as the "new world." His activities as viceroy and governor were not successful. He proved to be incapable of maintaining discipline in the Spanish colonies, committed cruelties against the indigenous peoples, and was actually accused of acts of theft. Nevertheless, with this extraordinary expansion of the known world on the part of Europeans, the period called "the modern age" is traditionally said to begin – although this notion is not accepted by everyone.

12. Portrait of Henry the Navigator (1394–1460), detail of the St Vincent altarpiece, attributed to Nuño Gonçalves, before 1460. National Museum of Ancient Art, Lisbon.

13. Eduardo Cano de la Peña (1823–1897), *Christopher Columbus in the Monastery at Rebida*, where he presents his plan for a voyage of discovery. Prado Museum, Madrid.

14. Naval battle in 1475 between the Portuguese and the Genoese, on an ex voto in the Church of San Pedro. Zumaia, Spain.

15. The routes of the great voyages of exploration.

16. Engraving from 1585, which shows the city of Santo Domingo, founded in 1497 by Bartholomew Columbus, brother of Christopher, on the island of Hispaniola.

15

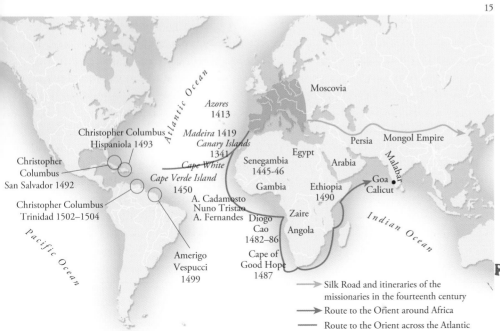

16

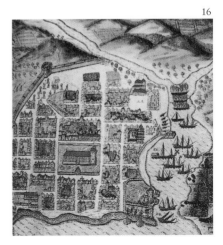

SELECTED BIBLIOGRAPHY

Abulafia, David. *Frederick II: A Medieval Emperor*. London, New York: Oxford University Press, 1992.

Ariès, Philippe. *Padri e figli nell'Europa medievale e moderna* (Fathers and sons in medieval Europe). Rome-Bari: Laterza, 1991.

Barbero, Alessandro. *Carlo Magno. Un padre dell'Europa* (Charlemagne, a father of Europe). Rome-Bari: Laterza, 2002.

Bloch, Marc. *La società feudale* (Feudal society). Turin: Einaudi, 1949 and subsequent editions.

Bloch, Marc. *Lavoro e tecnica nel Medioevo* (Work and technology in the Middle Ages). Bari: Laterza, 1973.

Bloch, Marc. *La servitù nella società medievale* (Servitude in medieval society). Florence: La Nuova Italia, 1975.

Bosl, Karl. *Modelli di società medievale* (Models of medieval society). Bologna: Il Mulino, 1979.

Boutruche, Robert. *Seigneurie et féodalité* (Seigneury and feudalism), 2 vols. Paris: Aubier, 1968–70.

Brooker, N.L. *Il matrimonio nel Medioevo* (Marriage in the Middle Ages). Bologna: Il Mulino, 1992.

Cantarella, G.M., Russo, L., and Sagulo, S., eds. *Enciclopedia del Medioevo* (Encyclopedia of the Middle Ages). Milan: Garzanti, 2007.

Capitani, Ovidio. *Medioevo passato prossimo* (Middles Ages as recent past). Bologna: Il Mulino, 1979.

Cardini, Franco. *Alle radici della cavalleria medievale* (The origins of medieval chivalry). Florence: La Nuova Italia, 1980.

Castelfranchi Vegas, *Liana. L'arte medioevale in Italia e nell'Occidente Europe* (Medieval art in Italy and in Western Europe). Milan: Jaca Book, 2007.

Castelnuovo, Enrico, and Sergi, Giuseppe, eds. *Arti e storia nel Medioevo* (The arts and history in the Middle Ages), 4 vols. Turin: Einaudi, 2002ss.

Duby, Georges. Guerriers et paysans, *VII-XII* siècle; premier essor de l'économie européenne*. (Early growth of the European economy: warriors and peasants from the seventh to the twelfth century). Paris: Gallimard, 1973.

Duby, Georges. *Le chevalier, la femme et le prêtre: le marriage dans la France féodale* (The knight, the lady and the priest: marriage in feudal France). Paris: Hachette, 1981.

Duby, Georges. *L'anno Mille: storia religiosa e psicologia collettiva* (The year 1000: religious history and collective psychology). Turin: Einaudi, 1992.

Eco, Umberto, ed. *Il medioevo* (The Middle Ages), 10 vols. Milan: Motta, 2009ss.

Frugoni, Chiara *Medioevo sul naso. Occhiali, bottoni e altre invenzioni medievali* (Books, banks, eyeglasses, buttons and other inventions of the Middle Ages). Rome-Bari, Laterza, 2003.

Ganshof, François-Louis. *Qu'est-ce la féodalité?* (Feudalism). Turin: Einaudi, 1989.

Huizinga, Johan. *L'automne du Moyen Âge* (The autumn of the Middle Ages). Paris: Payot, 1975.

Le Goff, Jacques. *La civilization de l'Occident médiéval* (The civilization of the West in the Middle Ages). Paris: Arthaud, 1964.

Le Goff, Jacques. *Pour un autre Moyen Âge: temps, travail et culture en Occident* (Time, work and culture in the Middle Ages). Paris: Gallimard 1977.

Le Goff, Jacques. *L'Europe est-elle née au Moyen Âge* (The birth of Europe). Paris: Seuil, 2003.

Minazzi, Vera, ed. *Atlante storico della musica nel Medioevo* (Historical atlas of medieval music). Milan: Jaca Book, 2011.

Modzelewski, Karol. *L'Europa dei barbari. Le culture tribali di fronte alla cultura romano-cristiana*, (The Europe of the barbarians. Tribal cultures in contact with Roman-Christian culture). Turin: Bollati Boringhieri, 2008.

Montanari, Massimo. *Alimentazione e cultura nel Medioevo* (Food and culture in the Middle Ages). Rome-Bari: Laterza, 1988.

Montesano, Marina. *Caccia alle streghe* (Witchhunts). Rome: Salerno, 2012.

Paravicini Bagliani, Agostino. *Il potere del papa. Corporeità, autorappresentazione, simboli* (The power of the popes. The pope's body, self-representation, symbols). Florence: Sismel, 2009.

Pernoud, Régine. *Visages de femme dans le Moyen Âge* (Images of women in medieval art). Saint-Leger-Vauban: Zodiaque, 1998.

Piva, Paolo, ed. *Arte medievale. Le vie dello spazio liturgico* (Medieval art. The forms of liturgical space). Milan: Jaca Book, 2010.

Pohl, Walter. *Le origini etniche dell'Europa. Barbari e Romani fra Antichità e Medioevo* (The ethnic origins of Europe. Barbarians and Romans from Antiquity to the Middle Ages). Rome: Viella, 2000.

Sergi, Giuseppe. *L'idea di medioevo* (The concept of the Middle Ages). Rome: Donzelli, 2005.

Toubert, Pierre. *Dalla terra ai castelli. Paesaggio, agricoltura e poteri nell'Italia medievale* (Land to castles. Landscape, agriculture and power in medieval Italy). Turin: Einaudi, 1995.

PICTURE CREDITS

The number not in parentheses indicates the chapter; the number in parentheses indicates the illustration.

INDEX